UNCHECKED POWER?

'Young is a meticulous and objective chronicler of our constitution. When she says it's time to worry, we should take that seriously.'
Meg Russell, Constitution Unit, UCL

'A brilliant and innovative account of the health of British constitutional democracy under the rule of Boris Johnson's Conservative government.'
Bojan Bugarič, University of Sheffield

'Liberal democracy means checks on the power of elected governments. Young provides a salutary, timely and readable reminder of why this matters.'
Anand Menon, UK in a Changing Europe

'An illuminating, insightful and timely account of the UK's post-Brexit constitutional problems – its special achievement is the way it captures and explores a number of important trends, connecting them while making them highly accessible to a wide audience.'
Mike Gordon, University of Liverpool

'Young understands constitutional law and practice and has a remarkable ability to communicate both the content and the importance of how we are governed.'
Lord Pannick KC

'Invaluable. A balanced and illuminating analysis of critical contemporary developments to our constitutional arrangements.'
The Rt Hon. the Lord Judge, Convenor of the Crossbench Peers, 2019–23

UNCHECKED POWER?

How Recent Constitutional Reforms Are Threatening UK Democracy

Alison L. Young

BRISTOL
UNIVERSITY
PRESS

First published in Great Britain in 2024 by

Bristol University Press
University of Bristol
1-9 Old Park Hill
Bristol
BS2 8BB
UK
t: +44 (0)117 374 6645
e: bup-info@bristol.ac.uk

Details of international sales and distribution partners are available at
bristoluniversitypress.co.uk

British Library Cataloguing in Publication Data
A catalogue record for this book is available from the British Library

ISBN 978-1-5292-3300-1 paperback
ISBN 978-1-5292-3301-8 ePub
ISBN 978-1-5292-3302-5 ePdf

Cover design: blu inc
Front cover image: Getty/PFE

Bristol University Press uses environmentally responsible
print partners.

Printed and bound in Great Britain by CPI Group (UK) Ltd,
Croydon, CR0 4YY

FSC
www.fsc.org
MIX
Paper | Supporting
responsible forestry
FSC® C013604

For Fiona Ross, without whom this book would not have been written.

Contents

About the Author

Alison L. Young is the Sir David Williams Professor of Public Law at the University of Cambridge, and Fellow of Robinson College, Cambridge. She is also Academic Associate at 39 Essex Chambers, a legal adviser to the House of Lords Select Committee on the Constitution and Emeritus Fellow of Hertford College, Oxford. She is the author of *Parliamentary Sovereignty and the Human Rights Act* (Hart, 2009), *Democratic Dialogue and the Constitution* (Oxford University Press, 2017) and *Turpin and Tomkins' British Government and the Constitution* (8th edition) (Cambridge University Press, 2021).

Acknowledgements

I often tell people that if they hear me say I'm going to write a book, they should stop me. My thanks go to those who, as usual, decided to offer encouragement and support rather than taking me at my word.

I was encouraged to write this book by a truly amazing group of women who, chatting to me after yoga, barre or Pilates, decided to ask me what I did. This led to many a conversation over coffee, particularly with Fiona, Nadine, Pam and Thea, about what was going on in Parliament and why it mattered. Their interest and support helped me to realize how many people wanted to know about what was going on, but never felt there was anyone they could ask, or thought that they needed to know too many things to fully understand it. Without their enthusiasm and questions, I would not have thought anyone would have wanted to read this book. I'd like to thank them for changing my mind.

Writing a book takes its toll. Any book is written around your day job. It sneaks into weekends and evenings. My thanks go to Duncan, Imogen and Bagheera. Duncan and Imogen are used to my early morning writing sessions, which often go on longer than they should. Duncan has probably made more cups of coffee than any husband should have to make, and Imogen has had to share her mum with the book on her visits home from university, especially over Christmas and Easter. Bagheera has made it clear that, while he's happy to be nearby to offer comfort and a welcome distraction, the provision of cat food always takes priority. Hayley is always there to listen to my complaining and Leah sends the best encouraging emails ever.

I am incredibly grateful to Becky, Grace, Helen and Kathryn at Bristol University Press for their help, support and encouragement, as well as the anonymous reviewers of both my book proposal and the first draft.

I also owe a debt of gratitude to everyone at Fresh in Ely. They stop me falling apart – both physically and mentally. Prosper is also THE best vegan café ever – not just in Ely! As ever, I owe a debt of gratitude to Muse, whose music keeps me going when I think I'm too tired to write. I may have listened a few too many times to *Will of the People* while writing this book. And, yes, I do have the T-shirt.

Preface

This book looks at constitutional change from the UK general election in December 2019 until the end of April 2023. It asks whether these changes have made things better or worse. There are claims that post Brexit, the constitution has become more populist. The people spoke in the referendum and the government needed to steer their will through Parliament. But, if all populism means is that the will of the people is respected, then it is hard to see why this is so problematic. Another way of viewing these reforms is to argue that these changes make the UK more democratic. The government can implement the will of the people free from interference from others – particularly experts – who may try and thwart the will of the people.

In some ways, working out whether the UK is more or less populist seems a bit pointless. Sometimes populism is nothing more than an insult, used to criticize the views or actions of those whose views we oppose. What is more important is why we criticize populism. The worry is that populist governments and populist leaders harm democracy. They do so by gathering more power for the government. They may limit the checks and balances over the actions of the government. They may change the style of government, focusing more on the use of rhetoric than reasoned argument. Populists define the 'will of the people' as if there is only one voice of the people, rather than trying to balance a range of interests of different individuals.

If we want to see if constitutional change has made the UK more populist, or more democratic, then we need to look more closely at what a government means when it says it is implementing the will of the people. We also need to see if the changes have given the government more power or added or removed checks and balances.

My worry is that the UK constitution is changing in the wrong direction. My hope is that by setting out my concerns, these changes can be discussed more generally by those for whom they matter: all of us living and voting in the UK, or anyone concerned that there has been a shift towards populism in their country.

There are some key events and changes in the UK that will be discussed across a range of chapters. It's helpful to do this so that we can see how the same change provides different evidence as to whether the UK has become more populist or more democratic. I've listed these changes here, so you can see where these are discussed in the book as a whole.

One event you will see discussed across the book is Partygate. We look at this in depth in Chapter 1. Issues relating to Partygate, and also Parliament's investigation into Boris Johnson's conduct, are discussed in Chapters 4, 6 and 8. We look at whether these events show that ministers, particularly the prime minister, are held to account for their actions by Parliament and the people, or whether the members or MPs of the political party the prime minister belongs to play the more important role.

Chapter 2 looks at the events of 2019 when Parliament did seem to check the actions of the government. Boris Johnson referred to the 2019 Parliament as a 'zombie Parliament'. Chapter 3 looks at what this might mean. One of the constitutional changes in response to the zombie Parliament was the Dissolution and Calling of Parliament Act 2022. This revived the power of the prime minister to ask the Monarch to dissolve Parliament and call a general election. This Act of Parliament is also examined in Chapters 2 and 6, looking not just at what it achieved, but how it was enacted and whether there was sufficient parliamentary scrutiny over such a constitutionally important Act of Parliament.

Chapter 3 focuses on the powers of the government, using examples of the rapidly changing measures used to implement lockdowns and other restrictions in response to COVID-19. Chapter 4 looks at the prorogation case, where the Supreme Court quashed an unlawful prorogation of Parliament. It also looks at the Owen Paterson affair. Chapter 5 looks at examples of whether legislation has been proposed that would contravene international law, including the UK Internal Market Bill, the Northern Ireland Protocol Bill and the Illegal Migration Bill.

Chapter 6 revisits some earlier examples of constitutional change, particularly the way in which Parliament enacted the Dissolution and

Calling of Parliament Act 2022, as well as focusing on Boris Johnson's first and last appearance at Prime Minister's Questions. Chapter 7 looks at how other bodies that can oversee the government saw changes to their role, as well as when these proposed changes fell away, such as the privatization of Channel 4.

Chapter 8 draws on all of these examples. It shows that both narratives fit the facts. Some will argue that the UK is more populist. Others will argue that the UK has become more democratic, with more political as opposed to legal checks over the action of the government.

It is this duality that is the problem. Populism can be disguised as democracy. In a constitution that can be so easy to change, often without the electorate realizing it, the 'will of the people' can become the will of the leader of the government. It can be used to stifle and not facilitate debate and participation. If we really are to empower the people, we need to make sure that the will of the people reflects all of the electorate, not just a few.

The UK constitution is changing rapidly. So much so that it almost becomes impossible to know when to stop. I've tried to ensure that the book, although focusing mostly on the post-Brexit constitution introduced by Boris Johnson, also takes account of events that took place under Liz Truss and Rishi Sunak, up to 30 April 2023. It also takes account of the report of the Privileges Committee that Boris Johnson deliberately misled Parliament. This runs the risk that some of the things described in the book will be out of date by the time you read the book. Such is the nature of any book that tries to look at contemporary events. Hopefully, as you spot what has and has not changed, this will keep the debate about these issues alive.

I'm writing this preface in the shadow of Ely Cathedral, on a bank holiday weekend which saw an eel (thankfully not a real one, though I was told that the spectacle was electrifying) parading through the streets of Ely, a craft and food fair, and the famous 'Foodie Friday' in the market square with local live music. There's something almost quintessentially British about these events, particularly as they took place a week before further celebrations of the coronation of King Charles III.

Similarly, it may be easy to think that the events described in this book are uniquely and typically British. While the events described took place in the UK at what may be seen as a turning point in

UK history, they are not isolated. The growth of governmental power, the restriction of checks and balances, and the equation of one group of society with the will of the people that must triumph over all are not unique to the UK. They may be used to describe events in other countries across the globe. While beyond the specific scope of this book, they are of grave concern. It should concern us as much as, if not more so, than the events taking place on one relatively small island.

Ely
April 2023

The Post-Brexit Constitution: Standing on a Constitutional Cliff Edge?

On 12 April 2022, Lord Hennessy, a historian and one of the foremost commentators on the UK constitution, wrote the following in his diary: 'Tuesday, the 12th of April 2022 will be forever remembered as a dark bleak day for British public and political life. ... I cannot remember a day when I've been more fearful for the well-being of the constitution.'[1]

When reading these words, it is easy to imagine that they refer to a catastrophic event. We might normally think of a coup. Did the army storm Parliament, rip up the constitution, and install military law? Did the UK Parliament enact legislation that removed the right to vote and install a dictator prime minister, after sacking the judiciary and replacing them with sympathizers of the prime minister?

Those events would indeed have been dark days for the UK constitution. Yet that is not what happened. Instead, the then Prime Minister, Boris Johnson, and Rishi Sunak, then Chancellor of the Exchequer, were both issued with fixed-penalty notices for breaching COVID-19 regulations. This may seem minor in comparison. But it marks the first time that a prime minister has been sanctioned for breaking the law while in office.

Both apologized for their actions. Both also agreed to pay the fine. This would seem to suggest that, while perhaps gloomy, 12 April was not such a dark day after all. So, what would prompt Lord Hennessy to be so fearful for the UK constitution? To understand this, we need to reflect further on 'Partygate', a political scandal arising from accusations that parties and gatherings had taken place in 10 Downing Street in breach of the strict Covid lockdown regulations. We also need to think about how far this led to the eventual resignation of Boris Johnson and his replacement with Liz Truss, who in turn, was replaced by Rishi Sunak.

When reflecting on these issues, we will focus on two possible narratives. Do these events show that the UK constitution is in a state of democratic decline, overtaken by populism? Or did the eventual resignation of Boris Johnson show that the UK constitution is in a good state of health, where politics does a good job of holding the government to account?

These two competing narratives will run through the book. While both are feasible, the book will propose a more subtle argument. The fact that these two interpretations are both possible shows that the UK stands on a constitutional cliff edge. While there may not be a danger of imminent democratic collapse, populist arguments are being used to change the nature of the UK constitution. This might not cause irreparable damage. But it nevertheless places the UK constitution in danger of undermining the mutual trust among governmental institutions, particularly as some of them fail to exercise necessary self-restraint. This combination of trust and restraint is fundamental to the UK constitution. If it is irreparably eroded, then 12 April 2022 may well prove to have been a dark day.

Partygate and beyond

Towards the end of November and early December 2021, the *Daily Mail* published a series of stories, some with photographic evidence, of parties and gatherings that had taken place in 10 Downing Street. During the Covid pandemic, a series of regulations had been introduced, preventing people from leaving their homes and prohibiting gatherings with members of other households. When some of these parties occurred, these lockdown measures were still in place, prohibiting gatherings of two or more people indoors unless they were reasonably necessary for work purposes. If there had been meetings of a large group of individuals responsible for dealing with emergencies that arose during the lockdown, then the gathering would have been reasonably necessary. Gatherings to celebrate birthdays or Christmas, or to mark the departure of individuals from their workplace, however, would not.

Stories of Christmas parties, leaving parties and birthday celebrations, therefore, struck a nerve, even more so when contrasted with the many devastatingly sad stories of those who had obeyed the rules. Many were unable to be with loved ones to comfort them through illness or their last moments of life, grieve for those who had died, or support a partner in the birth of their child. They had obeyed the strict lockdown regulations at considerable personal cost. If the stories were true, and those in power had been partying while the rest of us obeyed the rules, what did that tell us about our leaders? Could we still trust them to run the country?

The level of criticism surrounding Partygate prompted a reaction in Parliament. Once a week, the prime minister faces questions in the House of Commons. These are known as Prime Minister's Questions or PMQs. Currently, they take place once a week at midday on Wednesday, for at least half an hour. They are open to the public, who can apply for a ticket to come to Parliament and watch the debates in the House. They are also televised. Given the profile of PMQs, particularly the glare of the media spotlight, it is perhaps unsurprising that the leader of the opposition frequently asked the prime minister about the allegations of parties taking place in 10 Downing Street.

On 1 December 2021, the prime minister was specifically asked by the leader of the opposition whether 10 Downing Street had thrown a Christmas party on 18 December 2020. In response, the prime minister stated that 'all guidance was followed completely' in 10 Downing Street.[2] In other words, we should assume either that no party had taken place, or that the 'party' was reasonably necessary as part of a work meeting. The published photos of a gathering in 10 Downing Street, therefore, were not evidence that those attending had breached Covid guidance.

If that had been the end of the allegations, then this may have been the end of Partygate. However, two aspects of Partygate caused its elevation to a full-blown political scandal. First, more evidence emerged of other gatherings and parties. While one breach may have seemed like carelessness, a flurry of breaches looked more like the government was taking a cavalier attitude to the rules. Second, the story touched a nerve. It seemed to suggest that, while the rest of the population were making sacrifices for the greater good, those in government felt that the rules did not apply to them. It may have been one rule for the electorate, but it was another set of rules entirely for those in government.

This element of unfairness caused outrage and upset. For constitutional and political commentators, it raised an even deeper issue. It hinted at a disregard of a key principle of the UK constitution: the rule of law. This requires government according to the law. Those in power should follow the rules. Connected to this is a sense of fairness, or equality before the law. There should not be any special treatment. It cannot be one rule for us and another for those in power unless there is a justification for that difference in treatment. We do, for example, want to make sure that the police and the courts have the relevant powers to arrest, try – and when a guilty verdict is reached – convict, sentence and detain those who commit criminal offences, rather than granting these powers to everyone. Otherwise, citizens may take the law into their own hands, undermining the rule of law. But exceptions must be justified and set out in the law.

Over the next few days, more stories began to emerge of parties and gatherings taking place in 10 Downing Street. The most controversial was a video, leaked by ITV on 7 December 2021, showing Allegra Stratton, who was, at that time, the prime minister's press secretary, joking about the Downing Street Christmas party that was reported to have taken place on 18 December. The video, shot on 22 December 2020, was a recording of a mock televised press briefing. Parliamentary aides were asking Allegra Stratton questions, a standard means of ensuring that press secretaries are fully prepared for their role. One question concerned whether a Christmas party had taken place the week before. Allegra Stratton and others joked about the party and, in response to a practice question about the party, she laughingly stated that 'this fictional party was a business meeting, and it was not socially distanced'.[3]

Unsurprisingly, the video was raised in PMQs the next day. This time, however, the prime minister did not respond to a specific question as to whether parties and gatherings had taken place. Instead of routinely responding to the typical first question of any PMQs – a request for the prime minister to list his official engagements for the day – he began by saying he understood how infuriated the electorate must be, thinking that those who made the rules were not willing to follow the rules. He also stated that he was 'furious' to have seen the video clip and apologized 'unreservedly for the offence that it has caused up and down the country' as well as 'for the impression that it gives'. Boris Johnson then went on to say he had 'been repeatedly assured since these allegations emerged that there was no party and that no Covid rules were broken'. Nevertheless, he had asked the Cabinet Secretary, then Simon Case, to establish all the facts and to produce a report. He also promised that, were it to be discovered that rules had been broken, disciplinary actions would be brought against all of those who were involved.[4]

The cabinet secretary, the most senior civil servant in the UK who is based in the Cabinet Office, was asked to investigate three issues: first, the allegations of a gathering at 10 Downing Street on 27 November; second, a gathering at the Department for Education on 10 December 2020; and third the allegations of a gathering at 10 Downing Street on 18 December. He was tasked with determining whether these events took place and, if so, to ensure that disciplinary action was taken. Moreover, if evidence emerged of any breach of the law amounting to a criminal offence, the cabinet secretary was required to refer this matter to the police, pausing the investigation. If there was evidence of ministers attending these gatherings, then the cabinet secretary should follow the Ministerial Code, which provides guidelines as to the proper behaviour of ministers, to assess whether they had breached the provisions of the code. The cabinet secretary was also to make sure that the findings were made public, although any specific employment-related actions within 10 Downing Street would remain confidential.

Throughout December 2021, more accusations were made regarding further potentially unlawful gatherings in Downing Street. Allegations then emerged that the cabinet secretary had attended one of these events. He subsequently removed himself from the investigation, with Sue Gray, at the time a senior civil servant who was the second permanent secretary to the Cabinet, being appointed to take his place.

As Sue Gray carried on with her investigations, yet more information was revealed, leading to further situations in which the prime minister was asked questions about, or used PMQs to provide statements on, various gatherings that took place during lockdown. On 12 January 2022, for example, the prime minister apologized for a garden party that had taken place on 20 May 2020. He added that he believed stopping in the garden of 10 Downing Street for 25 minutes to thank staff was a work event. However, with hindsight, he accepted that he should have recognized that this was not the case and that 'even if it could be said technically to fall within the guidance, there would be millions and millions of people who simply would not see it that way'. Again, he offered his apologies and asked that Sue Gray be allowed to complete her inquiry.[5]

Later in January, the metropolitan police announced that they would be carrying out an investigation into the allegations of unlawful gatherings at 10 Downing Street. Finally, on 31 January, Sue Gray published a long-awaited update on her report, modified to take account of the police investigations. The interim Gray report investigated 16 separate incidents, taking place from 15 May 2020 to 16 April 2021. Twelve of these were also investigated by the metropolitan police. To ensure that the Gray report did not interfere with police proceedings, the report only made minimal reference to the incidents the police were investigating.

Despite its more restricted form, the update on the Gray report made some general findings that were highly critical and merit repeating in full:

> Against the backdrop of the pandemic, when the Government was asking citizens to accept far-reaching restrictions on their lives, some of the behaviour surrounding these gatherings is difficult to justify.
>
> At least some of the gatherings in question represent a serious failure to observe not just the high standards expected of those working at the heart of Government but also of the standards expected of the entire British population at the time.
>
> At times it seems there was too little thought given to what was happening across the country in considering the appropriateness of some of these gatherings, the risks they presented to public health and how they might appear to the public. There were failures of leadership and judgment by different parts of No 10 and the Cabinet Office at different times. Some of the events should not

have been allowed to take place. Other events should not have been allowed to develop as they did.[6]

The prime minister responded to the report by apologizing and promising to make changes to how Downing Street and the Cabinet Office operate to prevent future failings.[7]

The Partygate scandal continued to roll on, with more information emerging from the police regarding questionnaires that had been sent out and fixed-penalty notices that had been issued to those who had attended some of the events. The police finally concluded on 19 May 2022 that the prime minister would not face any more fixed-penalty notifications. On 25 May the Gray report was finally published in full. It confirmed the earlier initial findings, concluding that:

> what took place at many of these gatherings and the way in which they developed was not in line with Covid guidance at the time. ... It is also clear from the outcome of the police investigation, that a large number of individuals (83) who attended these events breached Covid regulations and therefore Covid guidance.[8]

Lord Hennessy believes that 12 April was a dark day for the UK constitution as neither the prime minister nor his chancellor resigned. Yet, for Lord Hennessy, the UK constitution would expect them to have resigned. By failing to do so, the prime minister breached the constitutional principles of good government. In particular, Lord Hennessy believes the prime minister did not follow the Ministerial Code. How can we argue that the UK's post-Brexit constitution is working if a prime minister can break the law and mislead Parliament, and yet remain in office?

Others, however, argue that Partygate does not show a failure of the UK constitution. They point to a wide range of mechanisms that could have been – and were – used to hold the prime minister to account. If the prime minister did not resign, this was merely because there was no need for him to resign. This reflects a fundamental aspect of the UK constitution. The UK has a predominantly political constitution. Political mechanisms determine whether a minister, including the prime minister, should resign. The political party to which the prime minister belongs can also keep its leader in check, with mechanisms that can be used to trigger a leadership election. Partygate did not remove any of these checks.

Indeed, they would argue that these checks are in a healthy state. After all, Partygate did eventually lead to a vote of confidence in Boris Johnson's leadership of the Conservative Party on 6 June 2022. Johnson won this vote by 211 votes in favour of his leadership and 148 votes against. If that were not enough, Johnson did eventually resign on 7 July 2022, due, at least in part, to the political fallout from Partygate. He also resigned as an MP on 9 June 2023.

Therefore, far from being a dark day, the 12 April merely shows that the prime minister was held to account but that there was no cause for him to resign. It did, however, form one of the many events that led to Johnson's resignation.

Who is right?

The prime minister, Parliament, party and the people

Partygate, and other events that led to Johnson's downfall, illustrate the array of political means through which ministers can be held to account for their actions. All form part of the UK's political constitution. Any member of the government can be held to account by the prime minister, who, in turn, is held to account by his or her political party, Parliament, and, ultimately, the people. This is the 'orthodox' account of the UK constitution. It upholds democracy, ensuring those in power act according to the wishes of, and are held accountable to, the electorate.

The prime minister

Ministers are appointed by the prime minister. The prime minister can also remove ministers from office. Sometimes this is to promote them to another ministerial role, rewarding them for their achievements or their loyalty to the prime minister. The prime minister may also fire and demote ministers. Again, this could be due to their lack of ability. Perhaps there had been failings in that ministerial department. It may also reflect a lack of party loyalty. It may even just be a desire to keep ministers on their toes or to change things around. These cabinet reshuffles have become a regular feature of UK politics.

As well as needing to perform well, ministers should also uphold good standards of government. Guidance on how ministers should conduct themselves can be found in the Ministerial Code. Like most things in the UK constitution, the Ministerial Code has evolved. It reflects past practices and constitutional conventions: non-legally enforceable rules and principles that guide how governmental institutions act and how they exercise their powers. The Ministerial Code also creates new guidance and can be modified by the prime minister. Each new prime minister normally reissues the Ministerial Code shortly after taking office.

It finds its origins in the Questions of Procedure for Ministers (QPMs), which were collated by Clement Attlee in 1945 from a series of directives on procedures for cabinet the government developed throughout the Second World War. The QPMs were originally unpublished, until 1992, when they were first published by John Major, the then prime minister. Following the general election in 1997, Tony Blair, recently elected as prime minister, published the first version of the Ministerial Code. This drew on both the QPMs and a parliamentary resolution. The current version of the Ministerial Code was published in December 2022 by Rishi Sunak.

The Ministerial Code contains an array of provisions. Some of them are principles. Others appear to be more akin to specific rules or restrictions. Some provisions focus on procedures: for example, setting out when ministers consult law officers or regulating the appointment of special advisers to ministers. The most relevant aspect of the Ministerial Code for assessing Partygate is found in paragraph 1.3.c: 'It is of paramount importance that Ministers give accurate and truthful information to Parliament, correcting any inadvertent error at the earliest opportunity. Ministers who knowingly mislead Parliament will be expected to offer their resignation to the prime minister.'[9]

Moreover, paragraph 1.3 states that the provisions of the Ministerial Code 'should be read against the background of the overarching duty on Ministers to comply with the law'. These provisions were part of the code at the time of Partygate and remain in the most recent version of the code. To assess whether the prime minister breached the Ministerial Code, we have to determine whether he 'knowingly misled' Parliament. If so, the code states that the prime minister would be expected to offer his resignation to himself, presumably implying that the prime minister would accept his own resignation.

The Ministerial Code cannot be enforced by the courts. There are only extremely limited circumstances in which courts can even discuss issues relating to the Ministerial Code. For example, a court was able to hear a case concerning allegations of bullying and whether these allegations had breached the Ministerial Code. However, courts cannot enforce the Ministerial Code itself. Rather, it was asked to look at the meaning of 'bullying' and 'harassment' set out in the code. As the interpretation of these provisions did not determine whether a minister should be removed from office or not, and related to a possible employment law claim brought by a civil servant, the courts were able to determine their meaning.[10]

Who, then, enforces the Ministerial Code? That role falls to ministers and, ultimately, the prime minister. Ministers are personally responsible for how they conduct themselves in the light of the Ministerial Code. As ministers only hold office for as long as they have the confidence of the prime minister, it is the prime minister who is the 'ultimate judge of standards of behaviour expected of a Minister and the appropriate consequences of a breach of those standards.'[11]

The Ministerial Code also sets out how the prime minister should enforce its provisions. When there is an allegation that someone has breached the Ministerial Code, it is for the prime minister to decide, after consulting with the cabinet secretary, whether to investigate the alleged breach. If the prime minister thinks that it does warrant investigation, then he or she can choose either to refer this to the Cabinet Office or the independent adviser on ministers' interests for further investigation. If investigated by the Cabinet Office, then the investigation would be carried out by civil servants.

The prime minister appoints the independent adviser on ministers' interests. As well as carrying out investigations, their role is to advise the prime minister on the operation of the Ministerial Code. The independent adviser may also initiate an investigation of an alleged breach of the code, but only after consulting the prime minister who will 'normally' give consent. The prime minister may, however, 'raise concerns' about such an investigation if there are 'public interest reasons for doing so'. This prevents the independent adviser from carrying out an investigation, although he or she may require the reasons for not pursuing such an investigation to be made public.[12]

The prime minister also decides on the consequences of a breach of the code. This may include resignation but need not do so. If the prime minister still has confidence in the minister in question, an alternative sanction may be imposed: for example, a public apology, removal of ministerial salary or other remedial action. The prime minister may ask the independent adviser for confidential advice on the appropriate sanction.[13]

While the code may provide a good means through which to check the actions of ministers, particularly when the press publicizes specific breaches of the Ministerial Code, it is only as strong as the prime minister's will to enforce it. The prime minister may also reinstate a minister who previously resigned for breaching the code. It is also hard to see how this can be used to check the actions of any prime minister who does not feel the need to follow the rules, particularly a prime minister who believes he or she has the backing of the people to stay in power.

Parliament

The Ministerial Code is not the only means through which ministers can be held to account for their actions. Ministers are accountable to Parliament. They may face questions and debates or be required to appear before parliamentary committees. We have already seen how PMQs may be used to pose embarrassing questions to the prime minister; in turn, the prime minister can use PMQs to defend personal conduct, or that of other ministers or Members of Parliament in the same political party as the prime minister.

Ministers are also Members of Parliament (MPs). Parliament has also endorsed principles that should guide how ministers should behave. In 1997, Parliament passed a parliamentary resolution on ministerial accountability. This was agreed to by both the House of Commons and the House of Lords. This resolution followed the publication of the Scott report, which investigated governmental failings surrounding the sale of arms to Iraq, and a series of reports by other parliamentary committees looking into the accountability of ministers. Ministers who are members of the House of Commons are subject to the codes and procedures governing the conduct of those members; for example, ensuring that they register their interests, as well as rules regarding lobbying and when an MP can carry on private work in addition to their work as an MP. An MP can also be held in contempt of the House. This applies to any situation in which an MP acts in a manner that interferes with or obstructs how Parliament or MPs perform their duties. This may include situations when a minister misleads the House. The parliamentary resolution on ministerial accountability states that 'It is of paramount importance that Ministers give accurate and truthful information to Parliament, correcting any inadvertent error at the earliest opportunity. Ministers who knowingly mislead Parliament will be expected to offer their resignation to the Prime Minister.'[14]

On 20 April 2022, the House of Commons agreed a resolution, without the need for a division, to ask the Committee of Privileges to investigate the actions of the prime minister. The committee looked specifically at whether Boris Johnson's statements to the House of Commons, that the rules and guidance had been followed and denying that a party had taken place, did knowingly or recklessly mislead the House. The Committee of Privileges is a select committee in the House of Commons. It has seven members, all of whom are MPs, and its composition reflects the composition of the House. As well as investigating the actions of the prime minister, the committee can make recommendations as to the appropriate punishment, should it conclude that the prime minister had committed contempt of Parliament by knowingly or recklessly misleading the House of Commons. These include fines and suspending a member from the House. However, to take effect, any punishment would have to be agreed to and voted on by the House of Commons.

On Wednesday 22 March 2023, the prime minister appeared before the Privileges Committee to make his case and to respond to questions from the committee. On 9 June 2023, Boris Johnson, having received a copy of the committee's proposed report for comment, announced his resignation as an MP, accusing the committee of being a 'kangaroo court', whose report was 'riddled with inaccuracies and reeks of prejudice'. He also stated that he had not lied and that he was 'being forced out of Parliament by a tiny handful of people'.[15]

The committee published its report on Thursday 15 June. It concluded that Boris Johnson had deliberately misled the House.

The committee reached the view that some of Boris Johnson's explanations were 'so disingenuous that they were by their very nature deliberate attempts to mislead the Committee and the House, while others demonstrated deliberation because of the frequency with which he closed his mind to the truth'.[16] The report noted that its original recommended sanction would have been to suspend Boris Johnson for a period that would have triggered a recall petition – that is, a suspension for ten days or more. This was in light of the serious nature of the misleading statements – both that these were from the prime minister and that they were on a matter of importance. However, in the light of Boris Johnson's resignation letter, the committee recommended that, if Johnson had remained as an MP, he would have been suspended for 90 days. The committee also concluded that Johnson's parliamentary pass as a former MP should be revoked. This was a conclusion of a majority of the committee. Two of its members wished to recommend that Johnson should be expelled from the House.

This higher penalty was in light of the further examples of contempt of the House committed by Johnson. First, he leaked information about the confidential interim conclusions of the committee, breaching confidence. Second, he had impugned the committee in his resignation letter, as well as being complicit in attempted intimidation of the committee and a campaign of abuse against the committee. The House of Commons voted to accept this recommendation on Monday 19 June by 354 votes to 7.[17]

Such events are unusual. But they are not the only means through which MPs can hold the government, or particular ministers – including former prime ministers – to account. Ultimately, if Parliament wishes to remove a government, it can do so by initiating a vote of no confidence in the government. By convention, if the leader of the opposition tables a vote of no confidence in the government, then parliamentary time will be found to hold this vote. However, as the events of 12 July 2022 show, difficulties can arise over the interpretation of the wording of a proposed vote. When Keir Starmer, leader of the opposition, tabled a motion of no confidence in the government and the prime minister, the government decided that this was not genuinely a vote of no confidence in the government, but a form of censure of the prime minister. Therefore, they did not have to find time for the vote.

Instead, the prime minister tabled a motion of confidence in the government, which was debated on 18 July 2022. Unsurprisingly, the government won this vote of confidence.

Votes of confidence are meant to be the ultimate way of holding the government to account. So much so that the most important convention of the UK constitution is often said to be that the government can only remain in power when it enjoys the confidence of the House of Commons. This would seem to provide a real means for Parliament to hold the government to account. If the government is failing, it can be voted out, triggering a general election.

However, in reality, this may be a weak control. On the one hand, it is too extreme. How many failures will it take before MPs think it is time to vote out a government? Any MP making this choice will also have to think about whether they are potentially prepared to lose their seat as an MP in the following general election. On the other hand, it is too weak. It is too blunt. If you try and use this to specifically challenge the behaviour of the prime minister, then the prime minister can construe this as a censure motion and refuse to allow time for a debate. Paradoxically, its strength is also a weakness. A majority government can easily ride out a vote of no confidence, relying on its backbench MPs who may not wish to run the risk of losing their seats and of losing the whip, not being selected as a candidate in any future general election, or even having their membership of the party revoked. The government can also use a confidence vote to ensure backbench MPs toe the line. A vote against a particular Bill may be turned into a confidence vote, thereby forcing MPs to either vote in favour of legislation they dislike or to face the possibility of a general election in which, again, they may either not be chosen as a future candidate or may lose their seat.

There is also no legal requirement that the prime minister should resign, or seek a dissolution of Parliament, triggering a general election, after losing a vote of no confidence in the Commons. What if he or she chose not to resign? It may be possible for the Monarch to use his prerogative power to remove the prime minister from office. However, the Monarch would be unlikely to do this unless he had a sense that this was desired by the House of Commons and there was a clear alternative prime minister who did have the backing of the House of Commons who could be appointed.

The Monarch may even be able to dissolve Parliament in these extreme circumstances, triggering a general election. However, again, the King would be unlikely to do so unless there was clear support from Parliament for this action, or if faced with an extreme constitutional crisis and he had been advised that a general election was in the best interests of the people.

Party

The prime minister is not only subject to checks from Parliament. They also face scrutiny from their political party. In the end, it was this form of accountability that provided the most effective check on the actions of Boris Johnson, leading to his resignation as Prime Minister.

Members of a political party can initiate a leadership challenge. This may also remove the leadership of the party from an incumbent prime minister, leading to a change of prime minister between elections. A prime minister may also decide to resign if they think they may be in danger of losing the confidence of their party, potentially facing a challenge to their leadership which they fear they may lose.

The effectiveness of this check on the prime minister depends on the procedures regulating the leadership of a particular political party. In the UK, there is no legislation setting out how political parties are to organize themselves, including how they determine their leader or remove a leader. Political parties can determine their internal regulations.

The rules of the Conservative Party state that a vote of confidence can be triggered if 15 per cent of current Conservative MPs write to the chair of the 1922 Committee, itself composed of all the backbench MPs of the Conservative Party, calling for the resignation of the leader of the party. The chair of the 1922 Committee receives these letters in confidence. Backbench Conservative MPs may disclose that they have sent a letter but they need not do so.

Having received the requisite number of letters, a vote of no confidence in Boris Johnson's leadership of the party took place on 6 June 2022, triggered, at least in part, due to concerns over Partygate. To remain in office, Johnson needed to obtain more than 50 per cent of the votes cast by Conservative Party MPs. He was able to do so – winning by 211 votes to 148. The rules of the Conservative Party meant that Johnson remained the leader of the party and, therefore, Prime Minister. Having won this challenge, no leadership contest took place and, in accordance with the rules, Johnson could not face another vote of no confidence in his leadership for 12 months – unless the Conservative Party decided to change its own rules.

Were Boris Johnson to have lost the vote of confidence in his leadership of the party, there is an expectation that he would also have resigned as Prime Minister. However, he is not legally required to do so. As we saw in the events that eventually led to Johnson's resignation, it can be difficult in practice for a prime minister to continue to govern without the support of their political party. It is this factor that, ultimately, led to Johnson's resignation as Prime Minister – not over Partygate, but due to further evidence of misleading his government, as well as Parliament, over the Pincher affair.

Christopher Pincher was Deputy Chief Whip of the Conservative Party. Reports emerged of an accusation that he groped two men at a London club. He resigned on 30 June 2022 following these accusations. This, alone, would not have been enough to remove the prime minister. Difficulties arose over the fact that the prime minister had renewed Pincher's position as Deputy Chief Whip. As further information about Pincher's behaviour emerged, further stories surfaced of earlier incidents of sexual misconduct. Did Boris Johnson know of these allegations when he reappointed Pincher as Deputy Chief Whip? The prime minister initially denied this, briefing his government to back his denial. However, a former civil servant provided evidence that this was not the case. The prime minister had been briefed on these allegations of misconduct when deciding whether to reappoint Pincher. The prime minister later stated that he could not recall being briefed and now regretted having made the appointment.

This proved to be too much for some Conservative MPs and ministers. As ministers began to resign, it became clear that Johnson had lost the confidence of his political party. It also became increasingly difficult for him to govern. Would he be able to find sufficient members of the party whom he could trust to run his government, steering through legislation in Parliament, appearing before committees and running their ministerial departments? In the end, it seemed that this would not be possible. On 7 July, Boris Johnson resigned, paving the way for a leadership election, which saw the appointment of Liz Truss as Prime Minister on 6 September 2022.

Liz Truss only remained in office for 45 days, making her the shortest-serving prime minister to date. It became clear that she too had lost the confidence of her party. This arose due to her economic policies, including a mini-budget which crashed the markets, and confusion over whether a vote on fracking was or was not a confidence issue. There were also accusations of some Conservative MPs being manhandled and bullied into voting on the issue. All this happened mere days after Suella Braverman, who was Home Secretary at the time, was forced to resign for breaches of the Ministerial Code as it emerged that she had sent confidential emails from her personal account. This combination of events became too much for Conservative backbench MPs. The pressure of their disapproval, communicated to the prime minister through the chair of the 1922 Committee, a committee composed of Conservative backbench MPs, led to Truss's resignation. This was followed by the swift appointment of Rishi Sunak as the next leader of the Conservative Party and Prime Minister. Suella Braverman was reappointed as Home Secretary by the new Prime Minister, a mere six days after she resigned from Liz Truss's government.

The people

Ultimately, it is the people who hold the government to account. Even if Boris Johnson had not resigned, eventually he would have faced a general election in which the electorate would have held him to account for his policies, his behaviour and his term in office.

As an MP, any prime minister will need to win a seat in Parliament. The voters in their constituency can decide to vote for a different MP. More generally, voters who cast their vote for the political party to which the prime minister belongs may decide to vote for a different political party, indicating their desire to change to a government of a different political persuasion.

If Johnson had lost the first leadership challenge but had then refused to resign as leader of the Conservative Party, this may have given rise to an early general election. The leader of the opposition could have tabled a vote of no confidence in the government which, if it had succeeded, should have caused the prime minister to resign or to call a general election. Failing this, the Monarch may have used his prerogative power to remove the prime minister from office or to dissolve Parliament and call a general election. Failing that, legislation currently limits the length of a government's term in office to a maximum of five years, triggering another general election when that term runs out.

However, if there is a large gap of time between the criticized actions of a prime minister and the next general election, it may be that the electorate has forgotten. If Johnson had not been forced to resign, would the Pincher affair have been forgotten, in a similar manner to the way that Partygate seemed to have been swept under the carpet? The electorate may be motivated by many issues when deciding how to cast their vote. A voter may not trust a particular prime minister but may still believe that there are other reasons for voting for the political party led by that prime minister. They may not even trust the political party but may nevertheless believe that it is better placed to run the country than any other alternative.

This may seem to provide a feeble role for the people. However, governments need to think about the need to win elections to stay in power. This may provide a brake on the actions of those in power. Did MPs and ministers resign over the Pincher affair because they did not like being misled by their prime minister, or because they were concerned that Johnson would no longer lead their political party to victory in the next general election, or both? Overall, does it matter if Johnson's downfall was due to his failure to uphold good standards or because of his potential failure to win votes? Either way, he was held to account for his actions.

A dark day for the British constitution?

We have discussed two of the events that triggered the resignation of Boris Johnson and looked at the different mechanisms through which the prime minister can be held to account by their party, Parliament and the people. But we still have not answered the deeper question: does it matter that Boris Johnson did not resign over Partygate, and survived a vote of no confidence in his leadership, only to eventually resign over his failure to recollect a briefing relating to his appointment of the deputy chief whip?

Some argue that these events show that the UK's predominantly political constitution works well. But what does this mean? We have already seen some aspects of this account. The prime minister's ability to check the power of his or her ministers, and the accountability of the government to its political party, Parliament and the people are all examples of the political constitution at work. We call this a political constitution as politics is the main way through which the UK keeps the government in check.

There are also other aspects of why we see the UK as having a predominantly political constitution. A key principle of the UK constitution is the sovereignty of the UK Parliament. The UK Parliament is the most important institution of the constitution. Parliament can make legislation on any subject matter that it wishes, at least as far as UK law is concerned. If the Westminster Parliament wished to ban individuals from smoking at the Eiffel Tower in Paris, it could do so. However, it may be difficult for the UK to enforce this law!

There are several consequences that flow from the sovereignty of the UK Parliament. It explains why the UK does not have a codified constitution – why you cannot find a single legal text called 'The UK Constitution' which collates a set of legally enforceable rules about the constitution. Parliamentary sovereignty also means that an Act of the UK Parliament is the most important form of law in the UK, not a constitution. Countries with a codified constitution tend to use the constitution to set legal limits on legislation enacted by parliaments. In countries with an entrenched constitution, courts can strike down legislation which breaches the constitution. In the UK, however, it is argued that the sovereignty of the UK Parliament means that we cannot have a constitution that would place legal limits on an Act of Parliament.

This is best explained through means of an example. Imagine that a government wished to provide stronger protection of human rights in the UK. It may decide to enact a new Human Rights Act 2023. This imaginary Human Rights Act 2023 states that human rights cannot be modified or removed unless there is a vote in favour of this modification or removal by two-thirds of the members of the House of Commons. A few years later, Parliament wishes to modify the imaginary Human Rights Act 2023. It enacts a new Freedom of Expression Act 2025, which weakens the protection of the right to privacy found in the Human Rights Act 2023. However, the Freedom of Expression Act 2025 is passed without a vote of two-thirds of the members of the House of Commons. The orthodox account of parliamentary sovereignty would argue that, by enacting the new Freedom of Expression Act 2025 with a simple majority, Parliament is deemed to have impliedly repealed the provisions of the Human Rights Act 2023 requiring a vote of two-thirds of MPs. Consequently, the attempt to provide stronger protection of human rights would fail. It could be overturned in the future by a simple majority vote in Parliament.

The importance of the sovereignty of the Westminster Parliament explains another key feature of the UK constitution. Many of the rules that regulate how institutions of the constitution should behave are not found in the law and are not enforced by the courts. We have already seen this when discussing the Ministerial Code, and how Parliament and political parties hold ministers and prime ministers to account for their actions.

Many of these rules are known as constitutional conventions. Not only do they set the rules that are meant to be followed, but they may also explain how governmental institutions exercise their powers. For example, the Monarch possesses the legal power to appoint a prime minister. By convention, he normally appoints the leader of the political party with a majority of seats in the House of Commons. Where this is not possible, he may appoint the leader of a coalition agreement between two parties as was the case during the 2010–15 Conservative/Liberal Democrat coalition agreement when the Monarch appointed David Cameron as Prime Minister. The Monarch may also appoint the leader of the party with more seats in the House of Commons than any other political party, even when they do not have a majority of seats, but where the leader of that political party would have a working majority. This was the case, for example, when the Monarch appointed Theresa May as Prime Minister following the 2017 snap general election.

The conventional limits on the Monarch serve two purposes. First, they ensure that the Monarch is kept out of politics as much as possible. His choice of prime minister is dictated by the outcome of a general election and the extent to which the House of Commons will support a particular prime minister and their government. Second, these limits uphold the convention of the UK constitution that a government only holds power to the extent that it enjoys the confidence of the House of Commons. This places political accountability at the centre of the UK constitution.

Do these political mechanisms work? Johnson did eventually resign. Therefore, the constitution would appear to be working well. Or is it? After all, Johnson did not think he had to resign in the immediate aftermath of Partygate, yet it seemed clear that he had misled Parliament and failed to follow the law. Surely the UK's political constitution should have held Johnson to account, and he should have resigned then, not later?

As with most things in the UK constitution, the answer to this question is – not necessarily. Did Johnson really breach the Ministerial Code or the similarly worded parliamentary resolution on ministerial accountability? This all depends on what we mean by 'knowingly' and 'mislead'. His statements appear to be misleading. The Prime Minister said he did not attend a party. However, the police concluded that he did. Yet the Prime Minister argued that he had not misled Parliament. He was given assurances that no parties had taken place and that no rules had been broken. Therefore, the Prime Minister did not mislead the House of Commons. He gave statements to the House of Commons that he sincerely believed to be true, even though they later turned out to be false.

Johnson argued that he could not have knowingly misled Parliament if he only said what he believed to be true at the time. However, arguably, he should have known better. Should he have done more to check that rules and guidance were being followed? Boris Johnson, in his evidence to the Privileges Committee, said that he had asked advisers, including those who advise on the media, about whether Covid rules and guidance had been followed. However, he had not asked members of the Government Legal Department or the law officers for advice. Perhaps, as prime minister, he should have behaved better and done more to ensure the rules and guidance were followed. He oversees 10 Downing Street. His government enacted the Covid regulations and guidance. He should have known that these parties were breaking the rules and should have checked this more thoroughly before telling Parliament that no rules had been broken.

In other words, was Johnson reckless about the truth when he said that no rules had been broken, even if he believed what he was saying was true? When it comes to ensuring Parliament is fully informed, don't we want MPs to take at least some measures to check that what they say is true, particularly when answering specific questions about their conduct?

If Johnson did not think he needed to resign over Partygate, why did he eventually resign following the Pincher affair? One possible explanation is that this was just the tipping point. A prime minister may be able to weather a few storms, but eventually, their accumulated force becomes so great that resignation is the only option. We may also expect it to take longer for a prime minister with such a large majority in the House of Commons to resign. The point is, it does not matter whether Partygate or the Pincher affair was the tipping point. Johnson was still ultimately held to account.

I would argue that it does matter. There are deeper issues at play. A lot of work is done by the Ministerial Code. Yet, as we saw above, the prime minister decides whether an alleged breach of the code is investigated and decides the appropriate sanction should a breach have occurred. Whether a minister is forced to resign or not may depend more on whether the prime minister has confidence in that minister, or can count on their loyalty, than on whether their behaviour merits reprimand.

The prime minister can also change the code's provisions. For example, modifications of the Ministerial Code relating to the role of the independent adviser to initiate investigations and enable sanctions other than resignation were introduced in the immediate aftermath of Partygate. The Gray report appeared on 25 May 2022. Boris Johnson issued the new Ministerial Code on 29 May 2022. Rishi Sunak kept the changes in this iteration when he reissued the Ministerial Code in December 2022.

Politics may be more important than good standards of behaviour when working out if a minister did, or did not, breach the Ministerial Code, or if the prime minister should, or should not, resign. All that appears to matter is whether the prime minister can still govern. The fact that Boris Johnson remained as Prime Minister after Partygate shows that he could. When making his assessment as to whether to resign, he assessed the political consequences of resigning or staying. This would have included an assessment of how far Partygate had damaged the Conservative Party's chances of winning the next general election. When Johnson resigned over the Pincher affair, he did so because that calculation tipped in favour of resigning. Too many of his ministers had resigned. He could no longer rely on the confidence of his party. Staying in power might also damage his party's chances of winning the next general election. This calculation may also explain why, although obtaining sufficient nominations, Johnson decided not to put his name forward as a candidate for the leadership of the Conservative Party following the resignation of Liz Truss.

This interpretation is worrying. Does it mean that the UK's political constitution is all about power and that good standards of government are immaterial? All that matters appears to be whether a prime minister can remain in power and lead his or her party to victory in the next general election. But how worrying is this interpretation if, ultimately, the electorate determines the next government by voting in the next general election? If Johnson had not resigned, and he had gone on to win the next general election, this just shows either that the electorate does not mind that he misled Parliament and his government, or that, in the grand scheme of things, this is less important than his policies.

Should we be satisfied with this explanation? Johnson's resignation could be seen as democracy in action. However, it can also be seen as a charismatic, populist leader being able to remain in power. This depends on what Johnson and others mean by 'the will of the people'. Is this the will of the electorate as a whole, or a group within the electorate that the prime minister thinks are representative of the will of the people – perhaps those he sees as his party's main supporters, or those who voted for Brexit, or who switched to voting for his party in the 2019 general election.

Did Johnson act in this way? There are signs throughout his term of office that suggest Johnson was a populist leader. After apologizing for Partygate, the prime minister made further statements that potentially show an appeal to populism. He stated that he felt 'an even greater sense of obligation to deliver on the priorities of the British people' when he appeared on television on 12 April 2022.[18] In his statement to the House of Commons on 19 April 2022, the prime minister again referred to his 'greater sense of obligation to deliver on the priorities of the British people', continuing his speech with a reference to the government's efforts in the war in Ukraine, and concluding by saying that it was his job 'to work every day to make the British people safer, more secure and more prosperous'.[19] In his response to questions, the prime minister also continued to refer to his desire to fulfil his purpose of working for the British people.

Johnson's resignation speech and his address to the Commons in the vote of confidence may also have populist overtones. He referred to his reluctance to resign because he felt he had a mandate from the people, particularly to get Brexit done. He argued that, given this large mandate, and the many achievements of his government, it would be 'eccentric to change governments'. If he had failed to persuade his colleagues in government, this was because 'at Westminster, the herd is powerful and, when the herd moves, it moves'. There was no expression of remorse. The prime minister never apologized. He never specifically said he was resigning. Instead, he said 'them's the breaks'.[20]

When introducing the vote of confidence in his government to the House of Commons in July 2022, the prime minister continued to give an account of what he saw as the triumphs of his government, often in colourful language. He referred to the 2019 election victory as having 'sent the great blue Tory ferret so far up their left trouser leg'. He also 'saw off Brenda Hale and got Brexit done'. Yet it is hard to see how this can be true, given that the Supreme Court, of whom Lady Hale was the president at the time, quashed Johnson's prorogation of Parliament.[21] It is hard to see how Lady Hale was seen off when she retired according to the rules setting out the retirement age of Justices of the Supreme Court at the time and is now, as Baroness Hale of Richmond, a member of the House of Lords.

This willingness to use rhetoric and criticize those whose role it is to hold the government to account is a further indication of populism. Populists believe that the will of the people is more important than the institutions of government – for example, Parliament and the courts – which are occupied by 'elites'. The government should only act in line with the will of the people. When the will of the people contradicts Parliament or the courts, the will of the people should prevail. Yet this will of the people is the will as determined by the populist leader, often using rhetoric which plays fast and loose with the evidence.

What is really going on?

When speaking in support of the motion of confidence in the government, Boris Johnson was interrupted by Kevin Brennan, the Labour MP for Cardiff West, who asked:

> Is not the essential problem that despite the litany of what he thinks are his fantasy achievements, the bottom line is that this country is supposed to operate on the good chap theory of government, but it does not operate when there is a bad apple at the core?[22]

Johnson's only response was to state that he was proud of his achievements. It is this failure that motivated Lord Hennessy's diary entry.

Lord Hennessy's work explains how the UK's political constitution relies on the 'good chaps' theory of government. It relies on self-restraint and respect for other institutions of the constitution. We do not need formal, legal means of enforcing the Ministerial Code if all those it governs accept that the code's guidelines and provisions are indicators of good behaviour that all should follow. There is no need to require people to act in line with what they accept is the right way to behave. Nobody needs to tell people to be polite, or to queue at the bus stop. They are just part of what it means to act in the right way as understood by those who are being polite and standing in a queue. No rules are needed to enforce these practices. But what happens when these guidelines are no longer accepted as the right thing to do, or when those in power think they should no longer limit their actions?

For Lord Hennessy, these guidelines are being undermined and too many ministers no longer think their actions should be limited.[23] While this was more prevalent when trying to achieve Brexit, implementing the outcome of the referendum, it has continued post Brexit. Lord Hennessy thinks that Boris Johnson was 'the great debaser in modern times of decency in public and political life, and of our constitutional conventions'.[24] Is he right? And why does it matter if he is?

I will argue that it matters because constitutions are not just about power. They are also meant to uphold good standards of government.

The electorate deserves a government that represents all its interests and that acts in a manner that upholds good standards. There are good reasons why we do not want ministers who knowingly mislead Parliament, or who think the rules do not apply to them.

While the Johnson era may have ended, this does not mean that the constitution is healthy. After all, if one prime minister can use populist rhetoric and ignore standards with apparent impunity, only resigning when his political party no longer trusted him to win the next general election, what's to prevent another prime minister, of whatever political persuasion, from acting in the same way in the future?

I don't think that the UK constitution is beyond repair, or that the only solution is to enact a written, codified constitution. I do think, however, that the post-Brexit constitution has overtones of populism. These signs of populism are potentially dangerous, particularly when they increase the powers of government and remove the ability of other institutions to hold the government to account for its actions. Moreover, in the UK's constitution, populism can erode principles of self-restraint and mutual respect, such that political checks no longer focus on upholding principled government.

What appears to be a potential weakness can also be a strength. If the electorate care about upholding principles of good government, then even if those in power are only concerned with maintaining power, their decisions will also have to take account of acting in the interests of good government. This is not to hold our institutions as blameless. More also needs to be done to ensure those who enter politics come from a more diverse range of backgrounds – be that socioeconomic, racial, gender (including transgender and non-binary), sexual orientation, religious or educational – as well as shoring up mechanisms through which we can hold those in power to account for their actions. The bottom line, however, is that the UK electorate gets the politicians and leaders it votes for. The more the electorate learns about how the constitution and government work, the easier it is for them to use their votes for those they believe deserve to govern as well as those they believe will best represent their interests and achieve the public good.

There may not be evidence of a clear plan of a populist leader in the UK to take over the constitution and, ultimately, to overthrow democracy. While some constitutional changes have increased the powers of the government and reduced checks and balances from Parliament and the courts, there is no evidence of an undermining of the key principles of the UK constitution.

There are, however, indications of the more subtle effects of populism. Most worryingly, there are signs that some of those in government do not accept that their actions should be limited by standards of good constitutional behaviour. Integrity gets in the way of getting things done. Self-restraint is not needed if you are charged with implementing the will of the people. Why worry about the rule of law if it stops you from doing what the people want? It is these more subtle changes that concerned Lord Hennessy so greatly.

Conclusion

The 12 April was a dark day for Lord Hennessy because the prime minister had 'broken the law', 'misled Parliament' and 'shredded the ministerial code'.[25] It showed that those in power did not behave as 'good chaps'. The standards of government were eroded and the constitution failed to hold the prime minister to account for his actions.

We are living in worrying times. The UK constitution is standing on the precipice of a constitutional cliff edge. But there is still time for our constitution to step back. To do so, it needs you. The UK constitution works best when the electorate understands its strengths and vulnerabilities. It needs both the institutions of the constitution and the electorate to work together to ensure those in power are not just concerned with implementing the will of the people, but with listening to all to help determine the public good, governing in a manner that respects good principles of constitutional government.

2

What Is Populism and Should We Be Worried?

It's hard to read about Brexit and its aftermath without seeing the word 'populism', or to see a leader or political movement described as 'populist'. Populism is not used neutrally. It's used as a criticism. Populism is bad. Populist leaders are demagogues in disguise. It's a small slide down a very slippery slope from populism to authoritarianism.

Is populism that bad? After all, the central element of populism is a desire to ensure that government is in line with the will of the people. If there is a conflict between the will of the people and the will of Parliament, then surely, we would want the will of the people to win. We vote for the members of the House of Commons. Members of Parliament should act in line with the wishes of the people. That, after all, is what we would expect in a representative democracy.

This tension between the will of the people and the will of Parliament came to a head in 2019. A majority of those voting in the Brexit referendum voted in favour of the UK's withdrawal from the European Union (EU) treaties. Yet, the majority of MPs were in favour of remaining in the EU. The referendum decision was interpreted as requiring the government and Parliament to implement the will of the people and ensure the UK withdrew from the EU treaties. This obligation did not come from legislation. The government and Parliament were not legally required to leave the EU following the outcome of the Brexit referendum. Nevertheless, Parliament conceded that the referendum created a moral or a political obligation to implement its outcome.

The process of leaving the EU, however, was regulated by law: the EU treaties. Article 50 of the Treaty of European Union set a clear timetable. Once the EU was given notice of a state's intention to leave the EU, the two-year clock started ticking down. The UK had until 29 March 2019 to negotiate a deal or automatically leave the EU, unless it could agree on an extension to the two-year time limit with the EU.

After extensive negotiations, Theresa May's government and the EU reached an agreement in November 2018, the first withdrawal agreement. The withdrawal agreement is an international treaty. Normally, treaties are ratified by the government. Any treaty is then laid before Parliament, which may vote against ratification. However, this does not provide Parliament with the power to veto the ratification of the treaty. Rather, it triggers a further 21-day period in which Parliament can vote to ratify a treaty. This process can go on indefinitely. Parliament may delay and potentially block but cannot veto the ratification of a treaty.[1]

However, Parliament was given a larger role with regard to the ratification of the withdrawal agreement in the provisions of the European Union (Withdrawal) Act 2018. The government could not ratify the withdrawal agreement unless the House of Commons voted in favour of ratification and also voted in favour of the framework for a future relationship with Europe. Also, an Act of Parliament was needed to implement the agreement. This gave the Westminster Parliament veto power. It could vote against the ratification of the withdrawal agreement. It could also refuse to enact legislation to implement the withdrawal agreement into UK law.

The House of Commons was also given further powers. If Parliament did not vote in favour of the withdrawal agreement, the government had to provide an opportunity for further debates in Parliament. These were referred to as 'meaningful votes', enabling Parliament to debate government statements and discuss how it wanted the government to proceed.[2]

This backdrop set the stage for what, at times, felt like a war between Parliament and the government. Some tension is usual in the Westminster Parliament. But the events of 2019 were different. This was not just a struggle between Parliament and the government. The government also argued that they were representing the people. The people had voted in favour of leaving the EU. The government was trying to implement that will. Parliament was not checking the government; it was arguably thwarting the will of the people by putting obstacles in the way of the UK's exit from the EU.

Members of Parliament, however, also claimed that they were representing the will of the people. While the referendum told us that a majority of the people wanted the UK to leave the EU, it said nothing about what the people wanted instead of EU membership. Concerns were raised in particular over the Northern Ireland Protocol. This protocol was needed to ensure that there was no hard border between Ireland and Northern Ireland. To achieve this, the protocol regulates trade between other parts of the UK and Northern Ireland, requiring those goods that may travel from Northern Ireland to Ireland to be checked before they leave Scotland, England or Wales to be exported to Northern Ireland.

Did the people want this protocol that effectively set up a border in the Irish Sea between the rest of the UK and Northern Ireland? Should the UK leave with a bad deal that may harm the public good or even no deal at all? Does it matter if this is what the people want? Surely, it is the job of MPs to ensure that all of their constituents are represented, and to check that the government are acting in the best interests of the UK electorate. But would this extend to preventing the UK from leaving the EU with a bad deal, or no deal, if doing so would harm the electorate?

Who was right? Was this just a tension between 'Leavers' and 'Remainers', or can we see this more as a tension between different understandings of democracy? If so, was one side best understood as populist and, more worryingly, did that side win?

Riding the 2019 parliamentary rollercoaster

Constitutional law does not normally make the headlines. In 2019, however, it seemed that it had taken over the airwaves. Having finally reached an agreement with the EU in November 2018, the stage was set. Problems first arose on 15 January 2019, when the House of Commons voted against the first withdrawal agreement by 342 votes to 202. This marked the largest governmental defeat since universal suffrage. It triggered a vote of no confidence in the government which took place the next day. Under the provisions of the Fixed-term Parliaments Act 2011, which was then in force, if the government had lost the vote of no confidence, there would have been a 14-day period in which a government could try and obtain a vote of confidence and, failing that, Parliament would be dissolved, and a general election called. However, although there was a majority of the Commons in favour of rejecting the withdrawal agreement, the majority of MPs still had confidence in Theresa May's government and the vote of no confidence failed.

This left the Prime Minister in a dilemma. She had very little time to get Parliament to agree to the withdrawal agreement to ensure the UK left the EU with a deal according to the original timetable. Theresa May also seemed reluctant to leave the EU with no deal but did not want to extend the negotiation period. A number of 'meaningful' votes took place, debating the Prime Minister's response. On 29 January, the Commons voted against leaving the EU with no deal. It did so again on 13 March. In the meantime, Theresa May had failed to get the Commons to endorse the withdrawal agreement, losing another vote on 12 March. Following a vote of the Commons in favour of asking for an extension on 14 March, the Prime Minister, on 20 March, asked the EU for an extension to the negotiation period. She agreed to the shorter of the extensions offered by the EU, resetting the Brexit deadline to 12 April.

Why did the Prime Minister agree to something she had originally refused? The simple answer is that she was put under political pressure from Parliament to do so. It was clear that Parliament did not wish to approve Theresa May's deal set out in the withdrawal agreement. It was also clear that a majority of MPs in the House of Commons were not willing to leave without a deal. This was clear from the outcome of the many meaningful votes. In addition, backbench and opposition MPs had tried to initiate private members' Bills – legislation that is started by MPs who are not part of the government – requiring the Prime Minister to ask for an extension of the Article 50 negotiation period. These attempts had failed. But they nevertheless ratcheted up the political pressure on Theresa May.

The first extension proved to be too short. On 25 March, the Prime Minister failed, again, to obtain sufficient votes in the Commons to support her withdrawal agreement. In a series of indicative votes on 1 April, the only consensus to emerge from the Commons was a desire that the UK should not leave the EU with no deal. Should the Prime Minister ask for a further extension?

This time around, the pressure placed by Parliament on the Prime Minister increased.

Yvette Cooper and Oliver Letwin succeeded in getting a private members' Bill through Parliament. They did so by using time set aside for a meaningful vote and succeeded in proposing an amendment to the government's motion. The Commons voted to suspend Standing Order No. 14, the internal rule of the House of Commons that prioritizes government business. In place of the government's agenda, the Commons voted to enact all three stages of the Cooper/Letwin Bill through the House of Commons in one day. The House of Lords then agreed to expedite the progress of the Bill. This became the European Union (Withdrawal) Act 2019. It required a vote in the Commons on whether the Prime Minister should seek a further extension to the Article 50 negotiation period. If the vote succeeded, the Prime Minister was legally required to seek an extension.

This pressure motivated the Prime Minister to seek a further extension to the Article 50 negotiation period, which she did after the Commons had voted on the Cooper/Letwin Bill, but before the Bill was approved by the House of Lords or had received royal assent. The government then agreed with the EU to an extension of the negotiation period until 31 October. Again, political pressure from Parliament forced the Prime Minister to act. The failure to obtain consent for the withdrawal agreement led to the Prime Minister announcing on 24 May that she would be resigning as leader of the Conservative Party on 7 June, staying on as Prime Minister until a new leader had been chosen. This triggered a leadership contest. Conservative MPs voted for a new leader of their party and, by doing so, also chose the next Prime Minister.

Boris Johnson became Prime Minister on 24 July 2019. After a brief hiatus, the battle lines were drawn again as the new Prime Minister sought to implement Brexit, stating from the beginning that the UK would leave the EU on 31 October 2019, even if this was with no deal. With a new Prime Minister came a new agenda and a change in approach. In late August, the Prime Minister advised Queen Elizabeth II to prorogue Parliament from a date between 9 and 12 September until 14 October. In 2019, the UK had fixed-term Parliaments that lasted for five years, unless there was an early general election. Parliamentary terms are split into sessions, which normally last for a year. Parliament is prorogued to bring one session to an end before a new session starts after the Monarch's Speech. When prorogued, Parliament does not sit. Bills introduced in a particular parliamentary session, but which have not been enacted before prorogation, normally lapse unless measures have been taken to carry over the Bill into the following parliamentary session.

The Prime Minister's prorogation was longer than usual. It was also suspected that Parliament was not just being prorogued to facilitate the writing of the then Queen's Speech. Was Parliament instead being prorogued to stop rebel backbench and opposition MPs from thwarting the Prime Minister's plans for Brexit? If so, was this acceptable as the Prime Minister was using prorogation to implement the will of the people, which Parliament was trying to frustrate?

Legal challenges were brought to the announcement of the decision to prorogue Parliament. Gina Miller, an investment manager and campaigner, brought her case to the English courts. Joanna Cherry, a Westminster MP, brought her challenge in the Scottish courts. Meanwhile, MPs returned to Parliament on 3 September 2019, following the summer recess, with prorogation hanging over their heads. That day saw Oliver Letwin propose an emergency debate, using the procedures of Standing Order No. 24. If the Commons votes in favour of a motion proposed in an emergency debate, this takes priority over the business of the government. Oliver Letwin used the emergency debate to propose a motion to suspend Standing Order No. 14, and, instead, set out a timetable to push through all three stages of a private member's Bill, proposed by Hilary Benn, which aimed to prevent the UK from leaving the EU with no deal. Having succeeded in pushing the Bill through the Commons, the Bill then went to the House of Lords on 5 and 6 September 2019.

In the meantime, the Prime Minister tried to achieve an early parliamentary general election. To do so, he needed to achieve a vote in favour of an early election from two-thirds of all MPs, a condition set by the Fixed-term Parliaments Act 2011. Although a majority of MPs did vote in favour of an early general election on 4 September 2019, there were not enough votes to satisfy the legal requirement of the support of two-thirds of the House of Commons. The Prime Minister tried again on 9 September. Again, too few MPs voted in favour of an early general election. Eventually, Boris Johnson prorogued Parliament on 9 September, but not before the Benn Bill received royal assent, becoming the European Union (Withdrawal) (No 2) Act 2019.

This Act went further than the one proposed by Yvette Cooper and Oliver Letwin. It set a deadline of 19 October 2019 for the Commons to either vote in favour of a withdrawal agreement or to leave the EU with no deal. If this vote did not succeed, then the Act required the Prime Minister to seek another extension of the negotiation period under Article 50 until 31 January 2020. An appendix to the Act set out the wording of the letter to be sent by the Prime Minister requesting this extension.

The legal challenge to prorogation succeeded in the Supreme Court on 24 September 2019. The Court concluded that the prorogation was unlawful and, therefore, should be quashed. Parliament thus returned on 25 September, only to be prorogued, this time lawfully, on 8 October, with a Queen's Speech starting a new session of Parliament on 14 October, a mere five days away from the deadline set by the European Union (Withdrawal)(No 2) Act. Parliament, unusually, sat on 19 October, a Saturday, to try and finally reach an agreement. However, the Commons refused to vote either in favour of the withdrawal agreement or to leave the EU with no deal. This left Boris Johnson with no choice but to seek a further extension under the terms of the Benn Act, although he did so reluctantly.

A further extension, however, did not resolve the dilemma. It only delayed the outcome. The Prime Minister introduced a new Bill on 21 October 2019 which aimed to implement the withdrawal agreement with a renegotiated Northern Ireland Protocol. The Bill had its second reading on 22 October. The Prime Minister hoped to get the Bill passed through Parliament in time to leave the EU on 31 October. Bills are normally accompanied by a programme motion, setting out the time allocated for deliberation on the Bill. The programme motion allocated just two days for the Bill's provisions to be discussed in a Committee of the whole house. The Commons did not think this provided sufficient time. A majority of MPs voted against this timetable, effectively placing the Bill in limbo.

On 28 October 2019, the Prime Minister sought a further early parliamentary general election and, once more, succeeded in obtaining a majority of votes, but not the two-thirds of MPs required. The next day, the Prime Minister introduced the Early Parliamentary General Election Bill 2019. This Bill provided for an early parliamentary general election on 12 December. As an Act of Parliament, a simple majority was enough to ensure the Bill was passed by the House of Commons. The Bill was pushed through Parliament in three days, receiving royal assent on 31 October. Parliament was then dissolved on 6 November, to prepare for the general election on 12 December 2019. Boris Johnson returned to Parliament as Prime Minister with a large majority of 80 as opposed to leading a minority government. He succeeded in enacting legislation to implement the UK's withdrawal from the EU, with the UK leaving the EU and entering the transition phase, governed by the withdrawal agreement, on 31 December 2020.

What are we to make of these events? They were certainly unusual. For Boris Johnson, Parliament was consistently 'delaying and sabotaging the negotiations, because Members do not want a deal'.[3] The Prime Minister, on the other hand, was trying to implement the will of the people, expressed in the referendum, to leave the EU. He blamed the opposition further for going to the courts to delay Brexit, rather than voting in favour of an early election and allowing the electorate to choose. As he put it most starkly in his statement to the Commons on 25 September:

> It is not just that this Parliament is gridlocked, paralysed, and refusing to deliver on the priorities of the people. It is not just unable to move forward. It is worse than that, Mr Speaker. Out of sheer political selfishness and political cowardice, Opposition Members are unwilling to move aside and give the people a say. They see MPs demanding that the people be given a say one week, and then running away from the election that would provide the people with a say. Worst of all, they see ever more elaborate legal and political manoeuvres from the Labour party, which is determined, absolutely determined, to say 'We know best', and to thumb their noses at the 17.4 million people who voted to leave the European Union.[4]

He then added that 'the electorate are being held captive by this zombie Parliament and this zombie opposition'.[5]

For the Prime Minister, therefore, the situation was clear. He stood for democracy. His job was to ensure that he implemented the will of the people. Parliament was not backing the will of the people. It was not democratic. Therefore, a general election was needed to allow the electorate to vote for a new Parliament that would back the will of the people.

Is this the only perspective? The alternative is to argue that the Prime Minister may have thought he was representing the will of the people, but, in reality, he was only representing those in the electorate who voted to leave the EU at any cost, including if this meant leaving with no deal. Yet, while a majority of those who voted in the referendum chose to leave the EU, this was not the same as a majority of the electorate as a whole. Not everyone voted in the referendum. To add further, and more serious complications, while a majority of those who voted in England and Wales voted to leave the EU, a majority of those who voted in Scotland and Northern Ireland wished to remain in the EU.

The majority of those voting in the UK as a whole may have voted to leave, but there was no consensus as to how the UK wished to leave, or as to the future relationship the UK wished to have with the EU. There were also huge divisions over the Northern Ireland Protocol, particularly as, while this avoided a border between Northern Ireland and Ireland, it imposed a border between the rest of the UK and Northern Ireland.

If we agree, Boris Johnson was not being democratic. He was being populist. His appeal was to a clear will of the people. Yet, the reality was more complex, particularly when discussing the will of the people of Scotland and Northern Ireland as opposed to the will of the people in England and Wales.

Moreover, Boris Johnson was a more charismatic leader than Theresa May. His statements tended to be more colourful, using dramatic analogies and metaphors, often appealing to the will of the people. This is seen by some as another sign of populism. Populist leaders tend to be charismatic. They tend to rely on rhetoric to win arguments, rather than through appeals to reason, or relying on consensus achieved through deliberation.

Additionally, Boris Johnson gave a strong criticism of Parliament. His decision to prorogue Parliament, and to criticize the judgment of the Supreme Court, could be interpreted as a belief that, as he is implementing the will of the people, there is no need for his actions to be checked by either Parliament or the courts. This, arguably, is a further sign of populism: a mistrust of experts and a willingness to reduce both political and legal checks over a populist leader, given that these checks too should not be allowed to limit the ability of the government to act in line with the will of the people.

Was Boris Johnson upholding democracy, or was he a populist? Does it matter?

What is populism?

Populism is notoriously difficult to define. Some of this difficulty stems from the fact that populism is often used as an insult. How can we tell when a party, movement or leader is populist or is just accused of being populist by their political rival as an insult, rather than a serious accusation?

If that were not bad enough, there is even disagreement about what populism is describing. Is populism a set of beliefs, a way of talking about politics, or a tactic used by leaders or parties to gain political power?

When used to describe a set of beliefs, populism is referred to as an ideology. In this sense, populism is similar to socialism, or principles of conservatism. Yet, unlike these other political ideologies, populism is not necessarily connected to right-wing, left-wing or centrist political ideologies. It is referred to as 'thin-centred'. This means there can be many different types of populism. For some, Jeremy Corbyn was a left-wing populist, with Boris Johnson a right-wing populist. For others, UKIP, or perhaps more clearly the BNP, are nationalist populists. Yet there is very little else in common between these political leaders and political parties, all of whom may be seen by some as populist. This can make it even harder to provide clear examples of those leaders or parties who advocate a populist ideology.

Populism may also refer to how we conduct politics. Understood in this sense, populism tends to be seen as inevitable. In multicultural societies, there will always be some minority groups whose voices are not heard. Populism appeals to these minorities. It explains how these groups are the 'real people' whose voices have been neglected. Politics is a form of communication. Populism is about communicating and empowering those who are ignored. All politics, in a sense, is populist. What changes is what we mean by 'the people'. Once one group has been brought into the mainstream of politics, another ignored 'people' is discovered and becomes the basis of another populist movement. Understood in this sense, it becomes even harder to distinguish between populism and politics more generally. It's also difficult to see why populism is problematic. Surely politics is meant to be about ensuring all voices are heard so that the decisions of political actors are truly representative and therefore more legitimate?

Populism as a tactic is perhaps the weakest definition of populism. It is neither setting out an ideology nor explaining how politics can be understood over time. Rather, it is a way of appealing to voters, or of winning general elections. Political parties or political leaders are populist because they appeal to the will of the people, knowing that to do so wins them political support. However, is this really being populist, or just being democratic?

All of these versions of populism are hard to distinguish from one another. How do we know if a political leader really believes in populism as an ideology, or is just using populism as a tactic? Is populism merely the same as normal politics, where groups constantly gain and lose political influence? If so, why bother defining populism at all and why worry about whether a particular leader is, or is not, populist?

This is why it is so hard to understand whether the Brexit referendum and the events of 2019 prove that the UK is populist. We know that Boris Johnson frequently referred to the will of the people and the need to get Brexit done. But this does not mean that the then Prime Minister believed in an ideology that prioritizes the will of the people over the will of the political elites. He is, after all, a member of that elite.

He may also have fervently believed that leaving the EU was the right choice for the UK. He campaigned for 'Vote Leave'. Appealing to the will of the people may well have been the best tactic to achieve Brexit. Even MPs who campaigned to remain in the EU recognized the need to implement Brexit once this had been backed by the referendum vote. The Prime Minister could also argue that this was all just politics as usual. MPs need to win votes. If a majority in a referendum vote to leave the EU, it's difficult to ignore that and still retain your seat at the next general election.

Populism may seem impossible to pin down. However, three common themes run through accounts of populism. First, populism focuses on the importance of 'the people' and of ensuring that politics implements 'the will of the people'. We saw this, for example, in explanations for why the events of 2019 should be spurned rather than welcomed. What happened in 2019 was not about the House of Commons taking control from the government. It was about MPs rejecting the will of the people.

Second, populism believes in popular and not parliamentary sovereignty. This does not mean that populism only believes in direct democracy, that the people should make all political decisions themselves through, for example, referendums or mass online voting. Rather, institutions should act in line with the will of the people as these institutions only have power because it has been granted to them by the people. Parliament may be sovereign in the UK. But that is because it is elected by the people – the true sovereign. When there is a battle between Parliament and the will of the people – backing Brexit, for example – in a referendum, it's the people who should win. MPs should vote for Brexit, as delegates of the people, even if this is not their personal preference.

However, different types of populism have different definitions of 'the people' who are, in turn, meant to be sovereign. They may be defined according to their social status; whether they live in rural or urban areas, or inside or outside the Greater London area; those who are 'British' as opposed to immigrants; or those who just get on with their lives, pay their taxes and don't cause trouble. During the 2019 crisis, 'the people' were those who had voted for Brexit in the referendum.

Third, populism believes there is an antagonism between the people and elite institutions. Elite institutions can be those that perform governmental functions: for example, Parliament, the government or the courts. They may also include experts who are known to advise the government, be they scientists advising the government on COVID-19 or climate change, economists advising on monetary policies, lawyers providing legal advice on domestic or international law, or academics advising on structures of government.

We can see this, for example, in the press reaction to the decisions of the court in the two cases brought by Gina Miller. In 2017, Gina Miller and others went to court to argue that the government did not have a prerogative power – a power inherited from the Crown whose limits are set by decisions of the courts, rather than given to the government by legislation – to inform the EU of the UK's intention to withdraw from the EU treaties. The divisional court agreed. The *Daily Mail* infamously reacted to this judgment with the headline 'Enemies of the People'. The article went on to state that there was 'fury' over the decision of 'out of touch' judges, who had 'declared war on democracy', defied the wishes of 17.4 million voters and caused a constitutional crisis.[6]

In 2019, Gina Miller and others went to court to challenge the Prime Minister's decision to advise the Monarch to prorogue Parliament. When Parliament returned, the Prime Minister, while disagreeing with the Supreme Court, nevertheless respected their decision. However, as discussed above, Boris Johnson did criticize Parliament. He accused the opposition of cowardice and selfishness because they were standing in the way of the 17.4 million voters who had voted for Brexit.

This antagonism between the people and the elites need not be real. What matters is how arguments are presented. Populism is antagonistic. Politics is about disagreement. But sometimes this disagreement can be resolved through discussion that leads to concessions, compromise, consensus and mutual understanding. Populism thrives on antagonism. It is 'us versus them'. There is no desire to achieve consensus. Compromise and consensus are weaknesses, not a strength. Brexit meant Brexit. It was all or nothing.

This definition of populism is deliberately broad. Other definitions also explain how populism focuses on the people, seeing the people as in conflict with elites and recognizing that the will of the people should override the will of these elites. However, they also add further elements. We can see this, for example, in Jan-Werner Müller's widely accepted definition of populism. Müller adds two further criteria: anti-pluralism and the use of rhetoric as opposed to deliberation in political discourse.[7]

What do these two additional elements mean? First, populism is anti-pluralist as it homogenizes the will of the people and dissuades or silences dissent. In other words, populism does not recognize that 'the people' can be made up of many different groups, all of whom have a different voice. Rather, populism tends to find one of the groups who make up the electorate, or the population, which is then selected as representing 'the true' voice of the people. We can see this throughout Brexit, in both the press reaction to the *Miller* decision and Boris Johnson's reaction to Parliament. The will of the people that was being denied was that of the 17.4 million who voted for Brexit.

While it is true that this group did vote for Brexit and that they did form a majority in the UK, they are only a majority and not all of those who voted. Nor are they a majority of the population in the UK. Some chose not to vote in the referendum. Others would not have been eligible to vote. We also do not know why those 17.4 million voted for Brexit. Did they all have the same reason? Would they have all wanted the same type of Brexit and the same future relationship with Europe? Also, should we recognize that the UK consists of England and Wales, who voted to leave, and also Scotland and Northern Ireland where a majority voted to remain in the EU? Populism does not ask these questions. It groups the 17.4 million as one voice, focusing on that one vote. It homogenizes the will of the people rather than recognizing a plurality of voices.

Second, as previously mentioned, populism often relies on charismatic leaders. These leaders tend to use rhetoric. This links to the distrust of elites. Populist leaders tend to reject expert advice. Experts do not understand the will of the people. If they cannot be trusted, why should we follow their advice? Populist leaders also tend to reject deliberation. There is no need to engage with arguments from the other side. The will of the people is the ultimate trump card in any political debate. If, for example, arguments were made in 2019 that leaving the EU with no deal would create chaos, or undermine the UK economy, the simple response would be to reject these claims as far-fetched and as having little or no worth in the face of the will of the people. If the people wish to leave the EU, then we have to leave the EU, regardless of any arguments anyone may try to make for staying in the EU or for delaying Brexit.

It is these extra elements that lead to the conclusion that populism harms democracy. If we are to assess whether the UK is populist, we need to look for signs that there is one will of the people and that, as the people are sovereign, this will of the people should override the views of others, particularly those of experts or the elites, including politicians and the courts. We should also look for signs of antagonistic debate, where one side takes all and consensus or compromise is avoided, and rhetoric triumphs over deliberation.

Undermining the UK's constitution?

Populism may endanger the UK constitution by undermining democracy. Like populism, democracy is a term that has many definitions. There are arguments as to the type of democracy that is valuable, as well as whether we think democracy is more, or less, important than other values – for example, human rights. This book is not the place to enter into these debates. But, as with our discussion of populism, they do suggest that we should proceed with caution. To say that populism may harm democracy is not enough. We need to think about how it may harm democracy and why this may be a problem.

One of the values of democracy is that it aims to take decisions that represent the will of the people – representative democracy. Legislation affects those living, working, visiting or conducting business in the UK. We can be punished if we fail to follow these rules. Laws may also set out how we should act if we want to achieve our life goals; for example, it can set out whom we can marry, and how this is achieved, as well as regulate how we buy or rent homes and enter into contracts to buy other goods and services. We want these laws to be enacted in a representative manner so that we have a say, albeit indirectly, in the content of the rules that we follow. We want to ensure we have a voice when legislatures balance different interests to tackle problems; for example, when deciding whether to prioritize the needs of older people, young people, or those living in deprived areas when determining which groups should benefit from extra payments during the current cost-of-living crisis.

Populism undermines representative democracy when it homogenizes the will of the people. We no longer have decisions taken to balance the interests of the electorate. Decisions are taken to represent the will of a group of the electorate selected as the people. By only recognizing one set of views as 'the will of the people' other voices are silenced. They are no longer represented.

Similarly, the homogenization of the will of the people can harm another reason why democracy is seen as valuable. Democracy enables the electorate to take part in decision making – participatory democracy. This participation may be through encouraging the legislature to enact rules on a particular topic, by taking part in consultations designed to help the government form policy choices, or by scrutinizing draft legislation. However, if there is only one voice of the people, individuals and groups wanting to present an alternative view may find that their contribution is ignored. The government and legislature can ignore those voices that do not chime with the 'will of the people'.

Democracy is also valuable as it may help to make better decisions. Two heads are better than one. Those with specific knowledge of a complex area are better able to take good decisions than those who do not share this expertise. The more we share information and expertise, the more likely it is that we will reach a good decision. This is deliberative democracy, which recognizes the importance of deliberation to facilitate the sharing of knowledge and to help make informed policy choices that balance a range of interests and seek to achieve consensus. For example, laws that tackle climate change are for the good of all to ensure the long-term future of the planet. It is important to ensure that people have a say in whether this is a valuable aim and can explain the impact of its achievement on their lives and businesses. It is also important to ensure that experts are able to explain how aims can be achieved, as well as take account of the interests of future as well as current generations.

Deliberation can help find solutions that aim to balance different rights and interests. To return to legislation about climate change, for example, good legislation will hear from those affected by climate change and by climate change measures, aiming to balance these interests to reach a consensus across a range of groups. Populism undermines deliberative democracy by rejecting deliberations based on evidence or expertise. It pitches 'the people' against elites, thus downgrading the use of expertise. Moreover, its antagonistic form of debate undermines the ability to balance interests and achieve consensus. Consensus may weaken the views of 'the people'. The people win. Others lose out.

As well as these potential dangers to democracy, evidence from other countries that have been influenced by populism suggests other ways in which populist leaders may harm constitutions. Populist leaders in government can use their position to increase their powers and reduce the ability of other institutions to check or hold governments to account for the use of their powers. To demonstrate these dangers, we often point to clear examples where populist leaders have been able to take control of governmental powers and then use these powers to change the constitution to make it more authoritarian. The two examples often referred to that are geographically closest to the UK are Hungary and Poland.

In both of these states, we can point to evidence of a move to a more authoritarian government, despite both of these countries still being classed as democracies, with a constitution and legal protection of rights and constitutional standards. Both countries made changes to enhance the power of the executive and to weaken checks over these powers. These changes were both formal and informal. Formal changes occur when the rules regulating the constitution are changed. Informal changes occur when those in power modify how they use the powers given to them, without changing the rules that set out these powers.

In Hungary, for example, Viktor Orbán, the leader of the Fidesz party and the Hungarian Prime Minister, introduced a series of constitutional amendments to strengthen the powers of his government. First, he made it easier to change the constitution – moving from a requirement of four-fifths of the members of the legislature to two-thirds. As Fidesz could command two-thirds of the votes in the legislature, the change in the rules meant that constitutional change could take place with just the support of one political party. This significantly increased the powers of the executive.

Having gained this power, Orbán introduced a series of measures that reduced the ability of other institutions to check the actions of the government and the legislation initiated by the Fidesz government. For example, laws that reduced the powers of the constitutional court to check the legality of budgetary and fiscal measures. In addition, the rules were changed to make it easier for the Fidesz government to appoint judges to the constitutional court who were loyal to the aims of the government. This was achieved by increasing the number of judges, allowing the new judges to be appointed by the Fidesz government, and reducing the retirement age of the judiciary. This made it easier to remove incumbent judges and replace them with those loyal to the government. Similarly, changes made it easier for the government to appoint members of other bodies that would check the actions of the government – for example, the election commission, the media and the ombudsmen.

A similar pattern can be seen in Poland. Here, changes to constitutional rules focused on undermining legal checks on the government's powers. This was achieved through 'court packing', ensuring that the members of the constitutional court, which alone had the power to check the constitutionality of legislation, were loyal to the government. This was combined with a series of formal changes to the rules, making it harder for the constitutional court to check legislation – for example, by requiring a two-thirds majority of the constitutional court to agree that legislation was unconstitutional. This was combined with taking over the media, with government-backed businesses and those loyal to the government buying independent media organizations. This ensured that the media supported government policies and could stifle or stigmatize those who were critical of the government.

This would seem to suggest a connection between populism and a potential slide to authoritarianism, as well as areas of concern for those worried about whether a particular country is populist and, if so, whether this is undermining the constitution. However, it is also important to recognize that, in many ways, focusing on whether the UK is populist or not is a red herring. While we can point to a pattern of behaviour in Hungary and Poland, and both are widely regarded as having embraced a form of populism, this does not mean that populism alone caused the perceived harms to these constitutions.

Both Hungary and Poland are said to exemplify a particular form of right-wing populism. They also both appeal to a particular identification of the 'real' people, which focuses on historical and national claims of identity, designed to differentiate Poland and Hungary from Western liberal democracies. Given this desire to distance from Western liberal democracies, it is hardly surprising if these populist regimes enact measures which will be perceived by those in Western liberal democracies as undermining democracy and constitutionalism. Would the same problems arise if the UK was populist, but was not wishing to distance itself from the values found in Western liberal democracies in the same way or to the same extent?

It's also hard to use some of these indications in the UK which has a very different constitution from Poland and Hungary. The UK is a parliamentary democracy where the Monarch, rather than a president, is the head of state. A prime minister has different powers from those of a president. Prime ministers are also elected indirectly as opposed to directly by the electorate. The Monarch has the legal power to appoint a prime minister. By convention, he appoints the leader of the political party which can command the confidence of the House of Commons. This is usually the political party that has the most MPs. There is no constitutional court that can strike down legislation, so court packing would have less of an impact on the UK constitution than in Poland and Hungary. If we are to think about the dangers to the UK constitution, therefore, we need to think more carefully about the particular type of populism that the UK may be prone to. What signs do we need to look for to determine if this type of populism exists and is potentially undermining democracy and the UK's constitution?

Practical populism and the UK constitution

As we saw in Chapter 1, one of the key defining principles of the UK constitution is parliamentary sovereignty. The UK Parliament can enact legislation on any subject matter it wishes. Unlike in countries with codified, entrenched constitutions or devolved parliaments, there are no legal limits on the law-making powers of the UK Parliament. Acts of the UK Parliament are the highest form of law in the UK. They often regulate key constitutional principles.

Any future Parliament can specifically or expressly overturn legislation enacted by an earlier Parliament – even legislation that regulates constitutional principles. The European Union (Withdrawal) Act 2018, for example, overturned the European Communities Act 1972. This was needed to secure Brexit. The 1972 Act was constitutional legislation designed to ensure EU law was implemented in the UK. The 2018 Act was also constitutional legislation, designed to implement the UK's decision to withdraw from the EU treaties. Acts of Parliament were used to change the constitution in one direction and then, later, change it back.

It is easier, therefore, for a populist leader in the UK to modify legislation regulating constitutional issues. This may appear to make populism more dangerous in the UK. Without constitutional safeguards, a populist leader may quickly enact legislation, using their parliamentary majority in the House of Commons, to undermine democracy or remove checks and balances over executive power, and remove or limit human rights. Equally, however, any such changes may be short-lived. Any populist leader will face a future general election and, if power is lost, a new government may quickly reverse the legislation of an earlier populist government.

It is also harder for any populist leader to enact legislation to extend the life of Parliament in order to enjoy power for longer. Any such legislation currently requires the consent of the House of Lords. The House of Commons cannot use the Parliament Acts 1911 and 1949 to overturn a veto of the House of Lords. To modify this requirement, any populist government would first need to change the Parliament Acts 1911 and 1949 – although, as was the case with the Parliament Act 1949, this can be done without the consent of the House of Lords. These provisions may slow down, if not prevent, a populist government from extending its term in office.

Parliamentary sovereignty also explains other key features of the UK constitution. The UK is regarded as having a predominantly political as opposed to a legal constitution. This means that a large proportion of the rules governing how the constitution operates is found in constitutional conventions or other non-legally enforceable rules. Also, the UK constitution tends to evolve. Legislation or other rules are created to respond to particular constitutional issues, providing a specific fix for a perceived problem. The Fixed-term Parliaments Act 2011, for example, established a five-year fixed term for the House of Commons, in part, because this was regarded as necessary in a coalition. Otherwise, the coalition agreement may have been undermined if the Prime Minister – typically a member of the coalition party with the most seats in the House of Commons – were to choose a date for a general election that favoured his political party but not that of his coalition partner. The Dissolution and Calling of Parliament Act 2022, which returned the UK to a system of maximum-term Parliaments of five years, combined with a discretionary power on the part of the Prime Minister to request that the Monarch exercise his prerogative power to dissolve Parliament and call a general election, was regarded by Boris Johnson's government as a necessary fix for the 'zombie Parliament' of 2019. Both Acts changed the constitution, at least in part, in reaction to events.

The UK has not had a recent event that triggered a national discussion and acceptance of constitutional principles underpinning the UK constitution. While it has experienced constitutional problems that have required constitutional change – such as Brexit – this has not triggered a broader discussion of the series of principles underpinning the UK constitution, or of how they should be applied to determine the relative powers of Parliament, the government, and the courts. It focused on the pros and cons of one decision – Brexit – and how to implement that decision.

The distribution of powers between the institutions of government also evolves. Differently composed parliaments may give relatively more power to the government or to Parliament. The larger the majority of the political party of the government in the House of Commons, the easier it is for that party to push through its legislative agenda. The relationship between the courts, Parliament, and the government also changes over time. The Human Rights Act 1998, for example, gave the courts a larger role in the protection of human rights in the UK. The now-withdrawn Bill of Rights Bill 2022–23 was designed to partly reverse that role, and redress a perceived imbalance of power between the courts and Parliament.

The evolutionary nature of the UK constitution would tend to suggest that, in the UK, populism is most likely to be used as a political tactic, rather than as an ideology. If populism resolves a particular perceived problem in the constitution, then we may see more populist leaders and political parties. Once this problem has been resolved, we can expect populism to dwindle. Populism may work in the aftermath of the Brexit referendum, where the referendum provided an example of direct as opposed to indirect democracy. But its popularity as a political tactic may wane, to be replaced with a new tactic that is more likely to appeal to the electorate or ensure a particular political party gains power in the aftermath of Brexit.

We may also expect to see different ideologies influencing populism, only to be replaced by other ideologies. For example, we may expect to see left-wing and right-wing movements alternate. It may also be less likely that populist leaders are driven by an authoritarian agenda given that any such agenda may be short-lived as new problems arise and the rules are changed – again – to resolve this new problem.

However, the pragmatic and evolutionary nature of the UK constitution may also exacerbate the dangers of populism. They may generate a form of populism which draws on a different form of ideology – one focused not on principles underpinning political policies, but on principles underpinning the nature of the UK's constitution. This may include principles as to the relative powers of the institutions of government. Should we favour a system that tries to balance the powers of these institutions or one which favours giving more power to Parliament or to the government or to the courts?

Populism may be combined with an ideology which advocates giving more power to the government. This may be motivated by a perception that courts and legislatures have claimed too much power, tipping the balance of power in favour of these institutions, and weakening the powers of the government. Powers need to be restored to the government to achieve a better balance of powers. It may also be based on an ideological argument that the government should have more power than the other institutions of the constitution. Powers do not need to be balanced. They should tip in favour of the government. Such arguments draw on how the government is accountable to their political party, Parliament and the people, as discussed in the previous chapter when examining Partygate and the eventual resignation of Boris Johnson as Prime Minister. This means that the government is, in reality, more democratically accountable than the legislature. It is more legitimate, therefore, for the government to have more power.

Populism may also have a longer-term impact on the UK's constitution. The UK's political constitution relies on self-restraint and mutual respect. The events surrounding 2019 illustrate this point. Problems arose with the prorogation of Parliament in 2019 because, arguably, the Prime Minister did not act according to constitutional principles that would have advocated self-restraint and an acceptance of the role of Parliament in the Brexit process. The prorogation of Parliament had, in the past, mostly been of a much shorter duration than the prorogation proposed by Boris Johnson. Also, prorogation is normally used to ensure sufficient time to prepare the Monarch's Speech at the opening of Parliament. In 2019, it was argued that Boris Johnson, instead, was using prorogation to silence Parliament, preventing the House of Commons from influencing the terms surrounding the UK's exit from the EU.

There was little that Parliament could do to prevent this use of the prime minister's prerogative power to prorogue Parliament. Some argued that maybe the Monarch could and should have intervened to prevent this prorogation – although this would have been problematic. It would have required the Monarch to get involved in politics. The principles of self-restraint and mutual respect underpinning the UK constitution argue that the Monarch should not intervene in politically sensitive issues. In the end, the Supreme Court concluded that there were legal limits on the power of prorogation. However, these were only triggered in extreme circumstances, designed to protect the powers of Parliament. Even these limits could be breached, provided that the Prime Minister gave good reasons for doing so. As no reasons were provided, the Supreme Court could only conclude that this use of the prerogative power was unlawful. The Supreme Court, too, had an awareness of self-restraint and respect for Parliament.

These principles of self-restraint and mutual respect help to ensure a good balance of power between the institutions of government. When they are removed, that can drastically alter this balance of power. This illustrates a further danger of populism in the UK. In some ways, it can be easier to change behaviour rather than to change rules. In other ways, however, such changes may be more difficult. When there are long-standing traditions and customs as to how individuals should behave, these can be difficult to modify – as anyone who has ever failed to join a queue in the UK will know. It may take strong reasons to override these customs and traditions, challenging their often deeply held values.

This challenge to the constitution may stem from an ideology that believes that the government deserves to be regarded as the most important institution in the constitution, combined with a charismatic populist leader who can justify the government's actions as being in line with 'the will of the people'. This combination may provide a means for behaviour to change, challenging self-restraint and mutual respect. Once this change is accepted, it may become a newly accepted means of behaviour that is harder to modify in the future. The more this behaviour is seen to succeed, the harder it may be to change. Also, the changes in behaviour make it harder for other institutions to hold the government to account. This, again, may make behavioural change harder to modify and easier to have a long-term impact on the UK constitution. As so many of the checks on the government rely on self-restraint and mutual respect, changing behaviour may have a larger impact on the constitution than changing the rules.

To see if this has occurred, it is important to focus on whether a change in the rules, or in how institutions of the government behave, has shifted the balance of power towards the government and away from Parliament. Does the government have more powers, or is it using its powers in a way that means it has more powers in practice? It's also important to see if those institutions that can hold the government to account are still able to do so. Again, this means looking at whether the rules have changed, or if the way these rules are applied has changed. We also need to look broadly at a range of institutions – the media and other bodies that can hold the government to account are just as important as Parliament and the courts.

More fundamentally, we have to ask ourselves whether there are signs of a shift in ideology. Not in terms of whether leaders are left-wing, right-wing, or more focused on the political centre, but on whether there is a prevailing belief that the government should have more power because it represents the will of the people. If this is the case, then tactical uses of populism may have long-term effects that may undermine democracy and the protection of constitutional principles.

Cause for concern?

It is hard to deny that populism was used tactically. Both the governments of Theresa May and Boris Johnson appealed to the will of the people to achieve their policies. It is also hard to deny that Boris Johnson was a charismatic leader, whose style frequently relied on rhetoric. Although he accepted the decision of the Supreme Court, he was critical of its role and stated clearly that he thought the Court's decision that the prorogation of Parliament was unlawful was wrong. He did, however, abide by that decision. He was also critical of the role of Parliament. Backbench and opposition MPs were holding the government to account, but in doing so they were thwarting the will of the people. These arguments were used as an attempt to shore up the powers of the government, helping the government to achieve its policy objective of getting Brexit done.

As we will see in more depth in later chapters, the events of 2019 promoted later changes in the rules. The Prime Minister blamed the Fixed-term Parliaments Act 2011 for creating a zombie Parliament. It made it more difficult for Boris Johnson to call a general election to allow the people to have a say. The Dissolution and Calling of Parliament Act 2022 makes it easier for the Prime Minister to call for a general election. This may give a greater role for the people – but it does so only as and when the Prime Minister decides. The changes in the rules, therefore, enhance the powers of the government. They also reduce the ability of both Parliament and the courts to hold the government to account as regards a decision to dissolve Parliament and trigger a general election.

Boris Johnson also changed the rules of behaviour. We saw this in Partygate. We can also see this in the way in which he appeared to be impervious to criticism. Why should he act with self-restraint, or respect the wishes of Parliament, if he has the backing of the people? However, as discussed in the previous chapter, Boris Johnson was also removed from power. Does this mean that any populist turn, if one even took place, was a mere blip, quickly corrected?

To answer this, we need to think more carefully about whether the UK government not only uses populist tactics but also advocates an ideology of a strong government. The events of 2019, and ensuing constitutional changes, could be regarded as a legitimate redressing of the balance of power in the UK constitution. The government is meant to take a leading role in the negotiation of treaties, with Parliament having a smaller role in how treaties are implemented. Yet, in 2019, Parliament had a larger role. It issued directions to the government, rejecting leaving the EU with no deal and requiring the prime minister to seek an extension to the negotiation period. Parliament rejected the withdrawal agreement, making it impossible for the government to ratify that agreement until it was renegotiated.

Similarly, the prorogation case saw the courts take a historically important decision, quashing the prime minister's advice to prorogue Parliament. While this particular decision has not been effectively reversed for the future, legislation has been enacted to ensure that a similar legal check cannot be used to challenge a decision to dissolve Parliament and call a new general election. We will look at this in more detail in Chapter 3. There have also been recent changes to the powers of the courts (discussed in Chapter 8), though these have made little difference to the powers of the courts, unlike the changes seen in Poland and Hungary.

This may show evidence of a move to increase the powers of the government and reduce the extent to which it is held to account for its actions. This may just be to restore the traditional balance of powers, preventing Parliament and the courts from having too much power. However, this may also provide evidence of a shift in ideology – one where the government believes it is legitimate for it to have more power than other institutions. This is because the government – and not Parliament – is more likely to represent the will of the people and, therefore, should have more power. This argument is easier to make when coupled with populism, where the will of the people is said to be the same as the will of those who voted for the political party in power at the House of Commons, rather than the will of the electorate as a whole.

The events of 2019 alone may not show that the UK constitution is in danger. But they do point to a potentially worrying trend. They show how, even when Parliament was able to push back, the government was able to enact the will of the people. As we will see in future chapters, the government was then able to further increase its powers, particularly over when to dissolve Parliament and hold a general election. The more we are aware of the specific dangers of populism to the UK constitution, the more we can be on our guard to protect democracy and the UK's long-standing constitutional traditions.

3

Is the Government Getting Too Big for Its Boots?

We've seen that the UK Parliament enjoys parliamentary sovereignty. There are no legally enforceable limits on the legislation that can be enacted by Parliament. Its powers are absolute and unlimited. All legislation, including legislation providing for the protection of human rights, or setting out the powers of the government, is enacted through a simple majority vote in Parliament. This feature is one of the main ways in which the UK constitution is unique.

However, we've also noted that the government is formed from the political party that has the most seats in the House of Commons. We would expect governments to be able to rely on their political party to vote for their legislation. In the House of Lords, whose members are appointed or have a seat as a hereditary peer or bishop, rather than elected, the government may not have a majority of sympathizers. However, the powers of the House of Lords are limited; rightly so, given its composition. It may propose amendments to legislation, but the House of Commons may reject them. When this is the case, the most the House of Lords can do is to delay the proposed legislation. The provisions of the Parliament Acts 1911 and 1949 mean that the Commons can enact legislation without the consent of the House of Lords, save for legislation designed to extend the life of Parliament. Given the dominance of the House of Commons, and the dominance of the government in the House of Commons, is Parliament really sovereign? Or is the government sovereign?

One commentator famously concluded that it was indeed the government and not Parliament that was sovereign, referring to the

UK constitution as an 'elective dictatorship'. He was concerned not just about problems arising from any government's dominance of the House of Commons, but also the enlargement of both the members of government and the range of governmental powers, as well as the change he saw occurring in the relative influence of Parliament and the government over legislation.

Who was this commentator, and was he right to be concerned? If so, are these concerns still valid, or have they become even more alarming in the UK's post-Brexit constitution?

Elective dictatorship?

Our mysterious commentator was first worried that the House of Commons had little ability to scrutinize and amend legislation proposed by the government. The party machine meant that backbench Members of Parliament (MPs) always vote in favour of the government. The whip system makes sure of this: dangling carrots of promotions through the party ranks and threatening sticks of languishing on the backbenches in perpetuity or even having the whip withdrawn, losing party support and not being selected as a candidate at the next general election. Such was the fate, for example, of some of those members of the Conservative Party who voted against Boris Johnson's government over Brexit.

If that were not bad enough, our commentator argued that political debate was best understood as a form of ritual dance or show. The government could curtail debate over Bills. The government is in charge of the timetable in the House of Commons. It decides which Bills are debated, when, and even how much time can be spent analyzing the provisions of a Bill. This means the government can rush legislation through the Commons with little, if any, time for scrutiny.

It could be argued that the relative power of any government to ensure it can enact its proposed legislation is unproblematic. After all, they were elected on a manifesto, voted on by the electorate. A government is formed because the political party its members are drawn from won a majority of seats in the House of Commons. Surely it has the right to push through legislation, given this must represent the 'will of the people', or at least the will of the majority of the electorate? Our commentator would point to two flaws in this argument. First, the UK's voting system means that even governments with large majorities in the House of Commons do not enjoy a majority of the votes cast in general elections. We can see this in Table 1, setting out the results of general elections from 1997 onwards.

Table 1: General elections 1997–2019

Year	Government	Simple majority	Share of votes (%)
1997	Labour	177	44.3
2001	Labour	165	42
2005	Labour	64	36.1
2010	Conservative/Liberal Democrat coalition	76	Conservatives: 36.9 Liberal Democrats: 23.6
2015	Conservative	10	37.7
2017	Minority Conservative	16 short of a simple majority	43.4
2019	Conservative	80	44.7

These figures provide an account of the simple majority, calculated on the date of the general election.[1] This is calculated by subtracting the total number of seats won by the other political parties from the total number of seats won by the government's political party. This figure differs from the working majority of the government. This is because some MPs do not vote in the House of Commons. The speaker and deputy speaker do not vote as their role requires them to be impartial. Also, members of the Sinn Féin party do not take up their seats in the House of Commons. This tends to mean that working majorities are larger than simple majorities. Working majorities can also fluctuate over time if by-elections need to be held. It is also possible for a member of one political party to defect to another political party, or to become an independent MP. Even taking account of these subtleties, the bottom line still stands. Governments can have a large majority in the House of Commons despite not receiving a majority share of votes cast by the electorate.

Our commentator was also sceptical of the role of manifestos. Far from being a clear document, read by and agreed to by the electorate, it was more likely to be akin to an advertising brochure, read by a small proportion of the electorate. Maybe it is time to pause and reflect on whether you read the manifestos of any of the political parties that stood in the last general election. Or when, if at all, did you last read a general election manifesto? Yet, the political system pays great respect to these manifesto promises. Any government will justify its power to push Bills through Parliament because to do so is to act in line with the wishes of a majority of the electorate who voted for the government because of its manifesto promises. Also, the House of Lords, by convention, will not vote against, or propose wrecking amendments to, legislation included in the government's manifesto.[2]

If this were not bad enough, our commentator is scathing of the reality of making manifesto promises. It would be rare indeed for any opposition political party, for example, to be fully aware of the current state of the country, meaning it may make rash manifesto promises that it may later become unwise to fulfil if this party is elected to power. Even when governments are re-elected, meaning their manifestos may have been more likely to be based on accurate information, no government can fully predict the future. This was so vividly brought to our attention through the Covid pandemic, Russia's invasion of Ukraine and the current cost-of-living crisis.

The size of the government was also a problem for this commentator. Legislation sets some limits on the number of ministers a prime minister can appoint; the maximum number of paid posts is 109, with no more than 95 ministers being able to sit and vote in the House of Commons.[3] There is no limit, however, on the number of ministers who can be members of the House of Lords. In addition to ministers in the House of Commons, we also refer to the 'payroll vote'. This is an informal term referring to those who have a role in the administration, paid or otherwise. This can include very junior roles, for example, parliamentary private secretaries (backbench MPs who are not paid an additional salary, and who keep track of backbench opinion but are not members of the government). Those who are part of the payroll vote are expected to vote in favour of the government or resign. The only exception is when the government allows a free vote on a particular issue. The payroll vote is, normally, around 20 per cent of the total number of MPs. Ministers also tend to dominate political debate, which is unsurprising given that they will be briefed on complex Bills by the civil service. Other MPs may struggle to keep up with the length and breadth of legislative provisions.

It's not just in the House of Commons that we see the ever-increasing size of the government. Our commentator, who coined the phrase 'elective dictatorship', was concerned about the ever-growing budget of the government, not to mention the centralization of power in England, with more decisions taken in Parliament rather than by local councils. The public expenditure budget appears to be on a continual upward trend, peaking in 2020–21 at 52 per cent of gross domestic product, although this may be artificially high due to the fall in gross domestic product during the same period, given the impact of COVID-19. The number of individuals who are members of political parties is dwindling. The government appears to be becoming ever more remote from the electorate and increasingly under the sway of its political supporters and pressure groups.

By now, I'm guessing most readers are becoming sceptical of assertions made by a mysterious commentator. I've deliberately hidden the identity of this commentator, not because they are particularly controversial but because of the date when these criticisms were made. The commentator was Lord Hailsham, a hereditary peer who relinquished his hereditary peerage to become a Conservative politician and MP. He also served as Lord Chancellor from 1970 to 1974 and from 1979 to 1987. What is perhaps surprising is when Lord Hailsham delivered this speech. It comes from his Dimbleby Lecture – a series of lectures then televised and now broadcast on BBC Radio 4 – given in 1976.

Lord Hailsham's criticisms are just as relevant today as they were nearly 50 years ago. They reflect themes that have run through the chapters of this book so far. Lord Hailsham's assessment of the UK constitution as an elective dictatorship is based on the orthodox account of the UK constitution, setting out features that were as common in 1976 as they are today. This raises a deeper issue. Should we just accept that this is just how the UK constitution works, pointing out that it works well, for the most part? After all, we need a strong government if we are to ensure that we can govern the UK and respond to crises as and when they arise. An elective dictatorship is better than an unelected dictator. Or should we be worried that accusations of populism, and particularly of the problems that arise from an overly powerful executive, are nothing new? This may make the picture even bleaker, suggesting that an elective dictatorship may be closer to the horror of an unelected dictator than it is to an elected accountable government.

It is difficult to conclusively argue in support of or against Lord Hailsham's classification of the UK constitution as an elective dictatorship. It does seem hard to square with Boris Johnson's criticisms of the House of Commons in 2019, which we looked at in Chapter 2. If the House of Commons was a zombie Parliament, it was precisely because backbench and opposition MPs were preventing the prime minister from achieving his government's policy of 'getting Brexit done', even if that meant leaving with no deal. Admittedly, the circumstances of 2019 were unusual. Johnson was in charge of a minority government. Brexit caused divisions within as well as across political parties. For some backbench MPs, the issue was so constitutionally important that it was worth running the risk of losing the government whip and of not being selected as a candidate in a future general election. To make matters even more difficult, the government was no longer fully in charge of timing in the House of Commons. Brexit took place against the backdrop of Article 50 of the Treaty on European Union, a provision of EU law which set a strict timetable that could not be unilaterally changed by the government.

Even when not faced with such extraordinary situations, it is not always the case that the government can push through its legislation with no criticism or push-back. Many of these amendments may go unnoticed. Backbench and opposition MPs can talk to government ministers to point out potential problems, leading to the government accepting changes and proposing amendments to legislation. An accepted amendment, therefore, looks like a governmental change, yet it may have only been achieved because to do otherwise may lead to the government potentially losing a vote in the House of Commons; the real source of the amendment may be backbench or opposition MPs. Also, as we saw with Partygate, discussed in Chapter 1, Parliament, the party and ultimately the public can hold even prime ministers to account for their actions and force a resignation.

Rather than try and resolve this dilemma, this chapter will look further at Lord Hailsham's concerns that the executive is ever-growing. Is this a sign of one of the dangers of populism, enabling a government, should it wish to do so, to become more authoritarian and undermine democracy? Or is this just a recognition that, as societies become ever more complex, larger and stronger governments are needed to govern the UK effectively?

To try and answer this question, we will look first at the range of powers in the hands of the government, before assessing two recent changes. The first change is a constitutional change made by the Johnson government, making it easier for the prime minister to decide when to dissolve Parliament and hold another general election. The second change is part of a gradual evolution, exacerbated by Brexit and the Covid pandemic, of the growing use of delegated legislation and other forms of executive rule making rather than using Acts of Parliament.

Just how big are the government's boots?

As with most aspects of the UK constitution, the concept of the government has evolved. Historically, the government was connected to the Crown. The Monarch would delegate specific offices to individuals to carry out the tasks of government. As the nature of the Crown evolved, these offices were given not just as a reward or gift, but also because of an understanding that those holding these offices would exercise their powers with integrity. This, at the time, provided a sense of legitimacy for the use of these powers.

With the establishment of democracy and a Parliament, the UK began to seek democratic legitimacy for those members of the government who were developing policies and making laws, but not for those whose task it was to implement and administer these laws on a day-to-day basis. Over time, the state became more centralized, with the establishment of a civil service. More recently, there has been a further division, separating out those who help ministers to shape and implement policy choices and the agencies involved in the day-to-day administration of those policies; for example, between civil servants shaping policies on welfare, determining who should be entitled to welfare assistance and social care, and agencies that ensure welfare benefits are distributed to individuals who should receive them.

This can make it difficult to provide a precise definition of the powers of government. We will focus on the powers of the prime minister, cabinet ministers and other ministers in Westminster. Ministers initiate legislation. This can either be legislation designed to implement manifesto promises, or legislation which aims to implement a policy developed by the minister or their department to either solve a particular problem or to achieve a particular aim. If the minister is to be successful in ensuring their legislation is initiated, they need to persuade a cabinet committee – the Parliamentary Business and Legislation Committee – to place their Bill on the legislative timetable. This committee decides which proposed pieces of legislation will become Bills that will be introduced to Parliament.

To become law, any Bill needs to be agreed by the House of Commons, the House of Lords and the Monarch. In the Commons and Lords, this requires the Bill to go through three stages. At the first reading, the Bill is introduced. At the second reading, there is a debate on the main policy issues in the Bill. Then the Bill goes to the committee stage. This can either be heard by the House as a whole or in a Public Bill Committee. Here the sections of the Bill are discussed in detail, which may lead to the Bill being amended. Following the committee stage is the report stage, where the Commons can vote on the provisions of the Bill and make further amendments. Finally, the Bill is read for a third time and voted on in its entirety.

The process is similar in the House of Lords. However, there are two main differences. First, the House of Lords normally sits as a whole for the committee stage, rather than forming a specific committee to examine the provisions of the Bill. Second, the rules setting out the procedures of the House of Lords are different from those in the Commons. These set out specific periods between different stages of a Bill, as well as reports that should be produced before the committee stage of the Bill to aid deliberation of the House of Lords. These provisions can be waived if the House of Lords agrees. This can make it harder for the government to push through legislation in the House of Lords, given that it does not have the same element of control over the timing of debates in general, or on specific programme motions for Bills.

We normally regard the consent of the Monarch as a formality. The Monarch has the power to veto legislation. However, by convention, the Monarch will consent to legislation, unless advised by ministers not to do so. The last time this happened was in 1708 when Queen Anne refused royal assent to the Scottish Militia Bill on the advice of her ministers.

Lord Hailsham's argument that the UK was an elective dictatorship was based on the power of the government to initiate legislation, to be able to push through legislation using the whip system to control votes in the House of Commons, as well as using its ability to take charge of the legislative timetable to ensure its legislation was enacted. A prime minister may also threaten to make a vote a matter of confidence, forcing potentially rebellious backbench MPs to choose between voting against the legislation and, in turn, triggering a potential general election, or voting in favour of the legislation and retaining their seat in Parliament.

However, these are not the only powers of the government. The government, as part of the state, is different from individuals. Individuals living in the UK have the power to act, provided that there is no rule preventing that person from acting. For example, I have the power to join a gym as no law would make this unlawful. I would not have the power, however, to steal from the gym, as laws exist that make theft a criminal offence. The rules for the government are different. Governments only have the power to act when this is granted to them, either from legislation or from prerogative powers or, more controversially, from the common law.

Most powers are given to ministers by legislation. We tend to divide these into duties, discretionary powers, and the power to make delegated legislation. For example, the Social Security (Additional Payments) Act 2022 requires the secretary of state to ensure that additional payments are made to those receiving universal credit or disability benefits. This is a duty placed on the minister, which they have to fulfil. It also empowers the minister to make regulations about the administration of additional payments or modifications to whom those payments are made. The minister has the power to make delegated legislation to ensure their duty is fulfilled. The Act sets out the procedure to be used when making these regulations. Here, the regulations are subject to the negative procedure. They can be annulled if either the House of Commons or the House of Lords passes a resolution voting against the regulations. This gives the minister, in practice, a discretionary power. They can decide how the payments are to be made, and when, setting this out in delegated legislation, which is then checked by Parliament which may vote against the regulation as a whole if it disagrees with its provisions.

The government also derives powers from two other sources. First, the government may exercise prerogative powers. These are powers that, historically, belonged to the Crown but which are now exercised by ministers. The scope of these powers is determined by the courts. These include, for example, the power to enter into and to withdraw from treaties, to declare war and to deploy the armed forces, and to issue passports. Some prerogative powers remain with the Crown. We refer to these as personal prerogatives. They currently include, for example, the power to appoint the prime minister, to dissolve and prorogue Parliament, and to give royal assent to legislation.

Constitutional conventions govern how the Monarch exercises these prerogative powers. We've already discussed how constitutional convention requires the Monarch to always exercise prerogative power to grant royal assent to legislation unless advised by ministers not to do so. By convention, the Monarch will appoint as prime minister the leader of the political party that, because of the number of its MPs in the House of Commons, can command the confidence of the House of Commons. The Monarch will also normally grant a request from the prime minister to prorogue or dissolve Parliament.

Second, and more controversially, the government has what we refer to as 'third source' powers. These stem from the fact that the Crown is recognized as a 'corporation sole'. This is merely recognizing that the Crown, as far as the law is concerned, operates in the same way as other companies. The Crown can legally act in its own name, distinctly from the powers of the King acting as an individual, or the powers of others who work for the Crown. In other words, we recognize that there is a difference between the role of the Crown and the individual who is currently the Monarch. The Crown has general administrative powers that have been transferred to the government. In a similar manner to individuals, the government can exercise these powers provided that this is not prohibited by legislation or the common law. The government can use these powers to enter into contracts, employ staff, convey property and perform other management functions.

There is a dispute among academics as to whether the 'third source' of power exists. Some argue that this third source needs to be connected to legislation, such that these powers should be limited even further, and restricted to those that are ancillary to legislation which grants powers to the government. This is because, to do otherwise, we may undermine the distinction between the government and individuals, treating the government as if it too has the power to act, unless there is legislation restricting its actions. Yet, the government is meant to be different. It is meant to only be able to act if it can find a legal power empowering the government to act. It should also only act within the scope of the powers given to it by the law.

Even with this limitation, the government still has a lot of power. However, we can see how these are necessary. If the government does not have this power, it would be impossible for it to do its job properly. The government would not be able to govern effectively if it could not enter into contracts, create agencies to implement policy decisions or oversee the acts of others. These powers are also checked by Parliament and by the courts. Judicial review is used to ensure that the government acts within the scope of its powers, as well as ensuring it exercises its discretionary powers fairly and follows fair procedures. Parliament also checks the government, not just through having the ability to approve delegated legislation, but also through holding the government to account for its policy choices.

Given the need for these powers, why was Lord Hailsham so concerned about an elective dictatorship? His main concern was that the government could push through legislation on any subject it wanted, using its political power to achieve its policy choices. However, the enactment of Acts of Parliament does provide MPs with the ability to scrutinize legislation, even having the potential to veto legislation, as well as provide amendments. These opportunities are reduced when it comes to delegated legislation. The executive can also enact other measures that determine how it will exercise its discretionary powers or set out how legislative provisions should be applied in practice; this is often referred to as guidance. These measures have no parliamentary scrutiny. A recent concern is that the government is increasingly using these powers, particularly post Brexit and throughout the COVID-19 crisis. This change led one House of Lords committee to refer to these activities as government by diktat.[4] The committee is not alone in raising such concerns. Does this show that the government is gaining even more power and, if so, is this legitimate?

Lord Hailsham was also concerned about how the government can control the timing of general elections. In 1976, at the time of the Dimbleby lecture, the Monarch had the prerogative power to dissolve Parliament. By convention, the Monarch would agree to a request from the prime minister to dissolve Parliament. This effectively gave the prime minister power to decide when to call a general election. The only limit on these powers is the legislation determining the maximum term of Parliament of five years. Lord Hailsham was concerned that this gave the prime minister too much power, enabling him to choose a date which maximized the chances of his political party being re-elected at the next general election. This provision changed in 2011 when the Fixed-term Parliaments Act 2011 set fixed terms of Parliament at five years. This made it harder for the prime minister to determine the date of the general election. However, this was reversed in 2022, with the enactment of the Dissolution and Calling of Parliament Act 2022. Are these changes and concerns further evidence of the government having too much power?

Government by diktat?

No government can govern through Acts of Parliament alone. There would not be enough time to enact all of these measures through Parliament without making parliamentary scrutiny ineffective. Granting ministers the power to enact delegated legislation is necessary, even more so when governments are trying to keep up with societal changes that seem to become ever more rapid. We want legislation to make important policy choices while allowing ministers to take regular decisions to ensure these policy choices are implemented. For example, we would want Parliament to decide the general policy as to how the UK should deal with climate change, set achievable targets and ensure the UK's compliance with its international obligations. Parliament may decide it wants to reduce river and air pollution and move from fossil fuels to renewable energy to achieve these objectives. It may also set the targets to be achieved and a timeframe for their achievement. Delegated legislation would be needed to enact specific measures to ensure that pollution was reduced, setting acceptable levels of pollution, perhaps through a series of moving targets to achieve Parliament's deadline, and setting out how fossil fuels are to be reduced and renewable energy increased. We would also expect legislation to empower bodies to enforce these rules, perhaps through using inspectors to check that pollution levels were maintained, or through administering grants to enable establishments to switch from fossil fuels to renewable energy. Why is it a problem, then, if we see governments using delegated legislation?

Problems can arise when measures that we think should have had parliamentary oversight are, nevertheless, taken by ministers alone. This is a problem because delegated legislation has less parliamentary oversight than primary legislation. There are two main ways in which Parliament can oversee delegated legislation: the negative and the affirmative resolution procedure. There are no legally enforceable rules setting out which procedure should be used for different types of delegated legislation. Rather, this is set out on an ad hoc basis. When legislation creates a power to enact delegated legislation, it sets out which procedure should be used. We refer to legislation setting out a power to make delegated legislation as a 'parent' Act.

Under the negative resolution procedure, delegated legislation comes into force unless either the House of Commons or the House of Lords votes against the measure coming into force. Parliament normally has 40 days in which to vote against the delegated legislation. Most delegated legislation is enacted through the negative resolution procedure, with little, if any, scrutiny. Under the affirmative resolution procedure, a draft of the measure is placed before Parliament. Both Houses of Parliament have to vote in favour of the draft measure for this to come into force. Again, the parent Act can set out the period during which the vote has to take place.

Other procedures can be set out in the parent Act. These may provide for more, or less, scrutiny. For example, sometimes the parent Act will set out that measures have to be enacted through the 'made affirmative' procedure. Here, a measure is enacted by a Minister and will come into force. However, unless both Houses of Parliament vote in favour of the measure by a date set out in the parent Act, the measure lapses and no longer has legal effect. This may seem like a provision that gives the government greater power and provides Parliament with less scrutiny. However, it could be used in a way that enhances the scrutiny of Parliament if it is used instead of the negative procedure. This can be particularly useful also for emergency measures, enabling delegated legislation to be enacted when needed, but empowering Parliament to remove these measures if they are no longer required.

Other rarer provisions of enhanced scrutiny may provide for a draft or a proposal for delegated legislation to be laid before Parliament, providing both Houses of Parliament with a chance to comment on these measures, before a final version is laid before Parliament. The parent Act may also include a 'sifting procedure'. This may empower a minister to decide whether a particular measure should be enacted through the negative or the affirmative resolution procedure. Committees in both the House of Commons and the House of Lords can then look at the measure in question and decide that, although the minister wishes this to be enacted through the negative procedure, the affirmative resolution procedure would be more appropriate. This was used for measures enacted to implement Brexit and is also proposed for measures to replace retained EU law. To date, the opinion of these sifting committees, however, has only been advisory. The parent Act may also require ministers to provide further information when enacting delegated legislation – for example, explaining why the measure is needed. It is also possible for delegated legislation to have no real scrutiny at all, only being required to be laid before Parliament.

Delegated legislation, therefore, does have some parliamentary oversight. But this is not as effective as the oversight over Acts of Parliament. There is normally no ability for MPs or members of the Lords to amend delegated legislation. This means that they are faced with an all-or-nothing situation. An MP may think that a piece of delegated legislation is, on the whole, good, but one section may have problematic implications. It is very difficult for the MP to vote against the delegated legislation in this situation. Delegated legislation is also laid before both the House of Commons and the House of Lords at the same time. This may make it harder for the two Houses of Parliament to enter into a dialogue, working together to craft delegated legislation that is better able to achieve a democratically acceptable policy objective.

If that were not bad enough, how scrutiny occurs is different from how it works for Acts of Parliament. Any delegated legislation enacted through the affirmative resolution procedure is sent to the Joint Committee on Statutory Instruments, a committee composed of members of the House of Commons and the House of Lords. The role of this committee is to check that delegated legislation is within the power granted by the parent Act. This is a good check, ensuring that the government only enacts delegated legislation when it has the power to do so. However, other procedures show how difficult it can be for MPs and members of the House of Lords to scrutinize delegated legislation.

Even when the affirmative resolution procedure is used, this is normally not scrutinized by the House of Commons as a whole, although it can be when this is of particular importance. Rather, the provisions of delegated legislation will be looked at by a delegated legislation committee, which is usually composed of 17 MPs. Any MP can ask to attend and speak at the committee, but only those members of the committee can vote on the delegated legislation. If the members of the committee vote in favour of the draft delegated legislation, then the approval process has been satisfied. It is even harder for the negative resolution procedure to be used to overturn delegated legislation. An MP needs to move a prayer motion. This may be dependent on the government granting time for this motion. It may also be difficult to ensure MPs attend to vote on delegated legislation. This may explain why the last time an affirmative resolution failed was in 1978, and the last time a prayer motion was moved to annul delegated legislation was in 1979.

The situation in the House of Lords is just as problematic. There are more opportunities for scrutiny in the House of Lords. The Secondary Legislation Scrutiny Committee looks at delegated legislation, scrutinizing its policy objectives. The committee can produce reports, drawing the attention of the House to issues arising from delegated legislation. The House of Lords as a whole votes on delegated legislation subject to the affirmative resolution procedure. It is also easier for a member of the House of Lords to succeed in obtaining a prayer motion to vote against delegated legislation subject to the negative resolution procedure.

However, it is equally rare for the House of Lords to vote against delegated legislation. Most members of the House of Lords believe that they should only do so in exceptional circumstances. We can see why this is the case. The House of Lords are not democratically elected and they see their role more as scrutinizing and proposing amendments, rather than as vetoing measures outright. Yet, the scrutiny over delegated legislation does not provide the House of Lords with this option. Members of the House of Lords may prefer to move a motion of regret. This sets out that, although the House of Lords is willing to approve delegated legislation subject to the affirmative resolution procedure, they regret having to do so.

The House of Lords did vote to delay, if not decline to approve, delegated legislation in 2015. This concerned tax credit regulations. A motion was placed before the House of Lords to decline to approve the delegated legislation. This was over concerns that the regulations, which were part of a set of austerity measures, would cause severe problems for poorer members of society. This motion did not succeed. Nevertheless, two votes did succeed which had the effect of delaying the tax credit regulations. These were motions to decline to consider the delegated legislation until the government had carried out a further review of the impact of the measures on poorer groups in society.

The government disapproved of this behaviour of the House of Lords, particularly as it was obliged to carry out a review before being able to bring the tax credit regulations into force. The government commissioned a review into the actions of the House of Lords, as well as asking more broadly what the role of the House of Lords should be regarding delegated legislation. This is known as the Strathclyde Review. The Strathclyde Review agreed that the House of Lords should keep its function in scrutinizing delegated legislation, although it also recognized that removing this scrutiny was an option that the government could pursue. It recommended the establishment of a new procedure, enabling the House of Lords to ask the Commons to consider delegated legislation again, but also recognizing that the House of Lords played a secondary role to that of the House of Commons.[5]

This would have removed the power of the House of Lords to veto delegated legislation. This recommendation of the Strathclyde Review was criticized by committees in both the House of Lords and the House of Commons. While it is true that the House of Lords should play a secondary role to the House of Commons in some areas, given that it is not democratically elected, this should be a concern when we are thinking about the relative roles of the House of Commons and the House of Lords more generally, particularly regarding the enactment of primary legislation. It should not apply when we are thinking about the role of Parliament in relation to the powers of the government, for example when Parliament is scrutinizing delegated legislation made by the government. It is right, therefore, for the House of Lords to only have a delaying power over primary legislation. It is not right for the House of Lords to only have a delaying power over delegated legislation, especially given the lack of scrutiny over these provisions by the House of Commons.

Why should we care that the scrutiny over delegated legislation is so weak compared to the scrutiny over primary legislation? It becomes a problem when matters that should have been enacted through primary legislation are, instead, enacted through delegated legislation. Admittedly, this is a very tricky line to draw. It is easy to argue that primary legislation should be used for policy choices and delegated legislation can be used for the implementation of those policy choices. But what does that mean in practice? Is it a policy choice, for example, to reduce river pollution, but for the administration to set the levels of pollution that are acceptable, or is setting the acceptable levels of pollution a policy choice? What about if the legislation sets long-term targets – for example, to reduce river pollution by 75 per cent in five years? Is it now more likely that the specific setting of annual targets to reach this aim is about the implementation of a policy choice, and so should be achieved by delegated legislation?

Determining when matters should be enacted by primary or delegated legislation is beyond the scope of this book. It is a long-standing problem. We can point, however, to growing trends in the post-Brexit constitution that appear worrying. First, two committees of the House of Lords have recently both noted a growing use of skeleton legislation and a greater use of Henry VIII clauses.[6] Skeleton legislation is where an Act of Parliament contains so many delegated powers that it is almost impossible to know what the Act is achieving other than granting delegated powers to the executive. It's almost as if Parliament is granting the government a blank cheque. This is concerning as it means that Parliament may be granting to the government the power to make policy choices that are not effectively scrutinized by either the House of Commons or the House of Lords.

Henry VIII clauses are concerning because they empower the government to use delegated legislation to overturn Acts of

Parliament. There are occasions when this may be valid. For instance, our example of legislation designed to protect the environment may create an environment agency to police river pollution. Other legislation may also refer to the environment agency; for example, there may be legislation designed to facilitate the insulation of homes which grants powers to the environment agency to oversee the administration of these grants and to check that insulation was carried out correctly. In the future, Parliament may wish to change the environment agency and create a new climate change agency that inherits the powers of the environment agency and also is granted new powers to protect against the impacts of climate change. A Henry VIII clause may be useful in this example to enable the minister to amend primary legislation to change references to the environment agency to references to the climate change agency, in case one of these changes is inadvertently missed.

However, they may also be used to grant wide powers. There is a growing tendency, for example, to use Henry VIII clauses in legislation to grant ancillary powers to ministers. These clauses are common in Acts of Parliament. They are designed as a fail-safe. What if legislation needs a minister to act to implement its provisions, but this was inadvertently missed from the Act of Parliament? An ancillary powers clause can empower the minister to act to achieve the aims and purposes of legislation in situations where the parent Act fails to grant the minister that power. These ancillary powers clauses, however, often contain a Henry VIII clause. Are these necessary?

There are also further worrying trends. In addition to delegated legislation, the two committees in the House of Lords also raised concerns about disguised legislation. Government departments can enact guidance and policies. Guidance can help to provide further information as to how legislation can be implemented in specific areas. For example, guidance may help explain how different types of factories can reduce pollution, these measures being different for factories making ice cream and those making bicycles. Policies can help explain how a minister may exercise discretionary power. They can help to provide clarity, so that those applying for a grant to insulate their home, for example, know how a minister will decide whether to provide a household with a grant. Problems arise, however, when these policies and guidance no longer help us to understand how legislation is to be complied with, or discretion exercised, and instead play the same role as legislation. This is what we mean by disguised legislation. To help understand this further, and to begin to understand a little bit more of the nature of this problem, it helps to provide an example. We will look at the range of delegated legislation and guidance used to regulate the Covid pandemic.

COVID-19 and disguised legislation

The Covid pandemic created a national emergency. The government needed to react quickly, and it did so, using its powers to enact an Act of Parliament and also to make delegated legislation. What is probably not so well known is just how much delegated legislation was used to regulate Covid. The Hansard Society, a charity which produces independent research on Parliament and parliamentary affairs, as well as providing advice on these matters, kept track of these provisions. According to their figures, 582 Covid-related pieces of delegated legislation were enacted between 27 January 2020 to 3 March 2022.[7] To put this in context, the Hansard Society counted 1,946 pieces of delegated legislation in total over that period, meaning about 30 per cent of all delegated legislation enacted in that period concerned Covid. According to Parliament's website, around 3,500 pieces of delegated legislation are normally made each year, with about a thousand each year considered in Parliament.[8]

When we look at the regulations made in response to Covid more precisely, 417 were enacted through the negative resolution procedure; 118 were made by the 'made affirmative' procedure, most of those under the provisions of the Public Health (Control of Disease) Act 1984, where legislation can be in force for 28 days without a vote from Parliament. Only 44 were enacted through the affirmative procedure, which provides Parliament with more scrutiny, with only one requiring enhanced scrutiny. Two were merely laid before Parliament. Given the need to act quickly, some delegated legislation came into force before it had been laid before Parliament. The Hansard Society's figures show that this happened for 66 pieces of delegated legislation, 11 per cent of the total made.

The lack of scrutiny did not only harm democracy. It also meant that some mistakes went unchecked. This meant that many measures had to be changed to deal with these inaccuracies. For example, the Health Protection (Coronavirus, International Travel and Operator Liability) (England) (Amendment) (No 17) (Amendment) Regulations 2021 had to be made three days after the original regulation, which had omitted 12 countries from the list of those whose vaccination certification was recognized. It's not only the number of measures that may be concerning. It's also what these measures were used to regulate. The regulations restricted your ability to leave your home, to go to work and to travel.

We got used to lockdown measures during Covid and the rapid change of rules in response to the pandemic. What was perhaps less well known was how so many of these rules were made by delegated legislation with little parliamentary scrutiny, despite their large impact on our day-to-day lives.

While we may find this concerning, it is understandable in times of emergency, especially one that posed such a threat to public health which was constantly changing as we learnt more about Covid. However, it becomes more concerning when these emergency provisions are used when there is no need. The Constitution Committee of the House of Lords, for example, noted that delegated legislation enacted to require the wearing of face masks on public transport was implemented using emergency provisions. It was made on the morning of 23 July 2020, laid before Parliament four-and-a-quarter hours later, and then came into force the next day. Yet, these requirements were linked not to imposing emergency measures in the face of an immediate crisis, but to providing a means of easing lockdown measures. Did this need to be enacted so quickly, or could there have been more time to check for potential mistakes before it was enacted? The Speaker of the House of Commons was so concerned over the pattern of delegated legislation used to implement Covid lockdown restrictions, that he made a statement to the House:

> The way in which the Government have exercised their powers to make secondary legislation during this crisis has been totally unsatisfactory. All too often, important statutory instruments have been published a matter of hours before they came into force, and some explanations why important measures have come into

effect before they can be laid before this House have been unconvincing; this shows a total disregard for the House.[9]

Problems arose not only because of how delegated legislation was used but also how this was combined with guidance. Rather than providing an accessible means of setting out legal requirements, guidance about Covid was often presented as if it was the law. Guidance even provided for measures that were more restrictive than the law. Yet, this guidance was not subject to any parliamentary scrutiny. Constitutional commentators were concerned that it was also undermining the rule of law, this time understood in terms of the need for citizens to be able to know what the law is to be able to follow it. Guidance caused confusion as to what the lockdown measures required, as well as causing individuals to believe that some measures were legally enforceable when they were not.

We can see this, for example, in the way in which the first measures implementing lockdown requirements came into force. On 23 March 2020, Boris Johnson addressed the nation, 'asking people to stay home during the pandemic'. He added that 'people will only be allowed to leave their home' for limited purposes; shopping for necessities, one form of exercise a day, any medical needs and travelling to and from work when this was absolutely necessary, and work cannot be done from home. This gave the impression that it would be against the law for people to leave their homes save for these restricted purposes. This was reinforced by a text message sent from the government on 24 March which stated: 'GOV.UK CORONAVIRUS ALERT. New rules in force now: you must stay at home. More info & exemptions at gov.uk/coronavirus. Stay at home. Protect the NHS. Save lives.'[10]

Even if you were not sure if it was unlawful to leave your home on 23 March, this text message the next day would appear to make it clear. New rules were in force. Surely that must mean it was unlawful to leave your home unless you fit into a narrow exemption. For most of us, we would then think that it would be right for the police to enforce these rules, making us return to our homes if we did not fit into one of these exemptions.

However, it was not unlawful as, at the time, no measures had been enacted to make it unlawful. The delegated legislation implementing lockdown requirements did not come into force until 26 March

2020 – at 1 pm, when they were made, and before they were laid before Parliament 90 minutes later. The measures were enacted through the made affirmative procedure, where they would be in force for 28 days and could only continue in force beyond that date if both the House of Commons and the House of Lords voted in favour of these regulations.

The guidance also caused problems as sometimes it seemed to impose restrictions that were not unlawful. Most of us think that the social distancing measures – which originally set out the need to keep two metres apart from others, even while outdoors, to stop the spread of the virus – were legal requirements. This was never the case. It was health advice. Yet, because the advice to keep your distance was often included in the information about the lockdown restrictions, it gave most of us the impression that it would be unlawful to stand too close to others. This influenced behaviour; even when taking a walk outside, many tried their best to avoid getting too close to others or to space themselves apart in supermarket aisles, for fear of breaking the law.

Confusion also arose when guidance gave the impression that lockdown laws were stricter than they were. For example, most of us believed that it was only possible to leave our homes to exercise once a day. Yet, for most of the country, this was only health advice. The lockdown regulations did not restrict the number of times you could leave your home to exercise, other than in Wales. However, repeated statements by ministers, including the prime minister, that you could exercise 'once a day' gave us all the impression that it would be unlawful to leave your home to exercise more than once a day.

The confusion over what was a legal requirement, what was just meant as guidance to help you understand legal requirements and what was just advice also extended to school closures. The Coronavirus Act 2020 empowered the government to issue notices to require schools to close. However, rather than using these provisions, the government first advised local authorities to close schools for all except vulnerable children and the children of key workers. The government did issue notices under other legislation, making it clear that, when schools were advised to close, it would not be possible to bring measures against parents for not sending their children to school. Guidance was issued to set out the definition of a key worker. This is an odd way of implementing rules. It can also bypass political scrutiny, as well as cause confusion. It also had the effect of making it harder to challenge the rules in the courts, with the divisional court (the court which hears claims for judicial review in the first instance) concluding that, as school closures were implemented through advice, the advice could not be the subject of a legal challenge for judicial review.[11]

It is understandable that delegated legislation was used, and that the government had to have the power to act quickly in an emergency. However, this did have the effect of transferring even more power to the government. It is also hard to see this as merely returning the UK to an orthodox understanding of the UK constitution, with more political as opposed to legal controls. The measures removed parliamentary checks over the powers of the government. The use of guidance and advice meant measures could be brought in by the government with no legal oversight at all.

Is this evidence of a populist government taking back control and moving the UK into an authoritarian state? Again, it is hard to see these measures as evidence of populism. What may be worrying, however, is how far televised statements of advice, alongside the use of guidance to give the impression that laws are in place, when they are not, or that laws are stricter than they really are, becomes a longer-term practice. When two parliamentary committees produce reports setting out their concerns about the use of delegated legislation and guidance, showing how guidance can be used as a form of disguised legislation in areas that are not related to Covid, we need to think carefully about whether the government is taking more power than it needs. Before we think about this further, there is another recent change that we need to investigate.

Stopping zombie parliaments

One of Lord Hailsham's reasons for arguing that the UK government was an elective dictatorship was because the prime minister had the power to determine the timing of a general election. In 1976, the Monarch had the prerogative power to dissolve Parliament. The prime minister could request that the Monarch dissolve Parliament. By convention, the Monarch would agree. The only exceptions were known as the Lascelles Principles (oddly, originally set out in a letter to *The Times* under the pseudonym 'Senex'). The Monarch could refuse to grant a dissolution if there was clear evidence that Parliament was still viable and capable of doing its job; if there was a time of crisis and a general election would be detrimental, particularly if it was detrimental to the national economy; or where there was evidence of an alternative government that would have the confidence of Parliament. This effectively gave broad discretionary power to the prime minister, or perhaps the prime minister and their cabinet, to time a general election. The only limit on this timing was legislation setting out a maximum parliamentary term of five years.

This placed what some argued was an important power in the hands of the prime minister. The prime minister could choose to hold a general election at a time that would provide their party with political advantage. This may be as simple as taking advantage of opinion polls showing that their political party was likely to win the next general election if this was held in the fourth year of a parliamentary term, rather than waiting until the end of the maximum five-year term. It may also provide the prime minister with the power to issue budgets or legislation likely to curry favour with the electorate or ensure bad news is published after a general election is held.

It also provided the prime minister with a possible threat to backbench rebels. The prime minister could determine that a particular issue was one of confidence. If the government lost the vote on that legislation, then the prime minister would resign and seek the dissolution of Parliament and a general election. This places a backbench rebel MP in a dilemma. Is this legislation worth the potential loss of your seat? Would you have any political future in your party if you voted against a confidence motion, not just in terms of your future promotion up the party ranks but also in terms of whether you would be chosen as a candidate for your seat in a future general election?

It could be argued that this power is more fictional than real. After all, global economics and situations outside the prime minister's control may play a large role, limiting the ability of the prime minister to perfectly time a general election. Even if this is the case, it is hard to argue against the claim that the ability, in practice, to set the time of a general election places the balance of power in the hands of the government. There is little the rest of the

House of Commons could do other than prepare for the inevitable forthcoming general election.

The balance of power was moved from the government to the House of Commons with the enactment of the Fixed-term Parliaments Act 2011. A promise to fix the terms of Parliament was found in the manifestos of the Liberal Democrat Party and the Labour Party for the 2010 general election. The 2010 general election produced a coalition government between the Liberal Democrats and the Conservative Party. The establishment of fixed-term Parliaments was argued to be even more beneficial for coalition governments. It could prevent the prime minister, typically appointed from the larger coalition partner, from choosing a general election date that would advantage his party, but disadvantage that of the smaller coalition partner as well as the opposition.

The 2011 Act removed the prerogative power of the Monarch to dissolve Parliament. It also changed the UK to a system of fixed-term Parliaments, rather than maximum terms, with a requirement to hold a general election every five years, the normal dates of general elections being set out in the legislation. It also tipped the balance of power even more in favour of Parliament as opposed to the government by providing for two ways in which it would be possible to call an early parliamentary general election. First, it would be possible for an early general election to be held if two-thirds of the whole of the House of Commons voted in favour of an early general election. This happened in 2017, when Theresa May, then Prime Minister, obtained enough votes to hold an early general election on 8 June.

Second, dissolution may occur after a vote of no confidence in the government. However, this process differed from the situation prior to 2011. The legislation set out the specific wording of a vote of no confidence in the government that would trigger a general election. A differently worded vote – for example, a vote of no confidence in the prime minister as well as the government – would not trigger a general election in the same way. It might, however, have triggered the resignation of the prime minister as leader of their party, or the prime minister might have used other means to trigger a general election, for example seeking votes for an early general election. Also, even if the specific wording was used, and the government lost a vote of no confidence, this would not automatically trigger a general election. Instead, there would be a two-week period in which it would be possible to hold a vote of confidence in a government, be that the existing government or a differently composed government. If there was no vote of confidence in that timeframe, then a general election would be triggered.

This tipped the balance of power in favour of the House of Commons. It made it harder for the prime minister to choose the date of an election to find a time more favourable to their political party. The events of 2017, however, questioned this conclusion. After all, even though the Conservative Party was winning in the polls at the time, Theresa May had no problem obtaining the votes she needed to hold a general election. The situation is almost akin to a game of political chicken. To fail to vote in favour of a general election looks like you are conceding that you do not think your political party would win. That is hardly a good position to be in at the start of your party's general election campaign. However, as the events of 2019 show, this is not always the case. Boris Johnson was unable to obtain the votes he needed to hold an early general election. This was an unusual set of circumstances, where MPs had to balance the prospects of winning or losing seats in the next general election against the prospect of a no-deal Brexit.

The prime minister was able to hold an early general election in 2019, despite not being able to obtain two-thirds of the votes of all MPs in the House of Commons. This was through the enactment of the Early Parliamentary General Elections Act 2019, which provided for the December 2019 general election as an additional date for a general election, partially amending the Fixed-term Parliaments Act 2011. As an Act of Parliament, only a simple majority was needed. This may seem to suggest that the balance of power remained with the government, even under the provisions of the 2011 Act. However, the Early Parliamentary General Elections Act 2019 specified the date of the next general election. The House of Commons and the House of Lords had to agree to this date. It would have been possible for either or both Houses to have amended the date chosen by the prime minister in the legislation. The Prime Minister, Boris Johnson, definitely did regard the 2011 Act as removing his power, complaining that it had created a zombie Parliament unable to get business done or to go to the electorate to break a parliamentary impasse.

The 2011 Act also limited the power of the prime minister to use a vote of no confidence as a means of securing the support of backbench MPs for controversial Bills. It was still possible for the prime minister to make an issue a matter of confidence. However, this would not satisfy the wording of the 2011 Act. Therefore, even if the government were to lose the vote, this would not lead to a general election. It would probably lead to a more embarrassing situation where the prime minister may feel obliged to resign as leader of the party, or where the prime minister may then face a vote of no confidence in their leadership of the party. This does not provide the same means of forcing rebellious backbench MPs to vote in favour of the government's policies. If anything, it may further incentivize backbench MPs to rebel, particularly if they see this as a means of changing the leadership of the party to an individual more in line with their particular political views.

The events of 2019, again, point to a possible way in which the prime minister may still use votes of no confidence as a means of bolstering support from backbench MPs. In January 2019, after losing the vote on the first withdrawal agreement setting out the UK's exit from the EU, the then Prime Minister, Theresa May, invited the opposition to table a motion of no confidence in the government. This is another form of political chicken. The leader of the opposition would look very weak indeed if they were to refuse to table a vote of no confidence. This motion was set out according to the requirements of the Fixed-term Parliaments Act 2011 and so could have led to a general election, after two weeks, if the government lost the vote. Despite suffering the largest governmental defeat since universal suffrage the day before, Theresa May's government defeated the vote of no confidence motion. This may have helped to boost support for Theresa May's leadership of the party and her prime ministership, even if it did not have the effect of ensuring backbench support for future votes on the withdrawal agreement.

Given Boris Johnson's concerns over the operation of the Fixed-term Parliaments Act 2011, it is hardly surprising that the Conservative Party's 2019 manifesto included a promise to repeal the Act. This was achieved through the Dissolution and Calling of Parliament Act 2022. This Act revives the former prerogative power enabling the prime minister to request the dissolution of Parliament and to hold a general election. The Act's provisions also make it clear that the court will not be able to review the exercise of this power by the prime minister. There is also no provision in the 2022 Act for a vote of the House of Commons before the dissolution of Parliament. As with the position in 1976, the only legal limit on the power of the prime minister to request the dissolution of Parliament is the reinstatement of a five-year maximum term of Parliament.

How are we to view this restoration of the power of the prime minister to request the dissolution of Parliament and the calling of a general election? On the one hand, it fits our narrative that the post-Brexit constitutional reforms are designed to return the UK to constitutional orthodoxy. Here, the reform removes a legal regulation of general elections, returning the decision as to when to hold a general election to one predominantly concerned with politics rather than one normally occurring when a set time has passed. It reinforces a fundamental convention of the UK constitution that the government is only in power to the extent that it can enjoy the confidence of the House of Commons by restoring the traditional role of the vote of confidence, removing a delay period where an alternative government may be formed.

It may mean that the prime minister has more power than before, tipping the balance of power in favour of the government. However, at the end of the day, any prime minister wishing to exercise this power faces the immediate judgment of the electorate. Get the decision wrong, and you face the ultimate price of losing the general election and, probably, the leadership of your political party. We also have to factor in that the Labour Party also promised to repeal the Fixed-term Parliaments Act 2011 in its 2019 manifesto, seeing this as propping up weak governments and stifling democracy.[12] However, this does not mean that they would have chosen the same replacement as the provisions of the 2022 Act.

On the other hand, we can read this as evidence of a shift of power away from Parliament and in favour of the government. Whether the facts show that governments always choose wisely or otherwise, the prime minister now has a choice he did not possess when we had fixed-term parliaments. The prime minister can request the Monarch dissolve Parliament and set the date of a general election without the need for the approval of the House of Commons. It also restores a means through which a prime minister can seek to quell a potential backbench rebellion.

Conclusion

It is hard to disagree with Lord Hailsham's assessment that the UK, or more accurately the Westminster Parliament, can be described as an elective dictatorship. The government does enjoy large powers. It would appear to be easy for the government to push through legislation, using its discipline to ensure that its MPs toe the line, even threatening to make an issue a vote of confidence, if needed, to quell a rebellion. However, it is also true that legislation does get amended. We often miss the extent to which backbench and opposition MPs, particularly when combined with the support of the Lords, may succeed in getting the government to propose its amendments to legislation along the lines of those proposed by backbenchers, the opposition or the Lords. It is important to recognize here, however, which of our trio of Parliament, the party or the people is providing the most effective check. The government needs the support of backbench MPs. Misuse a vote of confidence, or cause confusion over whether an issue is a matter of confidence, then, as Liz Truss's short term in office starkly illustrates, a prime minister can quickly lose power. The threat of rebellion may be an effective means of ensuring the government listens to its backbench MPs. In other words, the party, not Parliament or the people, appear to be the only effective means of checking a government intent on pushing through legislation, save for the exceptional circumstances of a minority government.

Recent changes to the UK's post-Brexit constitution would suggest that the powers of the government are growing. Even if the use of delegated legislation and guidance as a response to Covid was necessary for an emergency, this does not explain why two parliamentary committees both expressed their concern as to the growth of the use of these powers more generally, more widely than their use during the pandemic. Nor can Covid alone explain the continued use of skeleton legislation and guidance to regulate other matters post Covid. For all that the Dissolution and Calling of Parliament Act 2022 may restore the Westminster Parliament to one of maximum terms, alongside the prerogative power of the Monarch to dissolve Parliament at the request of the prime minister, this return to orthodoxy may also be seen as a retrograde step. The practical effect of the change is to reduce the powers of the House of Commons and to increase the powers of the government. While this may ultimately give power to the people in a general election, the timing of this general election may be used as a means to choose a moment when the people are more likely to give the government's political party the support it needs to win the next general election. Though, equally, the government may miscalculate this moment.

Is this sufficient evidence of populism? Not in and of itself. But it is worrying. What perhaps makes this more worrying is the extent to which the phrase elective dictatorship still seems apt. The UK constitution does not appear to have heeded Lord Hailsham's warning. It seems to have become widely accepted that the Westminster government can, for the most part, enact the legislation it wants, use delegated legislation and guidance to achieve its objectives and choose the date of the next general election.

If that were not concerning enough, in June 2023, the House of Lords was asked to approve the Public Order Act 1986 (Serious Disruption to the Life of the Community) Regulations 2023. These regulations provide definitions of when protests amount to a serious disruption to the life of the community. They have an impact on the right to protest, which we will look at further in Chapter 7. However, this is not why these regulations are concerning – indeed so concerning that they were referred to as a 'constitutional outrage' by members of the House of Lords.[13] This is because most of the provisions of this piece of delegated legislation had originally been proposed by government amendments to a Bill in the House of Lords. However, they had been rejected by the House and were not included in an Act of Parliament. In other words, the government is using delegated legislation, which received very little scrutiny in the House of Commons, to effectively overturn a parliamentary vote on primary legislation. Measures dropped from proposed legislation are then brought in through the back door through delegated legislation. There was no mention of such behaviour in Lord Hailsham's assessment – probably because such behaviour would not have been contemplated nearly 50 years ago. This suggests that, if anything, Lord Hailsham's assessment is even more apt now than it was in 1976.

Is it also widely accepted that this is how the Westminster Parliament should operate? If so, we are merely passively accepting that the government should be the dominant institution in the UK constitution, this being justified by the checks over its power by the party, Parliament and the people. Yet, in reality, many of these checks that are meant to be carried out by Parliament and the people are in the hands of the political party from which the members of the government are drawn. This tips the balance of power away from Parliament in favour of the government.

4

Checks and Balances or Crowing and Bolstering?

Nobody is infallible. This is why so many systems have checks and balances to try and prevent mistakes from being made. Authors of books have editors, copyeditors and proofreaders to spot and correct typing, grammatical and factual errors. Football matches have referees, linespersons and video assistant referee (VAR) systems to look over decisions, checking if players are offside and whether a penalty should, or should not, be awarded. These checking mechanisms may not be enough to stop every mistake, but it is hopefully better than having no checks at all.

Governmental systems are no different. Scrutiny over legislation and delegated legislation can help to spot and correct errors. Constitutions also provide for different checks and balances. Constitutional commentators refer to these as part of the separation of powers. The principle of the separation of powers argues that it is not a good idea to give all of the aspects of the powers of government to one institution. We normally see these elements as being the power to make law, to implement law, and to interpret, apply and resolve disputes about the law. The power to make the law belongs to the legislature. The power to implement the law belongs to the executive. The power to interpret, apply and determine disputes about the law belongs to the judiciary.

However, the lines between these powers are not clear. Also, the UK is well known for its fusion of powers between the executive and the legislature, that is, between the government and Parliament. We have seen this in the previous chapters. The government is composed of members of the legislature belonging to the political party that can form a government that will command a majority in the House of Commons, usually because this political party has more MPs than other political parties. It is also hard to draw the line between those measures that should be implemented through legislation, and so should be enacted by Parliament, and those that can best be implemented through delegated legislation, made by the government.

There is a clearer separation between the courts and the government and the courts and Parliament. The UK provides a strong protection of the independence of the judiciary. However, some argue that even these functions can be blurred. Courts can make the law by adding to the common law. They do this when they decide cases that come before the court. They do not initiate changes; rather, they respond to disputes brought before the courts by individuals. Courts can also only develop case law incrementally. Any new decision draws on past decisions, reasoning by analogy by looking at similarities and differences between the specific dispute before the court and previous cases decided by the courts. Courts can interpret legislation, and some would argue that, occasionally, the interpretations of the courts can stray into amending, rather than interpreting, legislation. Yet courts are keenly aware of their need to interpret and not amend legislation, often making it clear that they focus predominantly on understanding the text of the legislation.

These blurred lines and fusions between different institutions of government are justified because they can facilitate a different element of the separation of powers – checks and balances. It is easier for Parliament to hold the government to account for its actions when they frequently appear in the same place, where MPs can ask the government questions about its activities in a public arena. Courts, too, can check the powers of the government. In particular, they can uphold the rule of law, checking that the government does have the legal power to act and has only acted within the scope of that power.

These checks and balances are important. We mostly take them for granted. Occasionally, issues relating to these checks and balances hit the headlines – most recently in the prorogation case. This chapter will look at why this case was so newsworthy, using it to set the scene for our understanding of checks and balances and why they are important. We will then look at whether, as we would expect from a populist narrative, the checks and balances over the government are being reduced. Are there signs that, rather than holding the government to account, Parliament mostly supports the government? If so, is this further evidence of the UK becoming more populist, potentially harming democracy and the constitution, or is this just part of how democracy usually works in the UK?

A prorogation too far?

On 28 August 2019, the Monarch and the Privy Council, following a request from the government, made an Order in Council – a specific type of delegated legislation – announcing that Parliament would be prorogued at some point between 9 and 12 September until 14 October 2019. There is nothing unusual in proroguing Parliament. Parliamentary terms, which at the time were fixed at five years, are split into parliamentary sessions. Each session ends when Parliament is prorogued. This starts a new legislative programme, set out in the Monarch's Speech at the opening of Parliament.

However, this prorogation was unusual. It's not often that a future prorogation is announced so far in advance. The prorogation was also for a much longer time than usual. Normally, prorogation is for about a week, allowing the government time to prepare the Monarch's speech. The year 2019, as we have seen in Chapters 1 and 3, was unusual. Boris Johnson, who announced the prorogation of Parliament, had only recently become the new Prime Minister following the resignation of Theresa May as leader of the Conservative Party and Johnson's success in the ensuing leadership election. He was in charge of a minority government, supported by a confidence and supply agreement from the Democratic Unionist Party (DUP).[1] The DUP would vote for the Conservative government in a vote of confidence, or to support the budget and finance and money bills. The DUP also agreed to support the government on national security issues and Brexit. They were not required, however, to vote for the government on other issues. The new prime minister's desire to achieve Brexit, even if this was with no deal, did not have the support of a majority of MPs.

The unusual nature of the prorogation decision created a further novel situation for the UK constitution. Two legal challenges were brought against the Order in Council. One was brought by Joanna

Cherry, a Westminster MP who is a member of the Scottish National Party (SNP), in the Scottish courts. The other was brought by Gina Miller in the English courts. At first, both the English and the Scottish courts concluded that the courts could not examine whether the prorogation of Parliament was lawful. It was 'non-justiciable', a matter that the courts were not permitted to review. However, Cherry was successful in her appeal of this decision in the Scottish courts – an appeal to the Inner House. This appeal concluded that courts could review the legality of a decision to prorogue Parliament. Moreover, it concluded that the decision to prorogue Parliament was unlawful.

Given this divergence, the Supreme Court agreed to hear both cases. For only the second time in its history, the Supreme Court sat as a group of 11, the maximum number of Justices of the Supreme Court that can hear a case and still maintain an odd number to secure an outcome with the support of a majority, if not all, of the judges. Many of the arguments in the case concerned whether the court should have the power to review a decision to prorogue Parliament. Prorogation is a political decision. So, it should be controlled by politics and not the law. If the prime minister's party and Parliament are happy with a decision to prorogue Parliament, why should the courts get involved? To involve the courts would seem to give them too much power to limit the actions of a democratically elected government. Also, the prime minister, on behalf of their government, can only request the prorogation of Parliament. Only the Monarch can prorogue Parliament. If there were any serious constitutional issues of abuse, surely the Monarch would step in to prevent a wrongful prorogation of Parliament?

On the other hand, arguments were made that the power to prorogue Parliament could be open to abuse. What if the prime minister requested a prorogation of Parliament for such a long time that it would undermine the role of Parliament? In other words, could a government use its power to govern in a way that limited or even removed political checks over its actions? This would hardly be democratic – to put it mildly. Also, what if a prime minister were bribed to prorogue Parliament, or had requested a prorogation of Parliament to avoid a threat to their life?

It may also be difficult, and is normally impossible, for Parliament to check the government's decision to prorogue Parliament. Prorogation is normally announced in Parliament. This announcement brings the session of Parliament to an end. There is no debate or vote. Surely there is a need for some legal limits on the prorogation of Parliament to prevent abuse. Should we just rely on the Monarch here, or would this drag the Monarch into politics?

These questions relate to the need for checks and balances. These are means through which one institution of the constitution oversees the actions of the other institution. Checks and balances can help to prevent mistakes. What if a minister made a mistake in their mathematical calculations when proposing the budget? Parliamentary scrutiny over the budget proposals can help to find this error and correct it. They can also help to ensure one institution does not abuse its power. What if, hypothetically, a government wanted to use its power to initiate an Act of Parliament designed to halt a legal case looking at whether a prime minister had committed fraud, setting out in law that no fraud had been committed? We would hope that Parliament would check this action of the government as an abuse of the government's power. What if a minister enacted delegated legislation which they had no legal power to enact? We would want the courts to check this action of the minister, preventing them from acting unlawfully.

It can seem easy to set out why we want legal and political checks and balances. What is harder is working out when something is more suited to a legal or a political check. Should we trust Parliament or the courts to stop abuse of power? It is this issue that was at the heart of the legal cases brought by Joanna Cherry and Gina Miller. They argued that courts should check the power of the government to request the prorogation of Parliament. The government argued that it was the role of Parliament and not the courts to check this power. Who was right?

The Supreme Court concluded that the courts did have the power to review decisions of the government to request that the Monarch prorogue Parliament. However, the court was careful to set limits as to when this form of legal check and balance would be appropriate. Miller had argued that the Prime Minister, then Boris Johnson, had abused his power by advising the Monarch to prorogue Parliament for an improper purpose. The Prime Minister wished to prorogue Parliament to achieve Brexit. It was clear that Parliament did not want to leave the EU with no deal. Yet Boris Johnson wished to achieve the UK's exit from the EU on 31 October 2019, with no further delays. Proroguing Parliament would make it harder for the House of Commons to stop the Prime Minister from achieving his policy objective.

The Supreme Court concluded that the law placed limits on whether a prerogative power exists, and also on the extent of that power. We know that there is a prerogative power to prorogue Parliament. However, the Supreme Court concluded that there were limits to its scope. It relied on two principles of the UK constitution to set these limits: parliamentary sovereignty and parliamentary accountability. Parliamentary sovereignty recognizes that Parliament is the most important institution in the UK constitution and that the laws enacted by Parliament are the highest form of law. However, if Parliament is prorogued for so long that it cannot enact legislation, this would undermine parliamentary sovereignty. Parliamentary accountability refers to the need for Parliament to hold the government to account for its actions. However, if the government can request a prorogation of Parliament that prevents Parliament from sitting for a long period, how can Parliament hold ministers to account for their actions?

Therefore, it was not the case that the prime minister had a legally unlimited power to request a prorogation of Parliament whenever they wanted for as long as they wanted. That raises the deeper question, however, as to the legal limits over the power to prorogue Parliament. The Supreme Court set the limits as follows:

> A decision to prorogue Parliament (or to advise the monarch to prorogue Parliament) will be unlawful if the prorogation has the effect of frustrating or preventing, without reasonable justification, the ability of Parliament to carry out its constitutional functions as a legislature and as the body responsible for the supervision of the executive. In such a situation, the court will intervene if the effect is sufficiently serious to justify such an exceptional course.[2]

This decision means that the effect of the long prorogation of Parliament was sufficiently serious to justify the court intervening. It would frustrate or prevent Parliament from carrying out its functions at an important and exceptional time in history. Parliament would be prorogued for five of the eight weeks between Parliament returning from its summer break and the date on which the UK would be required to leave the European Union (EU), or to seek an extension to the negotiation period with the EU if it did not wish to leave the EU on that date. Yet, the UK's exit from the EU would mark a fundamental change to the UK's constitution.

The Supreme Court was then required to examine whether the government had justified this course of action. However, as no justification was provided, the Court could not conclude 'that there was any reason – let alone a good reason' to prorogue Parliament on these dates.[3] Having reached that conclusion, the Supreme Court quashed the Order in Council announcing the prorogation of Parliament. Once quashed, the law treats the Order in Council as if it had never been made. In effect, Parliament had never been prorogued. This meant, in turn, that Parliament was able to return, which it did the next day.

Commentators are still arguing about whether they agree with the Supreme Court. I am one of those who think that the Supreme Court got it right. The courts need to step in to ensure that legal limits over the powers of the government are enforced. Here, the court was not intervening to try and increase its own powers. Rather, it intervened to protect Parliament. Parliament's ability to hold the government to account was being undermined. It would be difficult for Parliament to do anything to prevent the prorogation of Parliament – especially in the usual situation where there is no gap between announcing that Parliament will be prorogued and the actual prorogation of Parliament. To rely on the Monarch to provide this check risks drawing the Monarch into politics, undermining their constitutional role.

More importantly, there have to be some legal limits over the power to prorogue Parliament if we are to prevent the possibility of any prime minister requesting the prorogation of Parliament for so long that they can effectively become a dictator. If there were no limits, it would be possible for a rogue prime minister to call Parliament to meet just to approve the budget and to pass an Act granting broad powers to the executive to implement the prime minister's policies, until Parliament met again a year later to achieve the same objectives. The limits set by the court were also ones that recognized the importance of Parliament and of political checks and balances. Their decision was designed to uphold these political checks. It's also important to recognize that the government had not given any reasons to the Supreme Court to set out why they wanted to prorogue Parliament for so long. The outcome may well have been different had the government been able to justify its decision.

This context helps us to understand why it is so important to ask whether there has been a decline in checks and balances over the actions of the government. If this is the case, then we may be rightly worried about the direction of travel of the UK constitution. We will look first at political and then at legal checks over the government. We will see that, since the prorogation decision, there is some evidence of a decline in both of these checks and balances. However, as with our assessment of the growth of governmental power, the UK constitution stands on a tipping point, where both of our competing narratives can be used to argue either that the UK constitution is working well or that it is on the verge of collapse.

Who should be checked by whom, and for what?

The Supreme Court wished to preserve parliamentary accountability, but what does that mean? Accountability is an odd concept. It relies on a series of relationships. As a professor at the University of Cambridge, I'm accountable to my university for the teaching I provide. Students can write appraisal forms on my courses and, if there are problems, I can be called to account for these issues to my employer – in my case that would be before the Faculty of Law at the University of Cambridge. There also need to be consequences when individuals fail. If I fail to provide the right teaching to my students, teach them inaccurate information, or fail to even bother to turn up to lecture, I could ultimately be removed from my position.

The Supreme Court in the prorogation case wanted to ensure that Parliament could meet so it could hold ministers to account for their actions. This provides Parliament with the opportunity to oversee the government's policy choices. Do we think ministers are making the right choices when it comes to tackling austerity, imposing Covid restrictions, protecting the climate, or ensuring a healthy economy? Ministers can also be held to account for the way ministerial departments achieve these policy objectives. For example, Parliament can ask questions to find out whether sufficient measures were put in place to ensure that equipment needed during the pandemic was purchased fairly and that medication, vaccines and personal protective equipment (PPE) were distributed properly to those who needed it.

Ministers can also be held to account for their behaviour. Are they acting fairly and honestly? Are we happy that they are being transparent about their activities and not engaged in lobbying?

There are various mechanisms in place to try and ensure that ministers are accountable to Parliament for their actions. MPs can ask written and oral questions of ministers. There can also be time for debates to scrutinize the actions of the government. Parliament also forms departmental select committees. These committees can scrutinize the actions of ministerial departments, calling ministers to appear before them to account for their activities.

The most obvious forum of accountability is Prime Minister's Questions (PMQs), which currently takes place every Wednesday. These provide an opportunity to hold a prime minister to account for their policies, their behaviour and the behaviour of their ministers. These exchanges are televised and are often reported on in news bulletins. They provide a means of ensuring Parliament and the electorate can hold the prime minister to account. However, there are no immediate consequences. Any accountability for policies will be at the ballot box and a general election could be up to five years away. They mostly provide a means for the government to defend its policies and the opposition to provide its account of policy alternatives. When you watch these debates, it can be hard to understand how there is any form of accountability – are they not merely opportunities for the government to crow about its achievements, bolstering support from its backbench MPs?

Boris Johnson's first PMQs took place on 4 September 2019.[4] Unsurprisingly, he was asked about Brexit. Jeremy Corbyn, the then leader of the opposition, asked whether the Prime Minister's negotiating strategy was to 'run down the clock' and, if not, whether he could 'provide the detail of the proposals he put forward to the EU'. The Prime Minister replied:

> Our negotiating strategy is to get a deal by the summit
> on 17 October, to take this country out of the EU on
> 31 October and to get Brexit done. The right hon.
> Gentleman's surrender Bill would wreck any chances of
> the talks. We do not know what his strategy would be
> if he took over. He is asking for mobs of Momentum
> activists to paralyse the traffic. What are they supposed
> to chant? What is the slogan? 'What do we want? Dither
> and delay. When do we want it? We don't know.' That
> is his policy. Can he confirm now that he will allow the
> people of this country to decide on what he is giving up
> in their name with a general election on 15 October?
> Or is he frit?[5]

It is hard to see this as a clear account of a policy choice. Rather, it
is a means of challenging the opposition, scoring points in terms of
witty remarks rather than being held to account for policy choices.
We will look more closely at the choice of language in later chapters,
focusing on whether rhetoric has become more important than
deliberation. Here, Boris Johnson is focusing on accusing Jeremy
Corbyn of being 'frit' – too scared to agree to a general election,
implying that it is clear that Corbyn knows his political party
will lose. The 'surrender Bill' was Johnson's nickname for the
Bill designed to require the then prime minister to seek a further
extension of the negotiation period with the EU should Parliament
fail to vote in favour of the withdrawal agreement.

Boris Johnson's last parliamentary questions took place on 20 July
2022.[6] After receiving a question from Keir Starmer, leader of the
opposition, about the unwillingness of future Conservative Party
leadership candidates to appear in a debate on Sky News, he replied:

> I am not following this thing particularly closely, but my
> impression is that there has been quite a lot of debate
> already, and I think the public have ample opportunity
> to view the talent, any one of which – as I have said
> before – would, like some household detergent, wipe the
> floor with the right hon. and learned Gentleman. Today
> happens to be just about the anniversary of the exit from
> lockdown last year, and do you remember what he said?

He said – *[Interruption.]* No, I am going to remind him. He said it was 'reckless'. It was because we were able to take that decision, supported by every single one of those Conservative candidates, opposed by him, that we had the fastest economic growth in the G7 and we are now able to help families up and down the country. If we had listened to him, it would not have been possible, and I do not think they will be listening to him either.[7]

Neither of these replies, however, shows parliamentary accountability at its best. These exchanges are designed for show. They are not the most effective means of ensuring ministers are held to account. They are also mostly used for debates about policies, where the ultimate accountability lies with the electorate.

MPs can also ask oral and written questions of any minister. On the same day as Boris Johnson's last PMQs, the President of COP26, Alok Sharma MP, was asked a series of questions on the COP26 (the United Nations Climate Change Conference, held in 2021) outcomes, the finance for loss and damage proposals from COP26, the remaining objectives for the UK's presidency of COP, and climate targets, as well as a series of more general questions.[8] These less publicized sessions provide a more effective means for MPs to obtain information – ministers can be called to account for their performance and provide information to MPs as to how well, or otherwise, their policies are progressing.

Departmental select committee hearings also tend to be less frequently reported – although any major issues arising from the appearance of a minister before a departmental select committee can often be more widely reported. These committees also write reports, which can include recommendations. While there is no obligation on the government to hold a debate on a report, or to implement its recommendations, reports are published and can be read by MPs and the electorate. This can put pressure on ministers to perform well. A failure to do so may lead to criticism in Parliament, and potentially by the electorate. It may also lead to criticism from within the minister's political party and government. Ministers are appointed at the discretion of the prime minister. If a minister fails to perform effectively or to provide support for the government's policies, then that minister can be removed and replaced. Ministers can be moved to other ministerial roles that are deemed less important, or even demoted to the back benches.

Debates on particular issues may also provide a means of raising awareness of where a particular minister had made bad policy choices or failed to ensure policy objectives were achieved. It can, however, be difficult for these debates to be held given Standing Order No. 14, one of the internal rules of the House of Commons, which prioritizes government business. However, this standing order also sets out the possibility of opposition days, where the leader of the opposition and the second largest opposition party can determine the agenda. Standing Order No. 24 also provides for emergency debates. Any MP can propose an emergency debate. However, for this to succeed, the MP needs to ensure they obtain the approval of the Speaker of the House and the leave of the House. Debates may also take place in Westminster Hall, another chamber of the House of Commons. These debates provide an opportunity for discussion of general topics, but no vote is taken.

While debates may provide a means of raising awareness of an issue or requiring a minister or the government to give an account of their actions, they too may not result in any specific immediate consequences should the minister fail to provide a convincing account of their activities. Debates need not lead to a vote. They may not be widely reported. As with questions, and the role of departmental select committees, problems arise when assessing how far there are consequences for ministers who fail to give an effective account of their activities.

Ministers are meant to be accountable to Parliament and the people. However, accountability tends to be in the form of giving an account of how they have performed. There seem to be few consequences other than through the ballot box. Yet, the further away a minister's bad performance is from the next general election, the less likely it is that the electorate will be able to hold that minister to account. Only those voting in the constituency of that minister can directly hold the minister to account. Others may only do this indirectly, deciding not to vote for the political party to which the minister belongs. However, any decision may not be straightforward. How bad must a minister's performance be to persuade a member of the electorate to vote for a different political party? Any reason to not vote for that minister has to be balanced against the reasons to vote for the party to which the minister belongs.

It is also difficult for Parliament to effectively hold ministers to account. While Parliament may call for a minister to resign, or put a minister under significant pressure, ultimately the main consequences for failures in policy and its implementation rest with the prime minister and the political party to which the minister belongs. Perform badly and a prime minister can not only remove a minister but also ensure that the minister is never offered another ministerial role. The prime minister may even try to prevent that minister from being able to stand for their seat at the next general election.

Ministers should also be accountable for personal conduct. The Ministerial Code sets out standards ministers are expected to adhere to. These are designed to ensure ministers uphold good constitutional principles. These include the seven principles of public life: selflessness, integrity, objectivity, accountability, honesty and leadership. The code also sets out the relationship between ministers and the government, their departments and the civil servants who work for the government, and Parliament. It also sets out how ministers need to separate their ministerial from their constituency interests, and when ministers can make appointments. There are also provisions ensuring there are no conflicts between government business and a minister's personal interests.

Breaches of the Ministerial Code can carry severe penalties. Ministers can be expected to resign for some breaches – for knowingly misleading Parliament, for example. Other sanctions include a public apology, remedial action, or the removal of ministerial salary for a set period. These sanctions can be more severe than those imposed through other means of accountability, which may suggest that the Ministerial Code can provide a more effective means of holding a minister to account. However, as discussed regarding Partygate in Chapter 1, the prime minister is responsible for interpreting and enforcing the code. This leads to a suspicion that ministers are more likely to be accountable when they cause embarrassment or harm the wishes of the political party to which the prime minister belongs. Is it politics rather than principles that govern when ministers are required to resign?

Finally, ministers are also accountable as MPs. Specifically, they are required to adhere to parliamentary resolutions on the conduct of ministers, which includes a reiteration of the principle that ministers, as well as other MPs, should not knowingly mislead Parliament. MPs are also required to disclose personal interests in the Register of Members' Financial Interests. There are also detailed provisions of the Ministerial Code regarding ministers' personal interests, including specific rules about travel and travel expenses.

Given this network of principles of accountability, why are there concerns about whether there are effective checks and balances over the behaviour of ministers? These concerns arise in two ways. First, when we look at the resignation of ministers, these tend to be more likely to be for reasons other than policy failings, or failures to comply with the standards of good behaviour set out in the Ministerial Code. They tend to be more due to issues of personal conduct or for political reasons.

In 2020, for example, there were ten ministerial resignations, only one of which related to standards – Conor Burns, the Minister of State for Trade Policy, resigned after the Committee on Standards concluded that he had used his position to intimidate members of the public. Five resignations were due to concerns over government policies, including Lord Keen of Elie, the Advocate General for Scotland, who resigned when it became clear that the government was intending to use powers under the Internal Markets Bill 2020 to break international law obligations. As a law officer and the government's legal adviser on Scottish law, Lord Keen felt the only option left available to protect the rule of law was to resign.

Of the five resignations from Boris Johnson's government in 2021, one, Matt Hancock, then Secretary of State for Health and Social Care, related to a breach of standards when it became clear that he had breached social distancing guidelines. Two further resignations followed due to disagreements over governmental policies and others resigned for personal or health reasons.

In 2022, the largest ever number of ministerial resignations occurred in 24 hours, with 54 resignations in total during Boris Johnson's prime ministership. Most of these were in response to concerns over the behaviour of Boris Johnson, following the resignation of Chris Pincher, then Deputy Chief Whip, over reports that he drunkenly groped two men in a private club. We looked at Boris Johnson's resignation in the first chapter and will touch on this again in Chapter 8.

These events may show that collective ministerial responsibility – the principle that ministers are collectively responsible for governmental policy and should resign when they are unable to uphold these policies – works well. This can help to shore up the government's policies and ensure that it can count on the payroll vote of its ministers to help steer these policies through Parliament. As 2022 demonstrated, however, these can also be an effective means of enabling the political party of the government to hold its leader to account, the en masse resignations leading, in turn, to the resignation of Boris Johnson as leader of the Conservative Party.

However, the same may not be true for individual ministerial responsibility – the principle that ministers resign when there are policy failings, or failings in the administration of their departments. This has become more of a principle of accountability. Ministers may have to give an account to Parliament for the performance of their departments, but they may no longer need to resign, reflecting the extent to which ministers have less day-to-day control over their departments and how much governmental business may be implemented in practice by next steps agencies – bodies that perform governmental functions but which are not under the direct control of the government – or other private bodies removed from direct ministerial control.

Second, there are concerns that not only did this trend continue in Johnson's post-Brexit constitution, but also that there is evidence of a weakening of these standards, particularly as concerns the mechanisms for holding MPs and ministers to account for failing to adhere to standards of good constitutional government. Two notable examples are the attempts of the government to interfere with the conclusions of the Committee on Standards in the Owen Paterson affair and the modification of the Ministerial Code following the publication of the Sue Gray report.

Owen Paterson: fairness or fudge?

On 30 October 2019, the then parliamentary commissioner for standards began her investigation into the conduct of Owen Paterson. The parliamentary commissioner for standards is appointed by the House of Commons. At the time of writing, the parliamentary commissioner for standards is Daniel Greenberg, who replaced

Kathryn Stone on 1 January 2023. The parliamentary commissioner for standards is independent and is tasked with overseeing the Register of Members' Financial Interests and the Code of Conduct for MPs. This includes the conduct of ministers who are also MPs, although where these requirements are replicated in the Ministerial Code, the Ministerial Code takes precedence.

The parliamentary commissioner for standards started her inquiry into the conduct of Owen Paterson on her initiative, following reports in the media that appeared to suggest that Owen Paterson had breached the rules of the House of Commons relating to paid advocacy, as well as rules prohibiting the use of parliamentary offices or parliamentary stationery for non-parliamentary business and potential breaches of the Register of Members' Financial Interests.

After carrying out her investigation, the parliamentary commissioner for standards provided her report to the Committee on Standards. This is a House of Commons committee composed of MPs and lay members. They are tasked with overseeing the work of the parliamentary commissioner for standards and overseeing complaints relating to the Code of Conduct for MPs. The committee may decide to uphold or reject the report and, if it agrees that there has been a breach of parliamentary rules, will agree on an appropriate penalty in relation to these breaches.

The Owen Paterson report took longer than most reports, with delays due to the tragic circumstances under which Mr Paterson's wife took her own life, as well as logistical problems arising due to the Covid pandemic. The parliamentary commissioner for standards concluded that Owen Paterson had breached the rules of paid advocacy, as well as regarding the use of parliamentary stationery and offices. While Owen Paterson accepted the conclusions relating to the use of parliamentary stationery, he rejected the conclusion concerning a breach of the rules on paid advocacy and the use of his parliamentary office for personal business. He also raised concerns about the process under which the parliamentary commissioner for standards had conducted her investigation. He was concerned that there had been too many delays and that the parliamentary commissioner for standards had adopted an inquisitorial approach. In particular, he felt that he should have been allowed to cross-examine witnesses. He felt that being unable to do so meant that he had not been able to raise a proper defence to the accusations made against him.

The Committee on Standards agreed with the parliamentary commissioner for standards and concluded that Owen Paterson had breached the rules on paid advocacy and had used his parliamentary offices to conduct personal business. It then went on to consider aggravating and mitigating factors when determining the sanction to be imposed for this breach. The committee concluded that 'this was an egregious case of paid advocacy' and recommended that Mr Paterson be suspended from the House for a period of 30 days.[9]

If the Owen Paterson affair had ended at this stage, then the outcome would support a conclusion that, at least as regards the investigation of this affair, there are good principles of checks and balances over the behaviour of MPs with regard to preventing paid advocacy and lobbying in the House. These provisions uphold democracy. They ensure that MPs are not paid to promote the interests of particular individuals or companies in Parliament, perhaps thereby procuring them advantages. Having been investigated and found to have broken the rules, the Committee on Standards imposed a sanction which, while recognizing the mitigating factors of grief, distress and mental illness, nevertheless also recognized a series of multiple breaches relating to paid advocacy.

However, problems arose as the report of the Committee on Standards can only recommend sanctions. For these to be imposed, the report, including the sanctions, needs to be approved by the House of Commons. On 3 November 2021, Jacob Rees-Mogg tabled a motion to approve the report and endorse the committee's recommendations. However, Andrea Leadsom proposed an amendment to the motion. Both Jacob Rees-Mogg and Andrea Leadsom were, at the time, members of the governing political party – the Conservative Party. Jacob Rees-Mogg was also a member of the government, holding the role of Leader of the House of Commons. Rather than approve the report and the sanction, the amendment asked the House of Commons to vote to note the report of the Committee on Standards and also to note 'concerns expressed about potential defects in the standards system'. Given these defects, the motion proposed that the House of Commons should decline to consider the report, resolving instead to appoint a select committee to look further into these matters. The select committee would look both at the general issue regarding the rules regulating paid advocacy and the procedures to be applied by the Committee on Standards to ensure fairness, and also would consider whether the conclusion of the Committee on Standards regarding Owen Paterson should be reviewed or reconsidered by the House of Commons.[10]

The motion also set out the composition of this select committee, including specifically naming the proposed chair of the committee, John Whittingdale, a Conservative MP. The committee would also have eight backbench members, four from the Conservative Party, three Labour and one SNP. Unlike the Committee on Standards, there would be no lay members and, as in common with other select committees, there would be a Conservative Party majority in the select committee, representing the composition of the House of Commons. The newly composed select committee would also have the power to appoint legal advisers and specialist advisers, as well as send for persons, papers and records. The Conservative Party also ensured that its members were whipped – in other words, its party members would be required to vote in favour of this motion or face the prospect of losing the party whip. Perhaps unsurprisingly given the large governmental majority in the House of Commons, the vote on this amendment succeeded.

There was, understandably, criticism. This undermined the authority of the Committee on Standards and of the parliamentary commissioner for standards. Even if there were concerns as to the Code of Conduct for members, or the procedural rules that should apply to investigations of the commissioner and the committee, these concerns needed to be kept separate from the specific matter of whether Owen Paterson had broken the rules. The use of the whip was also criticized. This, to say the least, provided the perception that, should a committee conclude that an MP who was a member of the government's political party had broken the rules, there would be means of enabling that MP to avoid any sanction, and to criticize an independent report which concluded that rules had been breached. Why worry about upholding good standards of government, even those like the rules against paid advocacy which are designed to uphold democracy and prevent possible corruption, if these rules can be modified to ensure individuals escape sanction?

Following extensive criticism in Parliament and in the media, Owen Paterson resigned. An emergency debate was timetabled for 8 November. During this debate, the government admitted that it should not have confused the individual case of Owen Paterson with the broader issue of whether the Code of Conduct and the procedural rules for investigating breaches of these rules should be changed. The government also admitted that it should not have whipped a vote on House business, such as the approval of a report and sanction of the Committee on Standards. The government also concluded that, as Mr Paterson had resigned from the House of Commons, there was no need to decide on whether to accept the report of the Committee on Standards.[11]

On 15 November, a motion was placed before the House of Commons to rescind the motion of 3 November establishing a specific select committee to investigate both the general issues and their specific application to Owen Paterson, to approve the report on the Committee on Standards relating to Mr Paterson's conduct, and to note that Mr Paterson was no longer a member of the House. This was originally timetabled as a motion with no debate. However, as one member of the House shouted that they objected to the motion, this required a vote to be held to agree on the motion.[12]

A debate and a vote took place on 17 November. This vote illustrated a change in tactics. Rather than appointing a specific select committee, it approved cross-party work, based on recommendations of the Committee on Standards in Public Life, to update rules regarding the outside interests of MPs. It also recommended that the Committee on Standards should undertake this work and bring forward recommendations to update the Code of Conduct for MPs.[13] This work was duly undertaken by the committee, which published a set of proposals for a revised code of conduct which were then reviewed by Ernest Ryder, a former Senior President of Tribunals.[14]

Following comments on the revised code, a new procedural protocol was approved for the MPs' Code of Conduct in October 2022.[15] This establishes a new set of formal appeals to an Independent Expert Panel. The new procedures retain the inquisitorial process of the parliamentary commissioner for standards. They do not provide for an ability for cross-examination of witnesses before the Committee on Standards. The new Code of Conduct also specifically prevents MPs from lobbying the Committee on Standards, the Independent Expert Panel, or the parliamentary commissioner for standards and his staff to influence their conclusion as to whether a breach had taken place, or a sanction should be imposed.

Does this event show a slide into the dangers of populism, leading to the weakening of democratic processes and undermining checks and balances? There is some evidence through the use of the amendment to the motion to approve a committee report, the use of the whip on a matter of House business and the confusion of general and specific matters. It is also evident in some of the statements of Owen Paterson regarding his innocence. He argued that his communication of information on behalf of companies that paid him consultancy fees had been justified as exceptional communications to pass on information about a serious wrong. For example, one of the communications made by Mr Paterson concerned testing procedures performed by Randox, one of the companies for which he was a paid consultant, which had found chemicals in milk that had not been detected by the standard testing procedures. The commissioner for standards and the parliamentary Committee on Standards had concluded that Mr Paterson had not just communicated information about a serious wrong but also went on to advocate for the services of Randox. For example, further email communications had advocated the superior testing facilities of Randox and sought to facilitate their approval as an official testing service.

Mr Paterson argued that, as he believed that he was only communicating information about a serious wrong, then he could not have been involved in advocacy in breach of the Code of Conduct. He also argued that, as an experienced MP, he had been elected based on his judgment and that, as he had judged his conduct to be within the code, this was strong evidence that he had not breached the code's provisions. Mr Paterson also made allegations about the integrity of the parliamentary commissioner for standards and her staff, including suggesting that the behaviour of the commissioner and her staff had played a role in creating the situation of extreme anxiety that had led to his wife's suicide.[16]

It is difficult to draw definitive conclusions, particularly given the tragic circumstances surrounding this investigation. However, these statements, combined with the actions of the government in response to the report of the Committee on Standards, could be interpreted as demonstrating a disregard for objective standards, with MPs being free to determine whether their conduct breached the rules. Politics, rather than standards, decide when conduct breaches the rules. If a prime minister wants to back an MP from their political party, they can do so, even if this means questioning the outcome of an independent investigation.

However, this narrative does not fit with subsequent events, which show how, in extreme circumstances, cross-party support can be used to unite MPs to force a change in direction in governmental policy. The government's attempts to conflate the specific circumstances of Owen Paterson and general concerns over procedure, and its desire to propose an alternative, less independent and impartial committee to investigate such issues was thwarted. The subsequent modification of the rules was conducted by the Committee on Standards and scrutinized by a process of independent review, leading to the establishment of an appeals procedure and a reinforcement of the need to refrain from intimidatory tactics during these investigations. Parliament was able to flex its muscles, ensuring there was an effective check and balance on what some saw as a breach of the rules of the game by the government.

This would suggest that, at least as regards the Owen Paterson affair, parliamentary standards won out. Not only did the normal processes of democracy prevail, but also, they improved checks and balances over MPs for breaches of the Code of Conduct. Democracy was enhanced, not diminished.

Modifications to the Ministerial Code

On 27 May 2022, shortly after the publication of the Sue Gray report into the events surrounding Partygate, Boris Johnson made three changes to the previous 2019 version of the Ministerial Code. The first change clarified that there was a range of possible punishments for breaches of the code, including public apologies, remedial action or the removal of ministerial salary. This was included in the recommendations of the Committee on Standards in Public Life. However, they were coupled with other recommendations that were designed to strengthen checks and balances over ministers. However, these recommendations were not fully implemented.

For example, the second change to the Ministerial Code was to modify the powers of the independent adviser on ministerial interests, an officer appointed by the prime minister to advise on matters relating to the Ministerial Code. The Committee on Standards in Public Life had recommended that the independent adviser should have the power to initiate investigations. However, the code was only changed to empower the independent adviser to initiate investigations after consulting with the prime minister. The prime minister may prevent this investigation if they assess that it would be in the public interest for the investigation not to take place. In that situation, all the independent adviser may do is ask for the prime minister to give reasons – although these reasons cannot be made public if that would also harm the public interest. The Committee on Standards in Public Life had also recommended that the independent adviser should have the authority to determine whether the Ministerial Code was breached, and that the findings of the independent adviser should be published eight weeks after the adviser sent their report to the prime minister. These recommendations were not implemented.

Third, Boris Johnson changed the foreword to the Ministerial Code. The foreword is not part of the code, but it does nevertheless set the tone and indicate how a prime minister views the importance and purpose of the code. The 2019 foreword referred to the need to 'uphold the very highest standards of propriety', including honouring the seven principles of public life and ensuring that there was no 'bullying or harassment'. These statements are not repeated in the foreword to the 2022 Code. There is, however, a new paragraph:

> Thirty years after it was first published, the Ministerial Code continues to fulfil its purpose, guiding my Ministers on how they should act and arrange their affairs. As the Leader of Her Majesty's Government, my accountability is to Parliament and, via the ballot box, to the British people. We must show every day that we are worthy of this privilege by keeping our promises and delivering on the priorities of the British people.[17]

Unlike our assessment of the Owen Paterson affair, these modifications to the Ministerial Code cannot be presented, in the long run, as a potential victory for democracy. It is also easier to fit these changes into the narrative of populism leading to democratic decline. The timing of these changes could be seen as suspicious, the Gray report having appeared a few days earlier. The Gray report had concluded that multiple gatherings had taken place in 10 Downing

Street during lockdown that had not complied with Covid guidance in place at the time. This might have suggested that other ministers who had attended these gatherings, or who had perhaps done little to ensure gatherings were within Covid guidelines, may have faced investigation under the Ministerial Code. Modifying the penalties for breaches of the code in this manner may suggest that, were this to be the case, these ministers may only need to apologize and nothing more.

The then prime minister also failed to modify the Ministerial Code to fully implement the suggestions of the Committee on Standards in Public Life, which were designed to ensure the code was reconstituted to have the sole purpose of providing a code of ethical standards of conduct, rather than also a set of discretionary powers given to the prime minister to hire and fire ministers at will. As well as failing to fully implement the recommendations for the changes to the role of the independent adviser, the then prime minister also failed to implement other suggestions that could have reinforced the code. For example, the Committee on Standards in Public Life also recommended changes to the definition of leadership, one of the seven principles of public life referred to in the code. Their proposal would have amended the definition to include a requirement to 'treat others with respect' and to 'challenge poor behaviour when it occurs' rather than being 'willing to challenge' such behaviour.

The new foreword to the May 2022 Ministerial Code suggested that the then prime minister did not see this as the sole purpose of the Ministerial Code. The revised Ministerial Code still included a reference to the need for its provisions to be interpreted against the background of the seven principles of public life. The then prime minister's foreword also stated that the code is meant to guide how ministers act. But the then prime minister also linked this to his accountability to the electorate. Boris Johnson saw his government as being worthy of governing if they kept their promises and delivered on the priorities the electorate wanted. There was no specific reference here to being worthy to govern through upholding good principles of government.

Rishi Sunak, who became Prime Minister on 25 October 2022, reissued the Ministerial Code on 22 December 2022. The changes made by Boris Johnson in May 2022 remain. There are, however, three changes made in the December 2022 version of the Ministerial Code. First, the most recent iteration of the Ministerial Code sets out more clearly that the Business Appointment Rules and the Radcliffe Rules continue to apply to former ministers after they leave office, by including a reference to these provisions in paragraph 1.5 of the Ministerial Code. This does not change the content of these rules, it merely stresses their importance. Second, the Ministerial Code has been updated to provide an accurate account of when and how ministers may take maternity and other leave. Third, the foreword to the Ministerial Code has changed. Rishi Sunak's foreword prioritizes his policies of economic stability and fairness. It also includes the statement that his government 'will uphold the Principles of Public Life, ensuring integrity, professionalism and accountability at every level'.[18]

The May 2022 modifications made to the Ministerial Code by Boris Johnson did not undermine its fundamental purpose. The code is still in place. It is still referred to by MPs and political commentators and provides a clearer means through which to hold ministers to account for their behaviour. The foreword to the December 2022 reissue of the Ministerial Code from Rishi Sunak suggests that, at least for this Prime Minister, integrity is important, particularly if his government is to 'earn the trust of the British people'.[19] This pressure can give rise to resignations from ministers who are alleged to have broken the Ministerial Code, without requiring an investigation from the prime minister. However, the stronger suggestions for change from the Committee on Standards in Public Life have still not been implemented. This continues to suggest that the Ministerial Code will continue to be tempered by politics in its application.

At the time of writing, the most recent resignation from a ministerial post was that of Dominic Raab, who before his resignation was Deputy Prime Minister and the Secretary of State for Justice and Lord Chancellor. His resignation occurred following allegations of bullying made by civil servants. At the time the allegations were made, the position of independent adviser on ministerial interests was vacant, so Rishi Sunak, Prime Minister at the time, appointed a leading barrister, Adam Tolley KC, to carry out an investigation. His report upheld two of the eight allegations of bullying.[20] Although Dominic Raab did resign, having stated he would if the inquiry found the allegations to be true, in his letter of resignation he criticized the findings. He argued, 'In setting the threshold for bullying so low, this inquiry has set a dangerous precedent. It will encourage spurious complaints against ministers, and have a chilling effect on those driving change on behalf of your government – and ultimately the British people.'[21]

On the one hand, we have a carefully written report, based on witness interviews, which concluded that Dominic Raab had used intimidatory behaviour that amounted to bullying, but which also recognized that other elements of his behaviour – for example, his interruptive and abrasive style – did not amount to bullying on the evidence provided. On the other hand, we have a response which could be interpreted as suggesting that ministers need to be able to act in a way they deem suitable to ensure the will of the British people is achieved, even if this may mean acting in a manner that some may (in Dominic Raab's view wrongly) perceive as intimidatory and bullying.

Whatever you conclude as to whether Dominic Raab should or should not have resigned, the hinted overtones of populism are hard to deny. Implementing democratically backed policies does not justify bullying. But using the 'will of the people' as a trump card and a tactic to achieve a government's policy, overcoming perceived interference from so-called experts, might appear to do so.

What about the courts?

Courts provide a different form of check over the actions of the government. They ensure that the government acts lawfully. If individuals feel that the government has acted unlawfully, they may go to court and bring an action for judicial review. Judicial review is designed to ensure that courts do not reassess the merits of a decision. Instead, courts check to make sure that the government is acting within the law, including ensuring that they adhere to principles of natural justice and do not exercise discretionary powers in an irrational manner.

The Conservative Party was concerned that courts had used their powers too greatly, particularly the conclusion that the 2019 prorogation of Parliament was unlawful. In their manifesto, the Party stated that it would update:

administrative law to ensure that there is a proper balance between the rights of individuals, our vital national security and effective government. We will ensure that judicial review is available to protect the rights of the individuals against an overbearing state, while ensuring that it is not abused to conduct politics by another means or to create needless delays.[22]

This was meant to have been done through the establishment of a constitution, democracy and rights commission.

Although that commission was not established, the newly elected Conservative government did commission two independent reviews, one looking at administrative law (the Independent Review of Administrative Law (IRAL)) and the other at human rights (Independent Human Rights Act Review (IHRAR)). Both independent reports suggested some minor recommendations for change but did not recommend broad changes to either administrative law or the protection of human rights. Both reports were also followed by government consultations on further reform, both of which recommended changes which went beyond those originally recommended by the independent reports. Following these consultation exercises, the Judicial Review and Courts Act 2022 was enacted and the Bill of Rights Bill 2022 was introduced to Parliament in June 2022.

The Judicial Review and Courts Act 2022 introduces very few changes. It removes one form of judicial review over tribunal decisions, replacing this with a far more restrictive type of review. It also clarifies that courts can issue suspended and prospective-only quashing orders. A quashing order is a normal remedy in judicial review. In the prorogation case, for example, the Supreme Court quashed the unlawful prorogation of Parliament. A quashing order means that the prorogation of Parliament was treated as if it had never happened. In the words of the Supreme Court – the prorogation order was a 'blank sheet of paper'.[23]

A quashing order can have consequences for third parties that have relied on an act of a public body which is later quashed as unlawful. A suspended quashing order can delay the impact of a quashing order. For example, the court could delay a quashing order such that it would take effect in three months, giving the administration time to enact a new, lawful, regulation on the same subject. A prospective-only quashing order would only affect the future. If the Supreme Court had issued a prospective-only quashing order in the prorogation case, for example, then the prorogation of Parliament up to the time of the decision of the court would have been lawful. It would have become unlawful after the Supreme Court delivered its judgment.

The rhetoric surrounding IRAL, the government's consultation and the new Act strongly fits a populist narrative. For example, in its response to the IRAL report, the government stated that the report 'identified a growing tendency for the courts in judicial review cases to edge away from a strictly supervisory jurisdiction, becoming more willing to review the merits of decisions themselves, instead of the way in which those decisions were made'.[24]

However, it is hard to find this conclusion in the IRAL report itself. The government's response also referred to reaffirming the role of courts as 'servants of Parliament', misquoting a statement of Lady Hale that judicial review is often the servant of Parliament, pointing out how most judicial review cases involve courts interpreting legislation, ensuring that governmental bodies act within the powers given to them in legislation so as to uphold the will of Parliament set out in that legislation.[25] This is coupled with rhetoric expressed by ministers in Parliament in response to the prorogation case, discussed above. This may give the impression of a desire to reduce legal checks and balances over governmental powers.

However, this is difficult to square with the reality of the legal changes made, or the careful manner in which the government responded to the submissions to its consultation on judicial review reform, which led to the Judicial Review and Courts Act 2022. The government also implemented an amendment to the Act that was made by the House of Lords. This amendment made it clear that the new remedies of suspended and prospective-only quashing orders were at the discretion of the courts. This was achieved by removing a clause that would have potentially created a default of requiring courts to use suspended and prospective-only quashing orders whenever this was an appropriate remedy unless there were good reasons for courts not to do so.

This may suggest that rhetoric about removing the powers of the judiciary is precisely that. It is much harder in practice to remove important legal checks and balances over executive power to uphold the rule of law, making sure that the government only acts within the law. However, the same may not be true regarding the powers of the courts concerning human rights. There were two relevant concerns with the Bill of Rights Bill 2022. First, the Bill tipped the balance of powers with regard to the protection of human rights away from the courts and towards Parliament. Second, and more concerning, many of the proposals in the Bill were adopted by the government even though these were often rejected by a majority of those who submitted evidence to the government's human rights review. This suggests a more worrying trend of ignoring expertise. However, at the time of writing, the current Lord Chancellor, Alex Chalk, has confirmed that the government is not currently planning to bring the Bill into law. This, too, may, in the end, be best explained as a rhetorical argument that may appeal to the electorate, but which does not modify the extent to which the courts can hold the executive to account.

Nevertheless, there have been concerning recent developments. In March 2023, the government introduced the Illegal Migration Bill to Parliament. Since the enactment of the Human Rights Act 1998, ministers make a statement concerning the compatibility of the Bill with 'convention rights': human rights found in the European Convention on Human Rights. Ministers either state that a Bill is compatible with convention rights, or that, even if the minister cannot confirm that the Bill is compatible with convention rights, the minister nevertheless wishes to proceed with the Bill. For only the third time since the enactment of the Human Rights Act 1998, the minister presenting the Illegal Migration Bill – Suella Braverman, Home Secretary – stated that she was unable to state that the Bill was compatible with convention rights.

The government also prepares a human rights memorandum, setting out how a Bill will affect the rights in the European Convention on Human Rights. The memorandum prepared for the Illegal Migration Bill sets out the provisions of the Bill which, although the government thinks they provide sufficient protection of convention rights, it may be that the courts would conclude that the balance between convention rights and other rights and interests has not been drawn in the right place.[26] This is particularly the case for those provisions which, by requiring the removal of illegal immigrants from the UK, may undermine the right to family life, the right to a fair hearing, or the right to life and the right not to be subjected to torture. The Memorandum also sets out how the provisions of the Bill may be applied in a manner compatible with convention rights, particularly those designed to prevent modern slavery, noting that:

> radical solutions are required to put a stop to the small boats crossing the Channel and the approach adopted in these provisions is therefore new and ambitious but taking such an approach means that the Home Secretary is unable to make a statement under section 19(1)(a) of the 1998 Act.[27]

In addition, the Bill's provisions remove one of the ways in which the Human Rights Act 1998 can be used to protect convention rights that may be limited by the provisions of the Illegal Migration Bill. Currently, clause 1(5) of the Bill states that section 3 of the Human Rights Act 1998 'does not apply in relation to provision made by or by virtue of this Act'. Section 3 of the Human Rights Act 1998 requires courts, so far as it is possible to do so, to read and give effect to legislation in a manner compatible with convention rights. So, for example, if a Bill gives broad power to a minister, the Human Rights Act 1998 can be used to read this power such that it cannot be used to restrict convention rights. The Illegal Migration Bill would mean that this would not be possible for its provisions, or with regard to the interpretation of any delegated legislation enacted by a minister under powers granted to that minister by the Illegal Migration Bill.

The Bill also provides a further means by which convention rights may not be followed. It may be possible for individuals, once they have exhausted their rights under UK law, to apply to the European Court of Human Rights in Strasbourg. This court may grant an interim measure. In other words, the Strasbourg Court may rule that, pending a full hearing of the case that this individual's convention rights may have been breached, the individual is not to be removed from the UK. The Bill provides that immigration officials, ministers and the courts are not to take into account the effect of interim decisions from the European Court of Human

Rights when deciding whether to remove an individual from the country, unless the home secretary has specifically decided that they should do so with regard to a particular individual.

The Bill also contains ouster clauses. These are clauses that remove the power of the courts to check whether the government is acting within the scope of its powers through actions for judicial review. The Bill also limits current forms of judicial review, including those designed to protect human rights or to enable individuals to claim asylum. The effect of these provisions makes it very difficult for individuals to bring legal actions to prevent their removal from the UK, even if this is because their removal may harm their convention rights or other human rights. The Bill provides more limited claims, aimed to prevent removal from the country when the decision to remove them was based on a factual error, or where they would face real, imminent and foreseeable serious and irreversible harm in the country to which the UK wishes to remove them. It also means that individuals can be detained for 28 days before being able to bring a legal claim to be released, or to be released on bail, unless they can bring an action for habeas corpus to show that they were illegally detained.

All of these measures are extremely concerning with regard to the ability of the courts to check that the government is acting within the scope of its powers, particularly in relation to the protection of convention rights. While the government may argue that its Bill does provide sufficient protection of convention rights, checks by the courts will ensure that the government is right to reach that conclusion. Removing the possibility of these checks will make it harder to ensure that the government is acting lawfully.

Another concern is the speed with which the Bill proceeded through the House of Commons. The programme motion for the Bill, setting out the time devoted to scrutinizing its provisions, provided that there would be two days of parliamentary time allocated to the committee stage of the Bill. Each day was limited to six hours of discussion. The government also introduced some of the Bill's provisions at a late stage – the report stage – and the House of Commons only had just over five hours to debate these provisions. Some of these provisions placed further restrictions on the ability of courts to check the legality of a decision to remove an individual from the country or to uphold human rights.

This is a controversial issue. It may be that a majority believe that the immigration crisis is so severe that it merits restricting the courts from checking on the actions of immigration officials and the home secretary to provide a sufficient deterrent. However, it is vitally important to ensure that this is what a majority of the electorate want. This includes providing Parliament with sufficient time to check the legislation – even more so when it will remove the ability of the courts to check decisions do not harm rights or undermine the UK's international law obligations to refugees and to prevent modern slavery and human trafficking.

Conclusion

The UK constitution does appear to have both political and legal checks and balance mechanisms over the Westminster government. This is particularly true when we take stock of the events of 2019, both in terms of the ability of Parliament to check legislation and of the courts to quash the unlawful prorogation of Parliament.

However, it is hard to escape the spectre of Lord Hailsham's assessment of the UK constitution as an elective dictatorship, discussed in Chapter 3. Not only have the government's powers grown, but the checks on its exercise by Parliament and, at times, the courts, appears to be diminishing. While we can see evidence of checks over the content of legislation, this tends to be mostly from backbench MPs who are members of the same political party as the government, not from Parliament nor from the people.

Our assessment has shown how a government can use a large majority in Parliament to evade scrutiny – though equally we have seen how, when things go too far, Parliament is willing and ready to step in. The more recent reiteration of the Ministerial Code by the current Prime Minister, Rishi Sunak, may also illustrate a recognition that the government cannot merely assert that it is implementing the will of the people. A government, to be worthy of the name, must also earn the trust of the British people.

Recent changes, however, also seem to provide evidence in support of our populist narrative. This is particularly true of the Illegal Migration Bill which plans to limit legal checks over immigration decisions. However, the claim that all post-Brexit changes have limited checks and balances and support a populist narrative is inconclusive. Though it is also hard to conclude that there are effective checks and balances over the government. Political parties, Parliament and the people may not always be able to perform effective checks over the government, particularly one that uses a large majority in the House of Commons to push through legislation limiting legal checks over its powers in the name of upholding the will of the people.

5

Constitutional Guardrails or Greasy Poles?

The UK constitution is often described as unwritten or uncodified. This may seem odd given that we have been looking at legislation which has changed the constitution, such as the Dissolution and Calling of Parliament Act 2022 which changed the Westminster Parliament from a five-year fixed term to a five-year maximum term. Yet unwritten and uncodified seem apt because of the extent to which the UK constitution relies on practices, the constitutional conventions governing how powers are exercised. Some of these, like the Ministerial Code, have been written down. Others, however, are unwritten. Yet these unwritten rules play an important role, not just in terms of accuracy, but also in terms of how the UK constitution upholds good principles of constitutional governance.

For example, every Act of Parliament has to receive royal assent if this is to become a valid law. Described in this manner, it means that the Monarch has a veto over legislation. If Parliament were to pass legislation the King disapproved of then, legally, he could just refuse to sign the legislation and prevent it from becoming a valid law. However, the King has not, to date, done this. Nor did Queen Elizabeth II ever exercise this veto power during her long reign. As mentioned earlier in the book, the last time royal assent was refused was in 1708, when Queen Anne refused to assent to the Scottish Militia Bill. This royal restraint is described as illustrating a constitutional convention: the Monarch assents to all legislation unless advised by ministers not to do so. Indeed, Queen Anne's refusal to assent to the Scottish Militia Bill was on the advice of her

117

ministers, concerns arising as to the loyalty of the Scottish militia in the light of changing circumstances led ministers to change their minds about the policy found in the Scottish Militia Bill.

As we have seen in previous chapters, constitutional conventions are not enforced by the courts. So why are they followed? There are a number of possible explanations for why the King will grant assent to legislation. First, there may be severe consequences for failing to adhere to a constitutional convention. What would happen, for example, if the King refused assent to legislation? Most constitutional commentators would see this as giving rise to a constitutional crisis. How such a crisis would be resolved may well depend on the circumstances.

What if the King refused to sign legislation that had been proposed by a popular government, had been voted in by an overwhelming majority in the House of Commons, including with the support of a least one of the major opposition parties, and had been resoundingly approved of by the House of Lords, where there was also wide evidence of general public support for the legislation in question? In these circumstances, it is hard to see anything other than widespread public disapproval of the actions of the King. Public criticism may transform into calls for a reduction in the powers of the Monarch, or the removal of public money supporting the monarchy, or even calls for a move from a constitutional monarchy to a republic in the UK.

What if the King refused to grant assent to legislation that had been pushed through Parliament by an unpopular government, perhaps with the use of the provisions of Standing Order No. 14 (the internal rule of the House of Commons that prioritizes government business) and programme motions for legislation to pass a Bill quickly through the House of Commons, with little if any scrutiny, often taking place at times when few people were present? Or what if the King refused to grant royal assent to legislation that was enacted without the consent of the House of Lords – using the procedure of the Parliament Acts 1911 and 1949 – and this legislation had been roundly criticized for either limiting fundamental human rights or breaking international law? In these situations, there may be more sympathy for the King's refusal to grant assent. This time, the criticism may be of the actions of the government and there may be calls for the prime minister to resign or to call a general election, rather than criticism of the King for refusing to grant his assent to a Bill.

As well as the serious possible consequences of failing to follow a constitutional convention, there may be good reasons for following a convention, particularly if this upholds good principles of constitutional government. The constitutional convention that the Monarch will grant assent to legislation, unless advised by ministers not to do so, upholds democracy. It is a key element of the UK's constitutional monarchy. This reflects what Lord Hennessy and Andrew Blick call the 'good chaps' theory.[1] It would not be the 'done thing' for the King to refuse assent. Like his late mother, the King has an excellent understanding of the UK constitution and its practical operation. He understands not only the consequences of acting contrary to this convention but also accepts the limitations that this places on his legal powers.

This element of self-restraint also contains an aspect of respect for the other institutions of the constitution. The Monarch respects the role of Parliament, the government and the courts. This respect is normally mutual. In the same way that the Monarch respects Parliament, there is a strong conviction in both the government and Parliament that the Monarch should remain politically neutral. The King is not to be drawn into politics. The King may enjoy the provisions of the so-called tripartite convention, empowering him to be consulted, to encourage and to warn the government. But there is no requirement for the government to follow the advice, warning or encouragement of the Monarch. If the government heeds advice or warnings, it is out of respect for the knowledge and experience of the Monarch, not out of duty.

Unwritten rules, alongside elements of self-restraint and mutual trust, are not unique to the UK constitution. They are present in written and codified constitutions as well. Levitsky and Ziblatt, for example, point out how they are also present in the US constitution.[2] They refer to them as constitutional guardrails. They stop those in power from using the rules for their own gain, or in a manner that would undermine democracy or good principles of constitutional government. A government that refuses to adhere to these unwritten rules or principles, without good reason, endangers the constitution. Examples of a government acting in this manner, therefore, would appear to fit our populist narrative. Why bother to restrain your power if you are acting in line with the wishes of the people? After all, it cannot be undemocratic if you are ignoring elitist principles of constitutionalism to uphold direct democracy. There is no need for a populist leader to respect the actions of other institutions of the constitution if those actions are restricting the ability of that leader to implement the will of the people.

If there is evidence of an erosion of these constitutional guardrails of self-restraint and mutual trust, then this would tend to suggest that there has been an erosion of democracy and principles of constitutionalism in the post–Brexit constitution. However, evidence that constitutional guardrails may have been dented or bent out of shape, but still managed to remain intact, would suggest that the UK constitution was robust enough to prevent the emergence of unchecked power, the post–Brexit constitution merely providing further evidence of business as usual and not a slide into populism.

We will look at two examples of where self-restraint and mutual trust on behalf of the government may appear to have been undermined. First, we will look at two situations in which it appeared that the UK government was prepared to act in contravention of international law. Second, we will look at two recent cases in the Supreme Court which suggest that there may be occasions when the government is acting in a manner that is not respectful of the courts. Finally, we will ask whether there is evidence of a further problem. The enforcement mechanisms for unwritten rules work well when there are independent bodies to which those following the rules are accountable. However, if there is evidence of the government having too much control over those to whom they are required to be accountable, it can be easy for any government to fail to uphold self-restraint and to act in a manner that respects other institutions of the constitution.

Ignoring international law

Following the UK's exit from the European Union at 11 pm on 31 January 2020, the UK government entered into negotiations to establish the UK's new relationship with the European Union. The timeline was tight. A deal had to be struck and implemented by the end of the year. In the meantime, EU law continued to apply in the UK to ensure a smooth transition to the new relationship. This also provided time for the UK to enact laws that would be necessary to fill in gaps left by EU law. One such gap was the regulation of the market in the UK.

The UK is a devolved nation. In addition to the Westminster Parliament, there are also legislative bodies in Scotland, Wales, and Northern Ireland. Unlike the Westminster Parliament, the Scottish Parliament, Senedd Cymru (Welsh Parliament) and the Northern Ireland Assembly do not have legally unlimited powers. Instead, each has a different set of powers, set out in legislation enacted by the UK Parliament. Each legislative body has a different arrangement, although over time all three have moved to a model where they can enact legislation in all areas save those that have been reserved to the Westminster Parliament. For example, all three of the devolved legislatures have the power to enact measures to protect health. This is why, during the Covid pandemic, there were differences between the lockdown measures in England, Wales, Scotland and Northern Ireland.

This ability for rules to diverge can have an impact on the sale of goods and services in the UK. For example, Scotland and Wales both used their powers to enact legislation to protect health to introduce a minimum price for alcohol. This means that it can be more expensive to buy alcoholic drinks in Scotland and Wales than it is in England. When the UK was a member of the EU, market divergences were regulated by EU law. Scotland, Wales and Northern Ireland did not have the power to enact legislation which contravened EU law while the UK remained a member of the EU. The EU's regulation of the internal market did allow for divergence, but only when this was for a legitimate aim and when the restriction on the free movement of goods around the EU would be proportionate. In this case, the EU was happy that the minimum alcohol price in Scotland and Wales was for a legitimate aim – protecting health – and that the price set was a proportionate restriction on the free movement of goods to protect health.

Post Brexit, however, the EU's regulation of the internal market no longer applies as the UK did not wish to be part of the internal market. During the transition period, as negotiations over the UK's future relationship with the EU were taking place, the UK needed to decide whether it too wished to have free movement of goods across the UK and, if so, how it would achieve this objective. This, in and of itself, was a difficult issue. It would require careful negotiations to respect the powers of Scotland and Wales to continue to enact laws on areas like health and the environment, while also thinking through how to ensure that these divergent provisions did not have an impact on the free movement of goods across the UK.

If that were not difficult enough, Northern Ireland posed unique problems that were proving almost impossible to resolve. Northern Ireland has a land border with the EU: the border between Ireland and Northern Ireland. The Northern Ireland peace process, which led to the Belfast Agreement/Good Friday Agreement, helped to remove this border. This was instrumental in smoothing over relations between Ireland and Northern Ireland and has given rise to aspects of an all-island economy, for example in agriculture and electricity. Yet, given the UK's exit from the EU and its desire to no longer take part in the EU's internal market, EU law would require a border between Northern Ireland, part of the UK, and Ireland, part of the EU. This is because, as the UK would no longer be part of the EU or the internal market, customs duties would need to be imposed on goods travelling from Northern Ireland to Ireland. These goods would also have to prove that they satisfied EU requirements relating to their production and sale. However, the imposition of a border could threaten the all-island economy and, more importantly and fundamentally, the delicate peace process in Northern Ireland.

The solution to this conundrum was the Northern Ireland Protocol. This provides for Northern Ireland to adhere to the same rules regulating goods and services as are found in the EU. It also regulates the movement of goods from the UK to Northern Ireland. Goods that are moving from England, Scotland and Wales to Northern Ireland which are likely to then move on to Ireland are subject to customs checks for compliance with EU rules and regulations before they leave the mainland and arrive in Northern Ireland. The Protocol also means that the rules relating to goods and services in the EU continue to apply in Northern Ireland.

These provisions ensure that there is no need for a land border between Northern Ireland and Ireland. Goods can move freely across the border without breaching EU law. However, it also has the effect of imposing a 'border' between Northern Ireland and the rest of the UK. This has proved highly controversial. It has also been difficult to fully implement the Northern Ireland Protocol and grace periods were created to ease this process, such that EU rules were not to apply to some areas of movement; for example, the transfer of chilled meats and sausages from supermarkets in England, Wales and Scotland to the same supermarket chain in Northern Ireland.

Against this complex background, the government introduced the United Kingdom Internal Market Bill to Parliament in 2020. This Bill was designed to establish an internal market in the UK, such that if a good could be lawfully sold in either England, Wales or Scotland, then it could be lawfully sold in all of these three nations. Existing arrangements, like the minimum price for alcohol, were allowed to remain as exceptions. There is also an ability for England, Scotland and Wales to enact further measures to protect health, for example, but these are harder to justify than they were under EU law. This is because the UK's internal market has a narrower definition of a legitimate aim that can be used to restrict the free movement of goods.

When the Bill was introduced, however, it contained clauses which would have empowered ministers to enact measures that contravened provisions of the Northern Ireland Protocol, both in terms of regulations for the movement of goods from other parts of the UK to Northern Ireland and with regard to state aids (the giving of grants from the government to businesses in Northern Ireland). The Bill also clarified that any regulations made by ministers that breached the provisions of the Northern Ireland Protocol would be lawful. No court would be able to declare these measures unlawful for breaching provisions of international or domestic law.

The provisions were widely criticized as they would empower a minister to enact measures that contravened international law. The UK has a distinct relationship with international law due to the sovereignty of the UK Parliament. The UK government has the power to enter into treaties with other states and international organizations such as the EU. These treaties, once ratified by the UK, are binding on the UK under international law. However, merely ratifying a treaty does not create any form of obligation or rights in UK law. This is because the UK adopts a theory of dualism. It regards international law as distinct from national law. Provisions of international law can only become part of domestic law if they are incorporated into UK law, normally through legislation, or delegated legislation when a parent Act empowers the executive to enact regulations to implement specific obligations arising under international treaties. This preserves parliamentary sovereignty. The government acting alone should not be able to create or modify rights and obligations in the UK unless authorized to do so by Parliament. It is for Parliament, therefore, to enact legislation to implement international obligations into UK law, or to give the government the power to incorporate specific international obligations into UK law through delegated legislation.

To bring in measures that would empower ministers to contravene international law is not unlawful as far as domestic law is concerned. Parliament is sovereign. If it wanted to enact measures to contravene international law, it could do so. However, to do so also undermines the rule of law: the idea that institutions of the UK are governed by law and act within legal limits. When it comes to the UK Parliament, this is an aspect of self-limitation. It may be legally possible according to UK law for the UK Parliament to enact measures which contravene international law. However, we would expect the government not to propose such legislation given its impact on the rule of law and the fact that this would breach international law. We would also expect Parliament not to agree to enact such legislation given its implications for the rule of law.

This element of self-limitation is even more important when it comes to enacting legislation empowering ministers to act contrary to international law. We have already talked about the Ministerial Code, particularly when discussing Partygate in Chapter 1. The Ministerial Code sets out principles of good government that ministers are expected to follow. This includes an overarching duty to comply with the law. The original version of the Ministerial Code, enacted in 2010, set out clearly that this included an obligation to comply with international law and treaty obligations as well as domestic law. This was removed from the 2015 version of the Ministerial Code and has not since been stated explicitly in the code's provisions. However, it was made clear in ministerial statements and case law that the change was not meant to remove the obligation to adhere to international law from the provisions of the Ministerial Code.[3]

Provisions in the Internal Market Bill 2020 appeared to transgress this self-imposed limit in three ways. First, international law was arguably breached from the moment the Bill was placed on the statute book. This was because it would contradict provisions of the withdrawal agreement, an international treaty between the UK and the EU that was binding in international law. This includes a provision of 'good faith', requiring the UK and the EU to comply with its obligations under the withdrawal agreement. Introducing legislation to empower ministers to act contrary to the Northern Ireland Protocol, part of the withdrawal agreement, undermined this obligation. The institutions of the EU in particular were concerned that the Internal Market Bill breached these provisions of the withdrawal agreement.

Second, the enactment of these provisions in the Internal Market Bill would further transgress the UK's international law obligations under the withdrawal agreement between the UK and the EU when they came into force as part of an Act of Parliament. The withdrawal agreement requires the Northern Ireland Protocol to have direct effect in domestic law. The withdrawal agreement also requires that to the extent provisions of the Northern Ireland Protocol clash with domestic law, including current and future legislation, the Northern Ireland Protocol is to be applied over and above conflicting provisions of domestic law. The Internal Market Bill, however, would, when it came into force, overturn the provisions of UK law providing for the Northern Ireland Protocol to have an effect on domestic law and override UK law.

Third, international law would be breached as and when ministers used their powers to enact measures that contravened the Northern Ireland Protocol or the withdrawal agreement. This would mean that ministers had made delegated legislation whose provisions breached specific elements of international law.

The fact that the Internal Market Bill contravened and could be used to contravene international law was confirmed by Brandon Lewis, then Secretary of State for Northern Ireland. When asked about the implications of the Bill in the House of Commons, he replied 'I would say to my hon. Friend that yes, this does break international law in a very specific and limited way. We are taking the power to disapply the EU law concept of direct effect, required by Article 4, in certain very tightly defined circumstances.'[4]

This makes it clear that the government accepted the second argument: that the Bill when it was enacted, would breach international law by removing an aspect of the requirement that the Northern Ireland Protocol be recognized as part of domestic law and be able to be relied on in domestic courts by individuals. This recognition of EU law by domestic law is known as 'direct effect' in EU law. However, Brandon Lewis argued that this breach of international law would only be in a 'very specific and limited way'. Only some aspects of the Northern Ireland Protocol and not all of its provisions would no longer have direct effect.

However, there was no mention in Brandon Lewis's statement that international law would be breached merely by proposing the Bill in the first place. Nor did Brandon Lewis argue that ministers were intending to use their powers to breach international law. Rather, the government argued that these provisions were part of the negotiation strategy with the EU. The government wished to secure a future trade agreement with the EU. However, in case that was not possible, the provisions enabling ministers to enact regulations contrary to the provisions of the Northern Ireland Protocol would provide a means of ensuring that the government 'can deliver on our commitment to the people of Northern Ireland'.[5]

In the end, the offending clauses were removed from the Bill. The United Kingdom Internal Market Act 2020 came into force and the Northern Ireland Protocol was applied, subject to specific grace periods that are still in place for some areas.

The willingness to enact legislation that breached international law, and which empowered ministers to act contrary to international law can fit with both of our narratives. On the one hand, it illustrates a willingness to ignore constitutional guardrails. Why bother complying with the rule of law if you do not have to, particularly when to do otherwise may mean you fail to implement the will of the people? If the people are sovereign, then the requirements of international law should not get in the way of their wishes. Brexit needed to be implemented to achieve the will of the people expressed in the referendum, even if that meant disobeying international law and undermining the rule of law. The Northern Ireland Protocol was unpopular, so surely it was acceptable to ignore its provisions to ensure the will of the people was upheld. Self-restraint is not needed. Upholding the will of the people is all that matters.

On the other hand, the specific and limited breach of international law was arguably justified given the complex backdrop of negotiations with the EU. There was no general disrespect of self-restraint or background constitutional principles like the rule of law.

The intention was never really to breach international law but merely to use this potential threat as a means of strengthening the UK's bargaining position. Exceptional circumstances justified a minor exception. There was no weakening or removal of constitutional guardrails, merely a threat to bend them a little to achieve the greater good in a difficult situation.

The reaction in Parliament, and from high-ranking government lawyers, however, supports the narrative that the government was not concerned about acting within the limits of its powers and was content to act in a manner that would breach the rule of law by undermining the rule of law. Jonathan Jones KC, then Treasury Solicitor, the highest-ranking member of the government's legal department, offered his resignation on 8 September, the day Brandon Lewis confirmed in Parliament that the Bill breached international law in a limited and specific manner. He did so because he believed that the Internal Markets Bill undermined the rule of law.

The Government Legal Department advises the government on the legality of its actions. As a civil servant, Jonathan Jones is bound by the civil service code and the Nolan principles, which set out standards in public life. As a barrister, he is also bound by the ethics of his profession. He regarded these codes as requiring him to find a way in which the government could achieve its policy objectives without breaking the rule of law. When it appeared to be impossible to achieve this, he felt he had no other option but to resign.

Lord Keen of Elie, the Advocate General for Scotland (a law officer who provides advice to the UK government on Scottish law), also offered his resignation, though at a later stage than Jonathan Jones. Lord Keen concluded that merely granting ministers the power to act contrary to international law would not be a breach of the rule of law in and of itself. Rather, a breach of the rule of law would occur as and when ministers exercised their powers in a manner that breached international law. However, when it became clear that the government did intend for ministers to exercise their powers in this way, Lord Keen felt he had no choice but to offer his resignation.

For two leading government lawyers to resign in this way seems to illustrate that the government were keen to enact legislation that would undermine international law obligations, even when those employed to advise the government on their legal obligations made it clear that the government would be acting in a manner that would undermine the rule of law by breaching international law. If the government is not willing to follow the advice of those appointed to advise them on the law, such that those holding these positions feel they have no choice but to resign, that would tend to suggest that the government is at least willing to bend, if not break, constitutional guardrails. Good principles of constitutional government can be easily sacrificed and self-imposed limitations ignored when they get in the way of the will of the people.

This narrative is reinforced when we explore further why the provisions were dropped from the Bill. Despite strong objections from the opposition in the House of Commons, the clauses remained in the Bill after the Commons had scrutinized and voted on its provisions, before sending these to the House of Lords. However, they did not survive scrutiny by the House of Lords. The clauses were widely condemned in the House of Lords, particularly in reports by the House of Lords Select Committee on the Constitution and the Delegated Powers and Regulatory Reform Committee. This led Lord Judge to table a motion of regret in the Bill's second reading in the House of Lords. The Lords voted in favour of the Bill and of Lord Judge's motion, which added 'but this House regrets that Part 5 of the bill contains provisions which, if enacted, would undermine the rule of law and damage the reputation of the United Kingdom'.[6]

Later, at the committee stage, the House of Lords voted to remove the provisions of the Bill that were contrary to international law. Following the Bill's return to the House of Commons, the government acceded to this amendment and the clauses were removed from the Bill. Even if the government was not willing to limit its actions, it was clear that the House of Lords were not willing to agree to legislation which would breach the UK's obligations in international law. The Lords were ultimately successful in ensuring, in the end, that international law was not breached. Even if the government does not act within the constitutional guardrails, other institutions are willing and able to ensure these guardrails remain in place.

It is difficult to know whether it was the actions of the House of Lords alone which led to the government removing the offending clauses from the Internal Market Bill. While the Bill was being debated in the House of Lords and following its return to the House of Commons, the UK government was continuing its negotiations with the EU. The government's decision to remove the clauses that breached international law took place after a meeting with representatives of the EU, which had also insisted that the clauses that breached international law should be removed from the Bill. An alternative narrative, therefore, is that the negotiation tactic succeeded, with the EU reaching an agreement with the UK and insisting that, as part of that agreement, the UK should not enact provisions that would contravene the Northern Ireland Protocol. Guardrails may have been bent in a time of emergency. But they did not break. Nor, according to this perspective, was it even the intention of the government that they should do so, such guardrails being meant to bend when required to achieve the will of the people.

As with most of the events in Boris Johnson's post-Brexit constitution, the narrative can be spun both ways. However, given more recent events, it is hard to conclude that the UK government is unwilling to propose legislation that breaches international law. In July 2022, the government introduced the Northern Ireland Protocol Bill. The Bill was also designed to stop provisions of the Northern Ireland Protocol from having legal force in the UK. The Bill also granted ministers the power to make delegated legislation to exempt other provisions of the Northern Ireland Protocol from having effect in UK law.

This second attempt to enact legislation that would breach the Northern Ireland Protocol was different. The government obtained legal advice to the effect that it would be lawful for the UK government to act contrary to its obligations under the Northern Ireland Protocol. This is because its actions were justified in international law according to the defence of necessity.[7] However, this argument was widely criticized.[8] It was accepted that the defence of necessity existed in international law and could be used to justify what would otherwise be a breach of international law. It is widely accepted that this defence exists when breaching international law is necessary to safeguard an essential interest against grave and imminent peril and normally only in exceptional circumstances. Much as there were difficulties with enforcing the Northern Ireland Protocol, as well as political controversy surrounding its application, it was hard to see this as giving rise to imminent peril. This was reinforced by the fact that there were mechanisms within the Northern Ireland Protocol itself that could have been used to suspend its application in the UK.

In the end, the Northern Ireland Protocol Bill was put on hold following the agreement of the Windsor Framework between the UK and the EU. This framework resolved some of the difficulties surrounding the transport of some goods from the mainland to Northern Ireland – for example, the movement of seed potatoes, processed meats and medicine. It also provides for the 'Stormont brake'. As discussed above, under the provisions of the Northern Ireland Protocol, Northern Ireland is required to follow certain EU laws, particularly those relating to the EU's internal market. However, when the EU makes laws post Brexit, this means that Northern Ireland is a 'rule taker', meaning it has to adhere to rules that were made by the EU institutions, but Stormont, the Northern Ireland Parliament, has no say in the content of these rules.

The Stormont brake enables 30 members of the Northern Ireland Assembly, from at least two political parties, to raise concerns about proposed EU legislation. This can only be used in exceptional circumstances when changes to EU law mean that provisions will be significantly different from the current law and are likely to have a persistent and significant impact on the lives of people living in Northern Ireland. When this succeeds at Stormont, the UK government is required to enter into discussions with the Northern Ireland executive and to raise these concerns in the EU if it agrees that the conditions for triggering the Stormont brake are met. If the EU agrees, then the measure is suspended. This then triggers a process through which the measure may be modified. If no agreement is reached, then Northern Ireland may decide that it will not adhere to the new law. If this were to occur, then the EU may take remedial measures in response.

Following the Windsor Framework, Rishi Sunak made a statement to the House of Commons confirming that the Northern Ireland Protocol Bill 'was only ever meant to be a last resort, meant for a world where we could not get negotiations going'. The Prime Minister went on to confirm that, following this negotiated agreement, 'the original and sound legal justification for the Bill has now fallen away [...] we will therefore no longer proceed with the Bill'.[9]

This approach does illustrate greater respect for constitutional guardrails. Rather than admitting that the government intended to breach international law, the government argued that its actions were justified in international law. However, given the widespread criticism of this justification, it could also be argued that constitutional guardrails are adhered to in theory, but not necessarily in reality. They have become weakened and warped, if not completely bent out of shape or removed.

It is also worrying that the government appears to see threats of breaching international law as a possible negotiation tactic. While this may have succeeded in helping to achieve a negotiated outcome in both instances, it is potentially damaging to the reputation of the UK government on the international stage. It is also not clear whether threats to break international law were necessary to initiate an acceptable negotiated settlement.

The Northern Ireland Protocol, however, is not the only international agreement that the UK appears to be willing to at least threaten to contravene. The recently proposed Illegal Migration Bill, discussed in Chapter 4, included a statement from the Home Secretary, Suella Braverman, that, even though she was unable to state that the Bill was compatible with convention rights, the government nevertheless wished to proceed with the Bill. The Illegal Migration Bill also prevents courts and immigration officers from using interim injunctions from the European Court of Human Rights to prevent an individual's removal from the UK, unless the home secretary determines that the interim injunction should be adhered to. There are also concerns that the Bill breaches the UK's international law obligations concerning refugees and those who are victims of modern slavery and human trafficking.

My concern is that these examples illustrate a change in culture and an acceptance that self-restraint is not needed. It is not unlawful, purely in terms of domestic law, for Parliament to enact legislation in breach of international law or which empowers a minister to act contrary to international law. It is, however, contrary to international law unless international law itself justifies this breach. We would normally expect governments not to propose such legislation and parliaments not to vote in favour of it, out of respect for international law and to uphold the rule of law. However, when breaching international law fits the will of the people, it would appear it can be ignored, be that to achieve Brexit as set out in the referendum or to deal with the problem of people travelling to the UK on small boats.

If these examples do illustrate a culture change, it is hard to deny their fit with a populist narrative. Self-restraint is not needed when implementing the will of the people. However, given the unusual and complex situation of dealing with Brexit, and the fact that often threats do not materialize, it could also be argued that these examples are merely exceptions to the norm and not evidence of populism. We may only know more if the Windsor Framework fails to resolve the problems surrounding the Northern Ireland Protocol or if the Illegal Migration Bill becomes an Act with the provisions that are and may be contrary to international law remaining, thereby becoming part of UK law.

Minimizing mutual respect?

There is clear evidence of rhetoric from those criticizing key constitutional decisions that were unpopular with the government. The most striking was the 'Enemies of the people' headline in response to the decision of the divisional court in the first *Miller* case, the case which looked at whether the government could use prerogative powers to notify the EU of its intention to withdraw from the EU treaties, or whether legislation was required. This came from the media, not the government, although some criticized the late response of Liz Truss, then Lord Chancellor, in failing to support the judiciary in response to these comments.

As discussed in previous chapters, Boris Johnson, when he was Prime Minister, also had strong words to say about the second *Miller* decision, the prorogation case. However, strong words are to be expected. Courts uphold the law and, in doing so, can strike down decisions of the government implementing key policy areas. Nobody likes being told they got it wrong. It can be even more infuriating if your error was not about whether you made the right policy choice, but because of the way you made that choice, or because you mistakenly believed you had the power to act when you did not.

Nor need strongly worded criticism undermine respect. While some saw judges as 'enemies of the people' for requiring Parliament to enact legislation to empower the government to trigger the Brexit process, the government respected the decision of the Supreme Court. In Prime Minister's Questions on the day of the Supreme Court judgment, the then Prime Minister, Theresa May, stated that 'following the Supreme Court judgment, a Bill will be provided for the House, and there will be proper debate on it in the Chamber and in another place'.[10] The following day, David Davis, the Secretary of State for Exiting the European Union, stated that the government would introduce a short Bill. During the second reading of the Bill on 31 January, he explained that the Bill was designed to implement and respect the decision of the Supreme Court.[11] Boris Johnson also respected the decision of the Supreme Court in the prorogation case. He did ensure that Parliament returned, despite disagreeing with the Supreme Court's decision. Mutual respect between the courts, the government and Parliament, therefore, remained intact, despite strong words.

However, three recent court decisions would suggest that there are signs of erosion in mutual trust, at least on the part of the government. Two illustrate a potential erosion of unwritten rules of respect. A third case potentially demonstrates a willingness to bend the guardrails, trying to find a way around a court order that did not suit the policy choices of a minister.

Declining to follow declaratory orders

Judicial review enables an individual with sufficient interest in a decision of a public body to go to court to challenge the legality of that decision. The usual remedy, if the decision is found to be unlawful by the court, is a quashing order. If a decision is quashed, then the law treats the decision as if it has never been made. Courts may also grant other remedies. For example, if a minister has failed to carry out a statutory duty, then the court might issue a mandatory order, requiring the minister to fulfil their duty. It may also be the case that an unlawful decision may harm the rights of an individual between the time the individual starts their claim and the court can hear the case. In these circumstances, courts may grant an injunction. This would prevent the public body from continuing to act in an allegedly unlawful manner until the court was fully able to hear the case.

The courts have discretion as to the remedies they can grant. Sometimes, particularly when a decision of a public body has an impact on those other than the person who brought the case, courts may decide to grant a declaratory order. This clearly states that the decision of the public body is unlawful. However, it does not quash the decision. Nor does the court require the public body to act in a particular way. For example, a planning authority may have granted planning permission for a café, only for it later to be discovered that they failed to give a full month for objections to the planning permission to be communicated to the planning authority, missing this required period by a day. It may have been that nobody was planning to lodge an objection on the missed day. However, one individual then brings an action for judicial review against the decision as they are concerned that, if corners are cut in one planning application, albeit one with near-universal support, they may also be cut in later, more contentious planning applications. In these circumstances, the court might issue a declaratory order to declare that the failure to have allocated the full month for consultations was unlawful but decide not to quash the decision to grant planning permission for this particular café.

Declaratory orders may also be used instead of issuing a mandatory order. This is what happened in the *Craig* decision.[12] The case concerned a request for the extradition of Mr Craig from the UK to the US to face charges of fraud. In particular, it was alleged that he had posted false information on Twitter about companies from Scotland. This information had reduced the value of the shares of these companies. He was then able to use this to profit from transactions on the US stock market.

Mr Craig argued that, as the bulk of his actions had taken place in Scotland, he should have been able to take account of the forum bar, set out in UK legislation. This would have provided him with the opportunity to argue against extradition, with any legal action being brought against him in the UK rather than in the US. However, he faced a problem. We often think of UK legislation as coming into force from the day on which it receives royal assent. But this is not always the case. Acts of Parliament may, instead, empower a minister to enact a regulation setting out when a statute, or certain provisions of that statute, are to come into force. We call this a commencement order. This was the case with the legislation setting out the forum bar. The minister had used this power to bring the provisions into force in England, Wales and Northern Ireland. However, measures had not yet been made to bring the provisions into force in Scotland.

Mr Craig first argued that the decision not to bring the provisions into force in Scotland was unlawful. He succeeded. The court concluded that the minister only had the power to issue an order to bring the forum bar into force for the UK as a whole. The minister did not have the power to choose to bring the forum bar into force for some parts of the UK, but not all of the UK. The court agreed and issued a declaratory order. This declared that it was unlawful for the minister not to have ensured that the forum bar came into force across the UK at the same time. However, the court did not issue a mandatory order requiring the minister to act to bring the forum bar into force in Scotland.

Despite this order declaring the action unlawful, the minister did not bring the forum bar into force in Scotland for another two years. In the meantime, Mr Craig's challenge to his extradition order came before the Supreme Court. He was arguing that the Scottish ministers did not have the power to comply with the extradition order. This is because an extradition order would harm his convention rights, particularly Article 8, the right to private life. Under the provisions of the Scotland Act 1998, Scottish ministers may not act in a manner that contravenes convention rights. To assess whether his convention rights had been harmed, the court could assess whether there were legitimate grounds to interfere with Mr Craig's right to privacy and, if so, whether this restriction on his rights had been according to the law and was a proportionate restriction on his right to private life. Although, by this stage, the forum bar had finally come into force in Scotland, this was too late to help Mr Craig. The Scottish ministers had not been able to use this provision as it was not yet in force when they decided to agree to extradite Mr Craig to the US to face charges. Consequently, the Supreme Court concluded that the decision to extradite Mr Craig was unlawful. It was not according to the law, as the ministers had not been able to consider the forum bar when they should have been able to, as this should have been brought into force in Scotland.

All of this may sound a little odd, especially given so many complex technical legalities in the case. What should strike the reader as particularly odd, however, is the fact that two years can pass between a court declaring that an action of a minister is unlawful and the minister doing something in response to this decision. This certainty struck the Supreme Court as odd. Lord Reed, the President of the Supreme Court who delivered the Court's judgment, stated that 'there is a clear expectation that the executive will comply with a declaratory order, and that it is in reliance on that expectation that the courts usually refrain from making coercive orders against the executive and grant declaratory orders instead'.[13] He went on:

> The Government's compliance with court orders, including declaratory orders, is one of the core principles of our constitution, and is vital to the mutual trust which underpins the relationship between the Government and the courts. The courts' willingness to forbear from making coercive orders against the Government, and to make declaratory orders instead, reflects that trust. But trust depends on the Government's compliance with declaratory orders in the absence of coercion. In other words, it is because ours is a society governed by the rule of law, where the Government can be trusted to comply with court orders without having to be coerced, that declaratory orders can provide an effective remedy.[14]

So, what went wrong?

As the Supreme Court noted, there had been some confusion as to whether it was legally possible to bring the forum bar into force at different times in different parts of the UK. This is understandable. But the declaratory order set the record straight. There was evidence of some reluctance on the part of Scottish ministers to introduce the forum bar. However, once a declaratory order is made, no matter how politically difficult the circumstances may be, ministers should adhere to the law. This may have required some time to liaise constructively with the Scottish ministers following the declaratory order, to maintain good relations between Scotland and England. But it is hard to see why this should have taken two years.

The UK government argued that the minister had to decide whether to bring the forum bar into force in Scotland, or to repeal the order which had brought the forum bar into force for the rest of the UK. However, Lord Reed concluded that the minister did not have this discretion. The Westminster Parliament had the power to bring the forum bar into force for the UK as a whole. Once the minister had decided to bring the forum bar into force, it was not possible for this to only apply in some but not all of the UK.

Nor could the UK government argue that a declaratory order could just be ignored, with there being no requirement on the minister to act unless someone went to court to obtain a coercive order in Scottish law or a mandatory order in English law, requiring the minister to act. Does this show an unwillingness to operate according to background principles of mutual trust, necessary to ensure the maintenance of good constitutional standards of government?

Candid or covert?

A similar example of a possible willingness to ignore these principles of mutual trust arose regarding immigration law. Over the last few years, a stream of people have crossed the channel in small boats from mainland Europe to the south coast. Some of these will be genuine asylum seekers who are not sure how else to get to the UK and ask for asylum. Others may have been trafficked, unknowingly lured into criminal activities or modern slavery. Some may be economic migrants seeking better jobs and wages in the UK. All will risk their lives to travel across the channel in these small boats, with others unlawfully profiting from these activities.

Without wanting to enter into the complex politics of immigration, it is understandable that any government would want to prevent lives from being put at risk and stop exploitation and unlawful trafficking. One of the means through which the government aimed to tackle this issue was to introduce a policy requiring those seeking asylum who arrived in the UK on small boats to surrender their mobile phones to the authorities. These could then be used to try and trace the individuals illegally transporting people into the UK. A legal challenge was brought as to the legality of this policy through judicial review in a case referred to as *HM*.[15]

Difficulties arose, however, when it came to bringing this action for judicial review. The government first denied that any blanket policy to seize all mobile phones existed, before conceding that the policy did exist. This denial breached the duty of candour. The duty of candour is another element of mutual trust between the government and the courts. Rather than requiring the government to disclose evidence, the duty of candour applies. The government is expected to reply honestly and openly during the pre-trial process of an action for judicial review. Failure to do so undermines mutual trust and can also undermine the rule of law. It can make it impossible for an individual to succeed in their case of judicial review, enabling the government to act unlawfully with no effective legal check over its power.

This lack of adherence to the duty of candour is unusual. The government apologized to the court for these actions. It was so unusual that the court, having concluded, as conceded by the government, that the blanket policy of seizing phones was unlawful, issued a further judgment evaluating the breach of the duty of candour.[16] In its judgment, the court expressed concern with 'a failure of governance which allowed an unlawful policy to operate for an unknown length of time'. The court was also concerned that, in the face of a challenge to the policy, 'those responsible for it failed to explain it clearly to the Government Legal Department lawyers and counsel who was instructed in the case'.[17] It was this failure of those working in the ministry to provide accurate information to the Government Legal Department that led to the government failing to adhere to the duty of candour. The court did note, however, that this may also have been due to the need to act quickly under pressurized circumstances, and the impact of the Covid pandemic which made it impossible for ministerial teams and the Government Legal Department to meet face-to-face.

Court order or suggestion?

Our final example is perhaps the most troubling of all. It demonstrates a failure to adhere to a court order. Court orders are mandatory, whether they are addressed to the government or individuals. Mr Majera was a Rwandan national who had travelled to the UK from Rwanda and had been given indefinite leave to remain in the UK. Following his conviction for serious offences, he was sentenced to an indefinite term, with a minimum of seven years. Following this conviction, a deportation order was granted against Mr Majera, which had not been implemented and was subject to a revocation order.

The Parole Board heard Mr Majera's case and decided to release him on licence, only for Mr Majera to then be detained under the Immigration Act by the home secretary. He applied for and was granted bail, enabling him to be released and to continue his voluntary work in a charity shop. However, shortly after the bail order was made, the home secretary sent a letter to Mr Majera stating that he was no longer to be detained, but that certain conditions would be imposed on Mr Majera. These included a prohibition on all work, including his voluntary work, and a requirement to adhere to a curfew.

As with the other two cases, this was another unusual example. The court had issued a court order setting out bail conditions. If the home secretary did not like these conditions, she could challenge the court order. She should not, instead, impose alternative conditions contradicting the court order. The home secretary argued, however, that she believed that the court order imposing the bail conditions was unlawful. As such, she was able to treat this as a 'nullity', a technical legal term which, if it applied to the bail order, would mean that the home secretary was able to treat the court order granting bail as if it had never been made. Consequently, she would be able to ignore the court order and impose her conditions on Mr Majera.

This argument did not persuade the Supreme Court. Lord Reed stated clearly that 'It is a well established principle of our constitutional law that a court order must be obeyed unless and until it has been set aside or varied by the court (or, conceivably, overruled by legislation).'[18] It is such a well-established principle of the law that it is almost impossible to think of situations in which this would need to be said. Yet, in this case, the Supreme Court was required to reinforce this message.

Court orders must not be disobeyed. This is a rule of law. Unlike our two previous examples, this is not merely something that the government is expected to do. They are legally required to follow court orders. This is necessary to uphold the rule of law – to ensure that government acts according to the law. If the home secretary believes that a court order is invalid, she should go to court to challenge the court order. She cannot just decide that, because she believes it to be unlawful, she no longer has to follow the court order.

To act in this way looks suspiciously like the act of someone who does not respect or trust a decision of the court or of the legal system to overturn an unlawful court order if challenged. It also looks suspiciously like the act of someone who thinks they can ignore an order they believe to be wrong. However, this is only one example and, as the Supreme Court itself recognized, this was an extremely rare occurrence.

Mutual respect or mistrust?

It is easy to see how these cases could be seen as signs of populism. Populist governments tend to distrust courts as part of the elite. If the people are sovereign, and legal niceties get in the way of ensuring the will of the people is achieved, then it is easy to justify undermining aspects of mutual trust to achieve the will of the people. It is perhaps also no surprise that these examples involve areas that tend to polarize public debate. Both *Majera* and *HM* involved immigration, a subject that is often used by populist leaders who benefit from a nationalistic narrative. *Majera*, *HM* and *Craig* also involved the state's response to crime. These subjects tend to be used by populists influenced by a right-wing ideology, promoting popular policies of being tough on crime, imposing higher penalties on criminals and reducing the rights of prisoners as these policies are seen to be the will of the people.

Of particular concern is the discussion in *HM* of a lack of communication between ministers and civil servants and the Government Legal Department. When these chains of communication break down it can be easier for policies to be developed that undermine the rule of law. As we saw when discussing Bills that were introduced that would undermine the rule of law by breaching international law, the law officers and members of the Government Legal Department can provide an effective means of ensuring government according to the law. When these relationships break down, those occupying those roles may feel that they have no other obligation but to resign. This has reached a particular level of constitutional concern when this gives rise to ministers thinking they can ignore a court order, as was the case in *Majera*.

However, in the same way that three swallows do not make a summer, three examples of a breakdown in mutual trust between the government and the courts do not illustrate a general disregard for the law or disrespect for the role of the courts. It is unusual for the court to have to deal with such problems, which is what makes these cases so noteworthy. As the courts themselves note, there were also explanations for some of these difficulties.

The duty of candour may have been undermined in *HM*, but this was unusual. The court noted that the duty of candour was very firmly embedded in the practice and culture of the Government

Legal Department. The minister also apologized for the lack of compliance with the duty of candour. There was also evidence of explanations of why this breakdown had taken place, focusing on the pressures of such a time-sensitive and contestable issue, and the difficulty of communications between ministers, civil servants and the Government Legal Department during the pandemic.

The government did take a long time to respond to a declaratory order in *Craig* and, at least in the arguments presented to the court, did suggest that, as there is no legal obligation to respond to a declaratory order, there was no need for the government to respond unless and until a court order was secured to require the government to bring the forum bar into force in Scotland. However, this may have been the best legal argument that could be made to justify a lack of action, rather than evidence of a general belief that governments should not respond to declaratory orders. It is also an accurate account of the law, as declaratory orders do not create legally enforceable obligations.

The deeper question is also whether this reflects a general attitude in government that the right thing to do is to ignore, rather than comply with, a declaratory order. That is a much harder question to answer. It is also harder to evaluate how far this accurately represents the culture of a particular ministerial department or the government as a whole. The situation in *Craig* can also be explained due to the misunderstanding of the legal position, and the complexities of maintaining good relations between the component parts of the UK when the law requires that a provision is brought into force for the UK as a whole, but there is divergence across Westminster and the devolved nations as to the desirability of bringing a particular legal provision into force.

It is harder, however, to explain *Majera*. The government is legally required to comply with a court order. If the government does not like the court order, it is open to challenge the court order through the law. It is not open to the government, or anyone else, to decide that because they think the court order is wrong, they can ignore its provisions. The extent to which this shows a general disregard for legal limits, however, is difficult to discern.

A further concern is another recent case decided in the first few months of 2023, which appears to show a lack of mutual respect for judicial proceedings. The then Deputy Prime Minister and

Secretary of State for Justice and Lord Chancellor, Dominic Raab, had made a regulation which, in certain key cases, required that experts providing evidence to the Parole Board were only required to present factual evidence and were not able to provide a view or make recommendations as to whether a prisoner should be released. Instead, the secretary of state for justice would provide a single view as to whether a prisoner should be released. The court concluded that the purpose of this rule change was to ensure that experts did not dissent from the single view of the secretary of state for justice regarding whether a prisoner should be released. This was an improper purpose, particularly as it was incompatible with convention rights, specifically Article 5(4) of the European Convention on Human Rights requiring that those who are deprived of their liberty can have the lawfulness of their detention reviewed by a court. The court concluded that the decision to make this regulation:

> was made as part of an attempt by a party to judicial proceedings to influence to his own advantage the substance of the evidence given by witnesses employed or engaged by him. By exercising his powers for that purpose, the Secretary of State was attempting to interfere with the way in which the Board exercises its judicial functions.[19]

In addition to changing the rules, the government also produced guidance setting out how experts were meant to provide evidence. This included directing witnesses that they should refuse to comply with directions of the Parole Board or refuse to answer questions put to them orally by the Parole Board at hearings if this would mean that they were presenting their view on whether a prisoner should be released in those cases where this view was meant to come solely from the minister for justice. The High Court concluded that this guidance was not only unlawful but that it also effectively instructed witnesses to commit contempt of court by refusing to comply with directions of the Parole Board.[20]

The court left open the possibility that proceedings for contempt could be brought against those who drafted or approved the guidance, although the court wished first to obtain more evidence from the minister for justice as to how the guidance was made and approved. If this were to lead to proceedings for contempt against a minister, or a member of their department, this would be yet more concerning evidence of a willingness to secure policy objectives, even when these objectives were not constitutionally sound. It may also provide further evidence of a lack of respect for the judicial process, in this instance the procedures of the Parole Board.

Greasy poles?

Lord Hennessy and Andrew Blick argue that the UK constitution relies on individuals behaving as 'good chaps' ('chaps' because most of those holding office in government are male, although the gender balance is becoming more equal over time).[21] We rely on those in power to accept the limits on their power and respect the roles of other institutions of the constitution, even when they place checks and balances on the powers of the government. If this is to work, those in power need to be motivated to act in a manner that upholds good principles of constitutional government, even if this is only to avoid being held to account by others. Are there incentives to act in this manner?

We have already argued that checks and balances imposed by other institutions may be reduced, as well as seeing evidence of this erosion, particularly of political checks over the government by Parliament. If the stick of accountability may not be there to provide an incentive, what about the carrot of promotion within the government?

Promotion is in the hands of the prime minister. This is understandable. Any prime minister needs a team they can trust to take on roles of responsibility and to support and implement the policies of the prime minister's political party. However, therein also lies the danger. If a prime minister is a populist leader, will they promote those who suggest that maybe the prime minister should uphold the principles of good constitutional government rather than implement what the prime minister perceives to be the will of the people? Would a populist prime minister listen to a minister advocating self-restraint, or respecting decisions of other institutions, particularly if doing so may slow down or modify a policy the prime minister believes reflects the will of the people?

It is not hard to imagine that challenging a populist prime minister may be difficult and may cost you your ministerial role. This may be all the more likely when dealing with a charismatic populist leader who has become prime minister and who may not believe they need the support of a team of ministers.

There are other checks and influences over cabinet appointments. As we have seen in previous chapters, prime ministers too have to act within the checks imposed by Parliament, their party and the people. Backbench Members of Parliament may have strong views about potential ministerial candidates which may be communicated to the prime minister. However, given that backbench MPs also need to catch the eye of the prime minister to be elevated to a ministerial position, this may merely provide a means of removing the incompetent or the unpopular.

The media, too, may report on ministerial behaviour. Newspapers report on ministerial failings when departments fail to fulfil their role. They also tend to report on personal misdemeanours or evidence of breaches of the Ministerial Code. This may incentivize ministers to maintain constitutional guardrails. However, what sells newspapers does not necessarily correlate with reports of behaviour of failing to maintain constitutional guardrails. Personal misconduct is much more interesting to the public. The UK's system of government may be more designed to facilitate career promotion and gain power than to ensure power is exercised in a manner that respects constitutional principles through the application of self-restraint and mutual respect.

Conclusion

Given their important role in the UK's predominantly political, unwritten constitution, any suggestion that guardrails can be easily bent out of shape needs to be taken seriously. Even if they can be bent back into shape, surely it is better to have robust rather than malleable means of upholding good principles of constitutional government. Any weakening of standards, even if of short duration and later corrected, may damage democracy and the principles of good government. A pattern of behaviour from a range of governments able to bend these constitutional guardrails may eventually cause them to snap. The more the guardrails are bent, the more we accept these minor changes as acceptable behaviour, meaning that each small dent can become permanent.

There is evidence of examples where the guardrails have been severely mangled. It should never be the case that government departments think they can disobey a court order, rather than challenge a court order they believe to be wrong through the courts. It should also only rarely be the case that the duty of candour is ignored in such a dramatic way as it was in *HM*, or it can take so long to respond to a declaratory order as it did in *Craig*. However, it is harder to establish whether this is evidence of a trend of a loss of mutual respect for the courts or a series of unfortunate events.

What is more worrying is the extent to which the UK constitution relies on self-restraint and how, as we saw in our earlier assessment of whether the Westminster Parliament was still best described as an 'elective dictatorship', this is just part of the orthodox account of the UK constitution. Orthodox or otherwise, self-restraint works only when those responsible for restraining their actions do so because they believe they should act according to good principles of constitutional government. My concern is that this leaves our system too open to populism, it being too easy for a charismatic leader to claim that he or she has the backing of the will of the people and that this is far more important than constitutional guardrails restraining their actions. After all, why should the will of the people be restrained by procedures imposed by elites that stop the government from doing what it knows the people want?

6

Getting Things Done or Putting on a Show?

The House of Commons in Westminster is a debating chamber. It's a place where ideas are discussed, policies are formed, and legislation is scrutinized to ensure all Acts of Parliament are of the highest standard. At least, that is our ideal. Yet, particularly when we watch highlights of debates on the news, it seems more like entertainment. Even the seating in the chamber gives an impression of a battle. The government versus the opposition. Two lines of green benches face each other, focused on the dispatch box from where ministers make their speeches. Those in government and the shadow cabinet sit on the front benches. Backbench Members of Parliament watch on from the rows behind, waiting for their moment to speak. The speaker sits on, refereeing what sometimes seems to be more of an exchange of insults than deliberation.

We would expect a charismatic populist leader to use rhetoric, focus on the big picture and constantly appeal to the people. A populist leader also has no need for detailed parliamentary scrutiny. Any government implementing the will of the people needs to be robust, ensuring that its legislation sails through Parliament with few amendments. After all, the people, not Parliament, are sovereign. Populist leaders get the job done, ensuring the will of the people prevails, particularly when challenged by experts or the parliamentary elite. Yet, the cut and thrust of debate is nothing new. The Westminster Parliament frequently produces strong governments. The electoral system means any one MP need only win one more vote than their opponents to win their seat in the

House of Commons. There is no need to receive a majority of votes cast overall in a particular constituency. This means that fewer votes across the country as a whole are required to achieve a majority in the House of Commons. Enacting legislation with few amendments from the House of Commons is nothing new, merely a return to business as usual from the rollercoaster ride that was 2019.

This chapter will look more closely at parliamentary debates. It will first look at Prime Minister's Questions, often the most televised aspect of parliamentary debate. However, much as this provides a showcase, it does not provide an accurate snapshot of the Westminster Parliament as a whole. We will then focus on the enactment of legislation, looking at the Dissolution and Calling of Parliament Act 2022. As mentioned previously, this Act returned the Westminster Parliament to a five-year maximum term as opposed to a five-year fixed term, as well as restoring the ability of the government to request that the Monarch dissolve Parliament, triggering a general election. This Act was chosen as it provides an overview of the backdrop to the UK's post-Brexit constitution. While it responded to the events of 2019 and the so-called zombie Parliament, discussed in Chapters 2 and 3, it was not directly related to polemical issues arising from Brexit. It also represents a more commonly shared policy goal. The Labour Party and the Conservative Party manifestos for the 2019 general election contained a commitment to repeal the Act's predecessor, the Fixed-term Parliaments Act 2011. Surely if any Act has a chance to demonstrate constructive deliberation, it is one that makes a clear constitutional change, with commonly shared policy aims. Yet, as we will see, detailed deliberation was combined with, and sometimes overtaken by, references to the will of the people and political ripostes.

There are also other ways in which the then Prime Minister, Boris Johnson, behaved that look more like the actions of a populist president than a democratically accountable prime minister. Prime ministers are expected to make announcements of major policy changes to Parliament, ensuring MPs can hear and comment on these announcements in debates. However, Johnson demonstrated a tendency to make these statements to the media rather than to the House of Commons, leading to criticism by the speaker. This tendency has been repeated for other policies by other prime ministers after Johnson. Is this further evidence of a move towards populism, appealing directly to the people rather than their elected representatives?

Populism and Prime Minister's Questions

Prime Minister's Questions (PMQs) currently take place every Wednesday, finishing in time for excerpts to make it onto the lunchtime news bulletins at 1 pm. No recent prime minister has seemed quite as capable of putting on a show as Boris Johnson, with his gift for rhetorical flourishes and charismatic delivery. As discussed in Chapter 4, Johnson's first question time took place on 4 September 2019 when he accused Jeremy Corbyn of being 'frit' for not wanting to vote in favour of an early general election. After the usual first question relating to listing his engagements for the day and paying tribute to PC Andrew Harper, who died in the line of duty, Boris Johnson faced questions on Brexit, the merger of the roles of cabinet secretary and the national security adviser, the provision of public services, the review of legislation to support autistic people, the planned prorogation of Parliament, community hospitals, the police, the need to increase the number of police officers, budgets for schools, the removal of the whip from Conservative MPs for voting against the deal with the European Union in the run-up to Brexit, the Watford job fair, the problems of drug addiction and obesity, retrospective loan charges, a request that the prime minister apologize for racist and derogatory remarks made in an article, and the role of Dominic Cummings, then special adviser to the prime minister.

Boris Johnson's replies, particularly on Brexit, included name-calling and nicknames. The day before, an emergency debate in the House of Commons, proposed by Oliver Letwin, had succeeded in ensuring that, on 4 September, the House of Commons would debate a Private Members' Bill, the European Union (Withdrawal) (No. 6) Bill. This Bill, which became the European Union (Withdrawal) (No. 2) Act 2019, required the prime minister to seek a further extension to the negotiation period with the European Union if, either the House of Commons failed to vote in favour of the withdrawal agreement, or voted in favour of leaving the EU with no deal, by 19 October. There is no wonder, then, that this unprecedented use of the emergency debate procedure, against the backdrop of the proposed prorogation of Parliament, meant tension was high and tempers a little frayed.

The Prime Minister frequently referred to this Bill as 'the surrender Bill'.[1] Johnson also referred to Jeremy Corbyn, the then leader of the Labour Party, as a 'chlorinated chicken'[2] and accused him of 'shameless scaremongering' about the consequences of leaving the EU with no deal.[3] He characterized Corbyn's policy for leaving the EU as 'Dither and delay'.[4] There is perhaps no wonder that the speaker had to frequently ask for order, and to caution the House of Commons:

> In the remaining minutes of this session, I appeal to colleagues to take account of the fact that we are visited by a distinguished group of Lebanese parliamentarians, at the invitation of the Inter-Parliamentary Union and the all-party group on Lebanon, which is chaired by the right hon. Member for South Holland and The Deepings (Sir John Hayes). We would like to set them a good example; I am not sure at the moment how impressed they will be.[5]

Heated debates about Brexit were, perhaps, to be expected. Nor did the insults only come in one direction. Jeremy Corbyn referred to the Prime Minister's negotiating strategy for Brexit as 'a complete fantasy',[6] and accused the Prime Minister of being 'desperate to avoid scrutiny'.[7] Ian Blackford, then leader of the Scottish National Party (SNP) in the House of Commons, started his contribution to the debate by stating, 'Today, we have seized back control from a Prime Minister who is behaving more like a dictator than a democrat.'[8]

Insults and reprimands continued on questions on other topics, even when these were not responded to by further references to Brexit. In response to a question on police numbers in London, the Prime Minister replied, 'I think it absolutely bizarre that a London Labour Member of Parliament should ignore the role of the present Mayor of London, who is, frankly, not a patch on the old guy. I left him £600 million and he has squandered it on press officers.'[9]

At his last PMQs, Boris Johnson faced questions on the importance of the seven principles of public life, the war in Ukraine, the campaign for a new leader of the Conservative Party, the cost-of-living crisis, the record of the prime minister, policies of the Mayor of London, freeports, the levelling-up agenda, the TransPennine rail system, the fire risks of disposable barbecues and Chinese sky lanterns, Scottish independence, the Windrush compensation scheme, the steel industry, the prime minister's legacy regarding Northern Ireland, economic growth in the UK, tariffs on white fish and investments in hospitals.

As with his first appearance on PMQs, Boris Johnson's replies include a series of insults, calling Keir Starmer, the leader of the opposition, 'a great pointless human bollard',[10] 'Captain Hindsight',[11] and 'one of those pointless plastic bollards you find around a deserted roadworks on a motorway'.[12] He went on to say, 'I can tell the House why the Leader of the Opposition does that funny wooden flapping gesture – it is because he has the union barons pulling his strings from beneath.'[13] He also characterized Ian Blackford, then leader of the SNP in the House of Commons, as 'talking a load of tosh',[14] before ending his last response with 'hasta la vista, baby'.[15]

This hardly illustrates democracy at its best. It is not unsurprising, therefore, that the Westminster Parliament is often used as the ideal illustration of an arena parliament as opposed to a transformative parliament. [16] Arena parliaments prioritise the cut and thrust of debates. While there may be a lot of discussions, with or without insults and rhetoric, there is little evidence of Parliament successfully proposing an amendment to legislation or providing scrutiny to improve the quality of laws made. The House of Commons may generate hot air rather than detailed legislative scrutiny. Transformative parliaments, on the other hand, show members of the legislature playing a larger role, scrutinizing legislation and succeeding in getting amendments agreed to, the implication being with fewer insults and more constructive deliberation.

As with most models, they are ideals that do not fully reflect reality. Nor is PMQs a perfect reflection of business in the House of Commons. However, it is concerning that this is often the only aspect of business in the Westminster Parliament that is widely publicized and seen by the electorate. The House of Commons may have many dramatic moments. It also has periods of deliberation and reflection, where debates and votes succeed in effectively scrutinizing and amending legislation. If we are to get a better account of how the Westminster Parliament operates, we need to dig deeper.

Scrutiny or support?

Until 2011, the Westminster Parliament had relied on a system of maximum terms, set for five years. The power to dissolve Parliament, leading to a general election, rested with the Monarch. The prime minister could request the dissolution of Parliament, which the Monarch would normally agree to, leading to a general election. As we saw in Chapter 3, the Monarch could decide not to dissolve Parliament if a parliament was still viable, if there was an economic crisis and a general election would be detrimental to the national economy, or if another prime minister could be found who could form a government that would enjoy the confidence of the House of Commons.

This changed during the coalition government of 2010 to 2015. Concerns were raised that the prime minister, drawn from the larger political party in the coalition government, could request that Parliament dissolve, and a general election be held at a time that would give a political advantage to his political party and harm the electoral chances of the coalition partner.

There had also been wider concerns as to the constitutional consequences of maximum-term parliaments. A prime minister could time a general election when it would be likely to favour the electoral success of their political party. Maximum-term parliaments can also create uncertainty. It may be hard to predict when a general election will be held, leading to speculation throughout the latter section of a parliamentary term, making it harder for any government to achieve its legislative agenda. It may also make it harder for businesses to predict whether future economic policies and other rules will be upheld or changed in future following a general election.

To deal with these concerns, the coalition government passed the Fixed-term Parliaments Act 2011. This provided for a fixed five-year term, setting the dates of future general elections. However, the Act also recognized that situations may arise when there is a need for an earlier general election. Under the 2011 Act, this could take place in two ways. First, the Act provided for a specifically worded vote of no confidence. If the government were to lose that vote, this would trigger a period of 14 days during which an alternative government could be formed. If the House of Commons were to hold a vote that granted confidence to this alternative government – or, less likely, the previous administration – then Parliament would continue. If not, then Parliament would dissolve and a general election would take place. Second, an early general election could be held if two-thirds of the members of the House of Commons voted in favour of a general election.

The Act changed the powers of the prime minister and the House of Commons. It reduced the powers of the prime minister in two ways. Before the 2011 Act, the prime minister effectively had a discretionary power to decide when to call a general election, given the rare circumstances when the Monarch would be able to refuse such a request. The 2011 Act removed this discretionary power. A prime minister wishing to hold a general election would need to use the Act's provisions to ask the House of Commons to vote in favour of an early general election and would need two-thirds of the House of Commons to support this request. The only other option would be if the prime minister were to initiate a vote of no confidence in the government, something that a prime minister would be unlikely to do.

Second, it reduced the ability of the prime minister to use a confidence motion to quell potential backbench rebellion. If an issue is made a confidence issue, then, should the government lose that vote, the prime minister should request the dissolution of Parliament leading to a general election. This can be an effective means of stopping backbench rebellion.

The Act increased the powers of the House of Commons as MPs were given a larger role in the decision as to whether to call a general election. First, they could veto the decision by voting against the motion. As two-thirds of the members of the House of Commons needed to vote in favour of an early motion for a general election, a group of 216 from 650 MPs could effectively veto a general election. Nor was it even required for these MPs to vote against the motion for an early general election. Merely failing to be present for the vote, or abstaining from voting, would suffice. As we saw in 2019 (discussed in Chapters 2 and 3), this can be an effective means for MPs to prevent the government from calling a general election. The House of Commons could also have more of a say in the formation of a new government, with MPs being able to vote their confidence in a different government to prevent a general election.

The Act also altered the powers of the Monarch. It removed the role of the Monarch from assessing whether to dissolve Parliament and trigger a general election. This has the advantage of ensuring the Monarch is not brought into politics. The Monarch is no longer placed in a position where he may have to decide whether there is evidence that Parliament could continue with a new government, or whether a general election may be detrimental to the economy, meaning that it would be better to avoid a general election. Instead, the 2011 Act provided for MPs to determine these issues when voting for an early general election, or on a vote of no confidence in the government or a vote of confidence in a new government.

However, the Act was subject to criticism, particularly during the 2019 'zombie' Parliament. The Act was criticized even before 2019. In 2017, it had been relatively easy for Theresa May to use the Act to call an early parliamentary general election. It is easy to see why when we think about the political context. While it is open to the opposition to vote against a general election, this can send the message that the opposition is not ready to face the electorate or is not confident of winning votes. This perception of weakness in the opposition may dissuade the electorate from voting for the opposition parties. The House of Commons veto, therefore, would appear to have little power in reality. Although it did succeed in 2019, this is best understood as arising in a unique set of circumstances. Voting to prevent the UK from leaving the EU with no deal was seen as justifying voting against an early general election. MPs may have seen this less as a sign of weakness and more as a sign of strength to prevent what they regarded as a bad outcome that may not have been in line with the wishes of the electorate. While the referendum was clear that the majority of those who voted wished to leave the EU, it was not clear whether there would be the same majority for leaving the EU with no deal as to the UK's future relationship with the EU.

Criticisms of the Act led to the introduction by the government of the Dissolution and Calling of Parliament Bill. The 2011 Act required a post-legislative review of its provisions. This had taken place before the introduction of the Bill. The government also relied on other reports from parliamentary committees that had looked at the operation of the Fixed-term Parliaments Act 2011. The Bill proposed a return to a system of maximum-term parliaments as opposed to fixed terms. It also revived the power of the prime minister to request that the Monarch dissolve Parliament, removing any requirement for a parliamentary vote to do so. It also overturned the requirement of specific wording for a vote of no confidence and the requirement of a delay between a vote of no confidence and the dissolution of Parliament before a general election to provide time for the formation of a possible alternative government, thereby avoiding a general election. Consequently, the prime minister would, once again, be able to turn a vote on a particular Bill into a vote of confidence to potentially quell a backbench rebellion.

Finally, the Dissolution and Calling of Parliament Bill contained an ouster clause, a provision that makes it clear that courts are not able to challenge the request of the prime minister to seek a dissolution of Parliament and call a general election. This arose following the prorogation case. If courts could review the extent of the prerogative power of prorogation, they could probably also review the extent of the prerogative power of dissolution. The ouster clause made it clear that the dissolution of Parliament could not be subject to judicial review.

The Dissolution and Calling of Parliament Bill, therefore, had constitutional significance. It altered the balance of powers between the House of Commons, the government and the courts. Despite this, aspects of the Bill's progress through Parliament reinforced the populist narrative that appeals to the will of the people. It can be used to silence discussion, even on constitutionally important matters, and rhetoric can be used rather than deliberation to facilitate a Bill's unchecked progress through Parliament.

Despite its constitutional importance, very little time was spent debating the Bill's provisions. In total, the Bill had just under six-and-a-half hours of debate in Parliament to go through all three stages, including a committee stage of the whole House and the response of the House of Commons to an amendment made by the House of Lords. This timetable was set by a programme motion proposed by the government and voted on by the House of Commons. The progress of the Bill through the House of Commons was such that the committee stage and the third reading of the Bill took place on the same day.

It is also hard to see the Bill's progress as demonstrating that Westminster can be a transformative parliament as opposed to an arena parliament. Nine amendments were proposed to the Bill, of which seven were selected for debate at the committee stage. None were successful – unsurprising, since these amendments all came from members of the opposition and were not backed by the government. One amendment did succeed in the House of Lords. This amendment would have required the prime minister to obtain a simple majority vote in the House of Commons before requesting the dissolution of Parliament leading to a general election. The House of Commons rejected this amendment and the House of Lords voted not to insist on the amendment, meaning that consensus was reached, and the Bill could be sent for royal assent.

There are also clear examples of statements in support of the Bill that appeal to the will of the people. When challenged as to whether the Bill was democratic, given that it removed the power of the House of Commons to veto a request to dissolve Parliament, Michael Gove, the minister who introduced the Bill to the House of Commons, replied that the Bill was democratic as 'it gives power to the people. Fundamentally, all of us sit here at the pleasure of and at the disposal of our electorates.'[17] When questioned about whether the Bill returned power to the government to decide the date of a general election, rather than the people, Gove reiterated that 'Ultimately, the decision about whether it is right to call an election and whether the Prime Minister and the Administration should return to power rightly rests with the people.'[18]

It may be that the prime minister makes the decision when to hold a general election, but the people ultimately decide whether that was a good call or not through their votes. However, this does not mean that the people decide when to hold a general election. The outcome of the general election will be used to judge whether the prime minister was successful in gaining re-election for their political party, part of which may have been determined by the date they chose for the general election. However, it is difficult to assess how far the electorate will choose to vote for the opposition because they believe the prime minister chose the wrong date for a general election.

There are also examples of the use of rhetoric on both sides. For example, during the committee stage of the Bill, the House of Commons discussed the ouster clause, with the opposition arguing that the clause was unnecessary as the courts would be unwilling to challenge a request to dissolve Parliament given the provisions of the Bill of Rights 1689, which makes it clear that the courts cannot question proceedings in Parliament. Lloyd Russell-Moyle, a Labour MP, asked if the ouster clause:

> is a bit like a red flag or saying to someone, 'Don't think of an elephant' – they will think of an elephant. It is saying to the courts, 'You can't touch this,' which would be a charter for clever lawyers and clever judges to start to think, 'Where can we start to look at this?' rather than using the long-established, age-old way of deciding matters: a vote here in Parliament.[19]

Cat Smith, also a Labour MP and shadow secretary of state for young people and democracy, agreed, stating 'In fact, it is probably like dealing with a toddler: if we tell them not to do something, we know fine well they will do it.'[20] Both of these statements came in the committee stage from opposition MPs, suggesting that rhetoric is endemic to political debate and is not confined to whichever political party is in government.

The clearest example of the use of rhetoric, however, was during the justification of the Bill as a response to the events of 2019. Those in favour of the Bill drew on the events of 2019 to explain why the Fixed-term Parliaments Act 2011 needed to be repealed, often using colourful language to describe the 2019 Parliament and the three failed attempts to secure a vote of two-thirds of the House of Commons to trigger a general election. Michael Gove referred to these events as 'the Parliament that prevented a Prime Minister from seeking dissolution';[21] a 'paralysed Parliament';[22] where 'parliamentarians sought to frustrate the Prime Minister seeking an election'.[23]

Chloe Smith, who as minister for the constitution and devolution led the government's statements at the committee stage of the Bill, spoke in a more measured tone, but still criticized the 2011 Act as it 'did not work', both because of the relative ease with which a general election could be called in 2017 and 'the threshold of a supermajority requirement for a general election and the statutory motions of no confidence, created an untenable situation in which the Government could neither pass vital legislation through

Parliament nor call a new election. The result was parliamentary paralysis at a critical time for our Government.'[24]

There was also colourful language from the opposition. Brendan O'Hara, an SNP MP, placed the Bill in the context of the post-Brexit constitution, referring to 'the irony of how taking back control supposedly has led us to a position where Parliament is being neutered by the Executive, and the people who were most loudly proclaiming "Take back control" are the people holding the scissors and doing the neutering.'[25]

When the House of Commons was considering the amendment of the House of Lords, Brendan O'Hara drew attention, again, to the ironical nature of the government arguing that Parliament was taking back control:

> let us have a look at who we will be handing those increased executive powers to. They will be given to a Prime Minister who has illegally prorogued Parliament, who sought to purge his party of all but his most loyal followers, and who had to remove the Whip from a long-standing and highly respected Member simply for being chosen to head a Committee over his preferred candidate. We will be giving greater executive power to a Prime Minister who, in defiance of the security services, ennobled the son of a former KGB officer turned billionaire Russian oligarch, a Prime Minister whose career three weeks ago was hanging by a thread and who has been revealed to be up to his neck in dirty Russian money, and a Prime Minister who is currently under investigation by the Metropolitan police.
>
> If Conservative Members vote to defeat this Lords amendment tonight, that is the character of the man to whom this House will be handing even greater executive power. I advise them to think very carefully about their decision, because this Lords amendment is there to protect the role of the House of Commons, to avoid executive overreach and, ultimately, to protect democracy.[26]

However, for all the rhetoric and name-calling, there is also evidence of legislative scrutiny and informed constitutional debate. The 2011

Act set out a process of post-legislative scrutiny. This was carried out by the Joint Committee on the Fixed-term Parliaments Act, which heard evidence, received written evidence and produced a report on the Act.[27] The Public Administration and Constitutional Affairs Committee in the House of Commons[28] and the Constitution Committee of the House of Lords[29] also produced reports. These reports were laid before the House of Commons and the House of Lords respectively. They were also published and are publicly available online.

Debates on the Bill also focused on whether its provisions really did give power to the people, or transferred power from Parliament to the government, weakening legal checks and potentially drawing the Monarch into politics. Chris Bryant, a Labour MP, also drew attention to the different understandings of the UK constitution, contrasting the position of a government that relies on votes of confidence and general elections, and governments that rely on consent earned in the arena of Parliament and not just through the general election.[30] Those arguing in response that Parliament failed had a different constitutional understanding of Parliament, the role of the House of Commons being to support the government, particularly when it is implementing the will of the people, rather than to scrutinize and check the actions of the government, which MPs believe may not be in the public interest, may not fully represent the views of the electorate or may have harmful consequences.

It was also clear in the debate that many MPs were well informed, drawing on reports, evidence given to committees that had looked at the Fixed-term Parliaments Act 2011, and their knowledge of the operation of the UK constitution and the practice of Parliament. This balanced debate may not have attracted headlines but did show clear signs of deliberation, and the concern, of some, to return Parliament to its constitutional role prior to the enactment of the 2011 Act, and of others as to the potential dangers of this transfer of power from the House of Commons to, effectively, the prime minister.

It also demonstrates that for all the rhetoric about returning decisions to the people, and the characterizations of 2019 as a paralyzed Parliament caused by the Fixed-term Parliaments Act 2011, part of the concerns were about a desire to return the UK constitution to its more traditional role. It may not have been populism that motivated the arguments, but a desire for a strong government, supported by a large majority in Parliament, able to enact legislation to implement its manifesto and backed by the will of the electorate as expressed in the outcome of the latest general election. The members of the opposition wished for Parliament to retain its role under the Fixed-term Parliaments Act 2011 to move the UK constitution to a different form, one where the legislature has more of a say in the enactment of legislation and where the government needed to seek support for its policies, not merely rely on the sheer force of numbers to ensure they are accepted and enacted. In other words, the arguments deliberated whether the Westminster Parliament should look more like an arena parliament or more like a transformative legislature.

Prime minister or president?

The UK has a parliamentary democracy, led by a prime minister. It is not a presidential state. The head of state in the UK is the Monarch, not the prime minister. The prime minister is also indirectly and not directly elected. The Monarch appoints a prime minister. By convention, the Monarch chooses as prime minister the leader of the political party that can form a government which can command the confidence of the House of Commons. This is normally the party with the most MPs following a general election. By voting for MPs from a particular political party, the electorate is also indirectly voting for a prime minister of a particular political persuasion.

There is no specific, separate election of a prime minister. As recent events have also very clearly demonstrated, the identity of the prime minister can change between general elections. The year 2022, for example, saw three prime ministers – Boris Johnson, Liz Truss and Rishi Sunak – and no general elections. Boris Johnson was the leader of the Conservative Party during the 2019 general election campaign. It can be more legitimate, therefore, to claim that he represented the will of the people. However, the same cannot be said for Liz Truss and Rishi Sunak. Both were elected as leaders by the members of their political party, the Conservative Party. Each political party determines its own set of rules as to how a leader is selected. None of the political parties, however, has the power to require that a leader can only be chosen following an election by the country as a whole. This can make it harder for the leader of any political party to justify that they represent the will of the people until their political party gains more seats at the next general election under their leadership. Different leaders may change the policies of their political party as well as their relative priorities. We would expect nothing less. How else can different candidates gain votes other than by setting out how their policies and priorities are different from those of their rivals?

Prime ministers, in contrast to presidents, are accountable primarily to Parliament as opposed to the people. Parliament represents the people through constituency MPs sitting in the House of Commons. We would expect, therefore, that the prime minister and other ministers would appear regularly before Parliament, setting out their policies and answering questions. Presidents, on the other hand, tend to appeal more directly to the people. After all, they need to appeal directly to the electorate if they are to be re-elected for another term.

During the COVID-19 pandemic, we got used to regular statements and updates from the Prime Minister, as well as the First Minister of Scotland, the First Minister of Wales and the First Minister and Deputy First Minister of Northern Ireland. These statements, made to the country and broadcast live, were crucial to inform everyone about the lockdown measures, as well as provide information about the pandemic and advice as to how best to minimize health risks. This was understandable given the context. The pandemic created an emergency. Lockdown measures meant that most of us were required to work from home. Parliament itself was regulated by lockdown measures, through hybrid measures to facilitate virtual attendance and social distancing rules in the chamber. In that situation, it made sense for the prime minister and leaders of the devolved legislatures to appear before the media to keep the country informed.

However, this also looks much more like a presidential than a parliamentary style of government. It's also not how ministers are meant to make announcements. The Ministerial Code states clearly that 'When Parliament is in session, the most important announcements of Government policy should be made in the first instance, in Parliament.'[31] The code also sets out a procedure for the making of oral statements. These should be shown to the opposition shortly before they are made. To facilitate this process, ministers should ensure that 15 copies of the oral statement are sent to the chief whip at least 45 minutes before the statement is to be made. The statement should also be sent to the speaker.[32] This facilitates parliamentary accountability. It also shows respect for the House of Commons.

However, there is evidence of these rules being bent – if not ignored – shifting to a situation in which policy statements are either leaked or announced to the media before they are presented to the House. During the Covid lockdowns, for example, concerns were raised in Parliament on 9 September 2020 that, on the previous day, the health secretary had made announcements regarding lockdown measures, before a statement had been made to the House, these measures having then circulated on Twitter. The speaker stated:

> I accept that decisions have been taken in a fast-moving situation, but timings for statements are known to Ministers. It is really not good enough for the Government to make decisions of this kind in a way that shows insufficient regard to the importance of major policy announcements being made first to this House and to Members of this House wherever possible. I have already sent a letter to the Secretary of State. I think the total disregard for this Chamber is not acceptable. I know that the Prime Minister is a Member of Parliament as well and that he will ensure that statements should be made here first, especially as this particular Secretary of State requests statements. To then ignore the major fact that he wanted to put to the country, and not put it before this House, is not acceptable and I hope he will apologise to Members.[33]

Similarly, the speaker raised concerns about the Covid roadmap plans being announced to the media before Parliament. This led Edward Leigh, the Conservative MP for Gainsborough, to state:

> It would have been perfectly possible for the Prime Minister to come to this Chamber at 3.30 and inform Parliament of what is going on. I quite understand that it is much easier for the Prime Minister to have a few

patsy questions from Laura Kuenssberg and her colleagues than to sit here for a whole hour and be grilled by MPs, but are we a presidential system or are we the House of Commons? Who runs this country? Is it the media or is it the House of Commons?[34]

The speaker noted he had been told that no decision had been taken, leading him to comment 'The fact is I am being misled – this House is being misled. It is not acceptable, and I would welcome them coming here before they make the press statement, as the press have already got an embargoed copy.'[35]

The issue of announcing policy statements to the media, rather than to Parliament, was raised again in September 2020, about statements made by the transport secretary to the media that rail franchises were to be ended and replaced by emergency recovery measure agreements. Tanmanjeet Singh Dhesi, the Labour MP for Slough, raised a point of order in the House in response to these statements:

In line with what seems to be common Government practice, at no point, despite being asked on numerous occasions, has the Transport Secretary, or any Government Minister for that matter, come to the House to make a statement on any of those issues. Instead, they have preferred to make announcements remotely through media outlets and press releases.

Mr Deputy Speaker, given that the Government keep talking about parliamentary sovereignty but seem set on disrespecting the House, what influence could you bring to bear to stop such abuse of the House and to stop the Government failing to make major policy announcements to the House? What influence can you bring to bear to ensure that the Transport Secretary comes to the House to announce such major transformational changes to our transport network?[36]

The deputy speaker noted, in response, that the House had received notification of a written statement from the secretary of state for transport, before going on to conclude that:

It is regrettable that such a major policy statement was made to the press before it was made available to the House. Mr Speaker has always been clear that such statements should be made to the House and that Members should have the opportunity to question Ministers on their policies.[37]

It is not just over Covid that concerns arose that announcements were being made to the press rather than to Parliament. Nor is this confined to the Johnson administration. On 11 January 2019, for example, concerns arose as to whether the work and pensions secretary had announced policy changes to the controversial two-child cap on universal credit. There had been reports in the media that the work and pensions secretary was going to make an oral statement to the House on this issue, as well as a radio interview in the morning. The speaker confirmed that he had only received notice of a written and not an oral statement. He had also not heard the radio interview, so was not in a position to comment on whether it had failed to comply with the provisions of the Ministerial Code. This led the speaker to state that:

> There has been considerable focus this week on Parliament and how matters should be handled. Let me say, for the avoidance of doubt, in terms so clear as to brook of no misunderstanding, that if a change in Government policy is to be announced, especially on a major matter that has been the subject of considerable controversy, it is proper for that announcement of a change first to be made to the House. A statement, of course, is a form of speech, but it is then customarily followed by substantial interrogation. If somebody can make a speech outside the House, it is perfectly open to that person to make a statement in the House. Respect for the House, and in particular for the Chamber, is a matter of the highest importance as far as I am concerned, and it should be so far as all Governments are concerned.[38]

On 2 March 2022, Angus Brendan MacNeil, an SNP MP, raised a point of order complaining that the government published information about a free trade deal between New Zealand and the UK, as well as briefing the media about this newly signed agreement before it was shared with the House of Commons International Trade Committee. This, again, undermines parliamentary scrutiny by select committees over these agreements.[39] There are also repeated concerns that budgetary measures are being announced first to the press before they are presented to the House of Commons. More recently, aspects of the government's planned Illegal Migration Bill were announced to the media in newspaper articles before the Bill received its first reading in the House of Commons on 7 March 2023. This included statements from interviews with both the prime minister and the home secretary. Similarly, changes to the Bill were announced to the press before being placed before Parliament at the report stage. On 11 May 2023, Kemi Badenoch, Secretary of State for Business and Trade, was reprimanded by the speaker for announcing important changes to proposed legislation on retained EU law to the media rather than to the House of Commons.[40]

Presentations to the media as opposed to Parliament may be necessary in a time of emergency. But this behaviour was not limited to the pandemic. It is also hard to see how this behaviour fits the narrative that the post-Brexit constitution is returning to its traditional form. The UK constitution has never been presidential. Both the Ministerial Code and the Cabinet Manual clearly state that important policy choices should first be presented to Parliament and not to the media, aiding parliamentary scrutiny. A shift to a presidential style of government may not seem, at first, to fit with a populist narrative either. Its link to populism stems from the use of the media by populist leaders. There is no need to appeal to Parliament if you can appeal directly to the people. There is no need for parliamentary scrutiny in a system of government that prioritizes popular sovereignty and rejects the views of the elite – which may include parliamentarians scrutinizing the actions of a populist government.

It is also hard to see this shift as accidental. There are too many instances of announcements being first made to the media or leaked to the general public, particularly of policies that may breach international law, but which the government regards as complying with the wishes of the people. It seems to suggest a more worrying trend of avoiding parliamentary accountability and appealing directly to the people, behaviour that fits more with populism than the orthodox account of the UK constitution.

Blame Brexit?

The Brexit referendum polarized the UK. Campaign tactics often appeared to appeal more to rhetoric than reasoned argument. We all remember the promises on the sides of buses and the wide use of slogans such as 'Take back control', 'Brexit means Brexit' and references to the referendum as an 'independence day'. Was it the use of a referendum that triggered a turn to rhetoric over deliberation, fuelling a turn to direct appeals to the people rather than parliamentary accountability?

Referendums can be a means of undermining deliberative democracy and facilitating populism. Populist leaders can use referendums to achieve their aims, determining which issues are put to a referendum, using campaigns to polarize debate and the outcome of the referendum to homogenize the will of the people. Referendums only ask 'yes' or 'no' questions, potentially oversimplifying complex issues. Referendum campaigns can rely on rhetoric to facilitate a simple answer, particularly when the referendum in question is focusing on an already divisive issue.

The referendum campaign of Vote Leave, one of the groups campaigning to leave the EU, focused predominantly on the need for the UK to remain independent and regain its sovereignty, and on the need for the UK to control its borders against a perceived flood of immigrants.[41] This message of the need to leave the EU to control immigration was then used by more mainstream politicians – for example, Boris Johnson and Michael Gove – in their pro-leave campaigning before the referendum. These sentiments were also echoed in pro-leave newspapers. The main focus of the Leave campaign was to 'take back control'.

Those in the Remain campaign, however, focused predominantly on the economy, setting out how leaving the EU would cause economic damage as opposed to focusing on economic benefits. Media outlets that were pro-Leave characterized these campaigns as 'Project Fear'.

This use of slogans, and a general lack of political awareness in the UK as to how the EU works, meant that it was easy for political campaigns to focus more on emotion than reason. Campaigners were free to appeal to a specific subset of the people. Unlike in general elections, there was no role of the Electoral Commission during the campaign to act as a fact checker, making it easier for campaigners to use rhetoric and hyperbole. The outcome of the referendum homogenized the will of the people by providing an overall majority outcome in favour of one response which was transformed into the will of the people to leave the EU.

This is not to argue that this was the right or the wrong outcome of Brexit. Rather, it is to point to how referendums, whatever their outcome, channel a range of responses into a majority in favour of 'yes' or 'no' to a particular policy choice. The same effect could have happened if the answer had been to remain in, rather than to leave, the EU.

However, this need not always be the case. Referendums can also promote democracy. They can provide a means of citizen engagement, particularly when there are clear campaigns designed to set out issues and educate the electorate, facilitating deliberation over rhetoric. It has been argued, for example, that this happened in the first Scottish independence referendum, particularly given the expansion of the franchise to 16- and 17-year-olds, and the fact that the Scottish government produced clear documents setting out the consequences of independence. There was also widespread discussion of these issues in schools, to facilitate the votes of 16- and 17-year-olds.

The Brexit referendum witnessed a growth in the use of rhetoric because of the nature of the question asked, not just because it was being resolved through a referendum. The issue of whether the UK should remain a member of the EU had split the Conservative Party. There were also divisions in other political parties about Europe. It had also seen the rise of emerging parties which threatened to poach traditional voters for the Conservative Party. A referendum initiated by the Conservative Party may have seemed like a good means of uniting the party and strengthening voter appeal. Instead, it merely transferred those divisions into society as a whole.

Having won the referendum through the use of rhetoric and slogans, it may have seemed all too easy to continue to use rhetoric once those campaigners for the winning side in the referendum gained political power. However, rhetoric has always played a role in the Westminster Parliament. For all the careful deliberation in committees, and government amendments to Bills that are made in response to perceived and actual reactions of opposition and backbench MPs, it is the theatrics of PMQs and the cut and thrust of political debate that attracts an audience. Rhetoric, as opposed to deliberation, is a fixed feature of the Westminster Parliament, even down to the layout of the chamber and the recognition of a government and an opposition.

Conclusion

Politics in the Westminster Parliament may be more for 'show' than for 'go' at times, although it depends on where you look. For all of the spectacle of PMQs, you will also find careful deliberation, particularly in the work of parliamentary committees and the less publicized work of scrutinizing legislation in public Bill committees.

Nevertheless, it is hard to deny a tendency for the government to try to appeal to the public, rather than to Parliament. This may be understandable. After all, any government will wish to seek re-election and it is the public, the electorate, to which it will ultimately be accountable, at least every five years. However, this tendency plays into the hands of populism. It makes it harder for Parliament to scrutinize policies. It makes it easier for governments to prioritize the communication of their policies in the media, gaining support for them before they are placed before Parliament, making it in turn harder for MPs to scrutinize these policies in depth. There is no equivalent of the speaker in the media to ensure the rules of debate are adhered to and to check when MPs of either political persuasion overstep the line. Rhetoric is more likely to sell newspapers, particularly when it appeals to the political leanings of that newspaper.

While it may be argued that this is nothing new, in one sense this is all the more worrying. A general tendency for 'us versus them' in debates makes it easier for a populist leader to deploy antagonistic tactics, pitching 'the people' against 'the elites'. After all, is this not just business as usual? It may also make it harder for MPs who wish to deliberate carefully, raising issues to make legislation better, or to point out potential flaws to reach a consensus. If an MP's deliberations can be characterized as 'ignoring the wishes of the people' they, in turn, can be used by the electorate to illustrate that the MP is 'out of touch' and does not deserve to be re-elected.

While we may not have found clear evidence to fit the populist narrative, nevertheless there is evidence that aspects of the structure of the Westminster Parliament may make it easier for a populist leader to deny accusations of being populist. After all, are they not just carrying on in the grand tradition of an arena parliament, where rhetorical flourishes, the occasional insult and doing anything to show your political party can win is more highly prized than reaching a consensus, which can always be classified as a weak compromise or, worse still, a U-turn?

7

Constitutional Watchdogs: Rottweilers or Lapdogs?

So far, we have been looking at how institutions hold the government to account. We've looked mostly at the Westminster Parliament, questioning how far the House of Commons in particular can hold the government to account for its actions. We've also noted the role of the courts in upholding the rule of law. Some of these checks stem from expectations that those in power are 'good chaps' who recognize the limits of their power and respect the decisions of others. These 'good chaps' are also meant to debate and deliberate fairly, scrutinizing legislation for errors and helping to reach informed policy choices. However, there is also evidence that 'good chaps' may not always occupy positions of power and that the Westminster Parliament may be more of an arena of rhetoric and winner-takes-all politics than a deliberative chamber.

These are not the only institutions that keep a check on the government. Moreover, the institutions we have looked at so far may carry out checks on the government for Parliament and political parties but may be less effective in carrying out checks on the actions of the government on behalf of the people. How do the people find out about what is going on in Parliament, or determine who they should vote for in a general election? The electorate needs information. This comes from the media, including social media. Do the media perform an effective watchdog function, providing the electorate with the information it needs? There are some examples of where this works well. But there are also concerns both as to how the media obtains the information it needs and its ability to remain independent.

The media is not the only constitutional watchdog. Other independent bodies can effectively perform this function. However, they are often created by Parliament, meaning their powers can be modified or reduced by those in power. These bodies also often create reports but it is up to political bodies whether to act on these reports or not. Does this hamper their function and is there any recent evidence of their powers being hindered or reduced?

One of the most important bodies is the Electoral Commission. This is an independent body that oversees elections. It plays an important role, checking on electoral expenses and political finance more generally. It also oversees referendums. Its role is important given the justification for the predominantly political controls over the government. Those who argue that the government is one of the most democratic institutions of the constitution do so because the actions of the government are checked by the political party from which the government is formed, Parliament and the people. The people control the government through general elections. If these are not conducted fairly, then the most important check on governmental power can be undermined. The role of the people is minimized in favour of checks by political parties or Parliament.

The people can also take matters into their own hands. Public protest can be an effective means of raising political salience by bringing an issue to the attention of Members of Parliament and, hopefully, instigating policy change. Public protests may also be a means of holding the government to account for its policy decisions. But these methods are only effective if an adequately protected right to peaceful protest exists.

This chapter will look at recent challenges to these alternative means of providing an effective check and balance on the government. Is there evidence of a reduction in the effectiveness of these constitutional watchdogs in the post-Brexit constitution? If so, does this fit our populist narrative of the UK constitution slipping into a more authoritarian populist regime, or do they merely illustrate the UK constitution in action? Before looking at these changes, we need to set the scene by giving an account of one instance where media reporting on Parliament did make a difference: the expenses scandal of 2009.

Duck islands and dodgy deals

In 2009, the *Daily Telegraph* produced a series of stories about MPs' expenses. Readers were equally fascinated and appalled by money spent on duck houses, moat maintenance, ride-on lawn mowers and porn movies watched by the husband of an MP during a hotel stay. It became apparent from the revelations that the expenses scandal was not limited to a few rogue MPs. It included a large number of MPs from a range of parties.

There also appeared to be a culture of using expenses to supplement MPs' salaries. At that time, MPs' salaries were set by Parliament. However, it is hard to justify voting for your large pay increase, particularly in times of austerity where MPs' salaries may not compare favourably with those paid for realistic alternatives for most MPs (for example, management consultancies, barristers or solicitors, or banking and finance employees) but still compare favourably with the average wages of voters, particularly those in predominantly working-class constituencies. MPs used a system of additional costs allowances. These were devised to enable MPs to cover the additional costs of needing a base in their constituency as well as in London so that MPs can work for their constituents and also attend Parliament. How far were these allowances being used to cover realistic costs and how far were they essentially being used to supplement MPs' salaries?

What was uncovered through a series of freedom of information requests and a leak, was a set of 'acceptable' practices to help supplement salary payments – acceptable, it would appear, to those working in Parliament, but deeply unacceptable to the electorate. This included the practice of 'flipping', where MPs would have two homes, one in their constituency and one in London, where they would swap which was their 'main' home and which was their 'secondary' home. This meant MPs could then take advantage of the expenses rules relating to second homes, including tax deductions on the mortgage interest payments, home maintenance and renovation. Another common practice that was unearthed was that of employing family members as office staff. It was also revealed that the rules surrounding claims through the additional costs allowance were opaque and under-policed, including the infamous 'John Lewis list' used to calculate reasonable expenses. For many of the electorate,

John Lewis is a high-end department store, not an indicator of the average expense of household items.

At the time, this was seen as the biggest political scandal of the age, probably the century. As we have seen, however, it has recently been eclipsed by Partygate. Where there are differences, however, is the reaction to the expenses scandal. Like Partygate, public outrage was centred on how MPs were 'different' from the electorate. It was one rule for the electorate, another for MPs. While the electorate was adhering to Covid lockdown rules or facing the consequences of austerity, MPs were holding parties or claiming expenses for items related to a lifestyle well beyond the means of most of the electorate. Few voters have duck houses and moats, or grounds that require a ride-on lawn mower, or two homes, or regularly shop in John Lewis for everyday house items.

The difference, however, was that Partygate soon became focused on the behaviour of a smaller group of individuals, from the same political party, all connected to the government, and on activities within 10 Downing Street, although other accusations were later made about opposition MPs. The expenses scandal seemed to touch nearly every MP, from all sides of the political divide, demonstrating a lack of transparency and accountability. This explains why the expenses scandal had such a large negative impact on the electorate's levels of trust in politicians.

It may also explain why the expenses scandal had a more tangible impact on checks and balances. Parliament commissioned an independent audit of additional costs allowances from 2004–08, chaired by Thomas Legg, a retired senior civil servant who was then a member of the Audit Commission and the House of Commons Audit Committee. There was also a report from the Committee on Standards in Public Life. Criminal charges were made against three MPs and one member of the House of Lords, some of whom were convicted. Legal changes were brought into effect, creating the Independent Parliamentary Standards Authority. This body determines the salaries to be paid to MPs, as well as setting out an allowance scheme for MPs and administering the payments. A compliance officer was also established to investigate complaints relating to the payment of MPs' allowances. The Bribery Act 2010 also codified the criminal offence of bribery. The revelations also led to the resignation of the speaker, as well as MPs who decided to stand down at the next general election.

It is hard to assess, however, how far the expenses scandal had an impact on voter turnout or votes in the next general election. The scandal created a general malaise against politicians. In some senses, populist parties can exploit such a situation; smaller, newly emerging parties could have made political gains, appealing to the electorate as being in touch with the people and not part of the corrupt elites occupying Parliament. However, there is little evidence of this taking place. While the UK Independence Party did see a rise in support, it is hard to assess whether this is due to a reaction against the political elites, or a general swing in favour of the anti-European platform on which UKIP's electoral campaign was mainly based. As the criticism was more general as opposed to individualized, it is also harder to assess whether discontent with the behaviour of their MP led members of the electorate to switch political allegiances at the next general election.

What the expenses affair does illustrate, however, is that, if we are to assess whether checks and balances over the government are being reduced, we also need to take account of the role of other constitutional watchdogs, those institutions that oversee the actions of politicians generally and the government more specifically. The expenses scandal and Partygate, in particular, show the impact of the media. This impact can be particularly severe when the media reveals a scandal over a longer period, with coverage from a range of media institutions. If we remember duck islands and the lockdown parties in 10 Downing Street, it is because of the extent to which broad media coverage over a long time brought these to our attention. We may more easily forget individual examples of ministerial misconduct, even if they lead to the resignation of the minister in question.

For the media to act as an effective watchdog, however, it needs to have access to information and be sufficiently free to publicize stories which criticize those in power, including the government. A politicized media whose information only comes from 'official' sources, or one which is constantly criticized and attacked by those in power, is less able to perform its job effectively.

Unlike the concerns that were raised in the US during the Trump presidency, there are no immediate concerns about the independence of the media in the UK in terms of a political takeover, with one media outlet being chosen by the government as the only true vehicle of 'the truth'. Nor is there evidence of the government widely using the media purely for propaganda. Concerns were raised recently to the Commissioner for Public Appointments about the appointment of the chair of the BBC. Following an investigation led by a barrister, Adam Heppinstall KC, which concluded that the then BBC chair, Richard Sharp, had inadvertently failed to disclose a relevant interest to the appointment panel, Mr Sharp resigned.[1]

It may be harder to fit the role of the media in the UK into a populist narrative. Indeed, some of the examples of rhetoric against the media may suggest that the media is capable of holding the government to account. Would we be writing books on Partygate, Owen Paterson and Chris Pincher, or the rapid turnaround of prime ministers in 2022 had the media not been able to freely report on these events?

Nevertheless, there are some recent developments that some may see as concerning, particularly in terms of their potential to undermine the independence of the media and its ability to publish information that is in the public interest, even if this is not interesting enough to the public to facilitate the selling of newspapers, media subscriptions or advertising space needed for some media outlets to survive.

Channel 4: public or private?

For the media to provide an effective check on governmental activity, they need access to information and sufficient protection of media freedom to ensure they can publish material critical of the government. This can be compatible with regulations to prevent the media from abusing their position, or to protect the rights of others – for example, the right to privacy. The post-Brexit constitution has seen little change in these areas. It may seem possible to conclude, therefore, that the constitutional watchdog role of the media remains intact. Nevertheless, one proposed change to media regulation may give weight to suspicions that the post-Brexit constitution – at least under the government of Boris Johnson – was willing to act to potentially reduce the watchdog role of the media.

In July 2021, the government launched a consultation on the future ownership of Channel 4. Channel 4 is a public service broadcaster, launched in 1982. It is a self-financing public corporation. This means that it is publicly owned, but commercially run, obtaining its revenue predominantly from advertising. Part of its role as a public service broadcaster means that it has a specific remit to produce distinctive and innovative programmes. Channel 4 regards its purpose as creating change through entertainment. In particular, it aims to ensure that minority views and unheard voices are represented, particularly the content produced by and designed for diverse communities. Channel 4 also aims to hold power to account in an impartial and balanced manner. Channel 4's licence will expire in 2024, so holding a consultation exercise from 2021 to 2022 was a timely way of getting information about Channel 4 in time for a decision about its licence renewal.

The government was concerned as to whether Channel 4 was still able to serve its remit in the ever-changing media market, particularly in light of the growth of digital and video-on-demand services since the establishment of Channel 4. The government believed that the best way of achieving these aims was to privatize Channel 4, transferring it from public to private ownership. In particular, the government argued that this would enable Channel 4 to access a wider range of funding opportunities, with greater access to capital. This would enable Channel 4 to take advantage of strategic partnerships and acquisition opportunities, enabling it to expand into international markets and future-proofing itself through diversification of its revenue sources.

Those opposed to the privatization of Channel 4 were concerned that this would mean that Channel 4 would have to trade off content for profit making, a commercial entity being more concerned with generating profit than generating diverse content. There was particular concern that this would prevent Channel 4 from pursuing its agenda of diversification, ensuring representation from a wide range of voices. The desire to enter into international markets to maximize profits may, arguably, undermine the ability of Channel 4 to produce content representing minority UK views and minority UK cultures. There was a fear that this would lead to the homogenization of content. There were further concerns that Channel 4 would also lose its independence, depending on the identity of its potential buyer. Concerns also arose that this could give rise to a reduction of in-depth, impartial news coverage and groundbreaking documentaries that enable the media to hold the government to account.

Following this consultation exercise, the government concluded that it would continue with its plan to privatize Channel 4. On the same day as the government published its response to the consultation exercise, it produced a white paper, a policy document, setting out this decision. The white paper also included plans to introduce a new public service remit for public service broadcasters and empower Ofcom (the independent media regulator) to produce a code to regulate harmful content on video-on-demand services.

These are complex issues. What is concerning, however, is not necessarily the government's choice following the consultation exercise, but how the outcome was reached. The government's consultation exercise focused on six specific questions. Even if we only look at the responses that were gathered from the website and from those who sent responses in through the post (discounting those that were gathered from a public interest group who translated the questions and gathered responses) there was overwhelming support for rejecting the privatization of Channel 4. The gov.uk survey, for example, received 15,329 responses. Of these, 89 per cent were against privatization. Only 5 per cent were in favour of privatization.[2] Yet, despite this response and the concerns expressed, the government was convinced that privatization of Channel 4 was still the best option, citing concerns that continued public ownership of Channel 4 could place too much risk on the government and, ultimately, on the taxpayer, or potentially lead to an increase in public sector net debt.[3]

In response to concerns that privatization might undermine Channel 4's ability to provide content for a diverse audience and continue to provide independent and critical news coverage, the government gave assurances that it would seek to find a buyer who would continue to uphold these aims. The government also noted that Channel 4 would continue to be a public service broadcaster and, therefore, would still be subject to regulations which apply to these broadcasters. Channel 4 would also remain subject to oversight from Ofcom to ensure that its news coverage would continue to be independent and impartial.[4]

It is easy to see how this response fits with a populist narrative. Channel 4's content is not likely to be such that it would please a populist government. This is not because of its political leanings – Channel 4 is and remains politically independent. It is because

Channel 4's remit and purpose is to represent diverse and minority views. Any government wishing to succeed needs to obtain the support of the majority of the community. This may not be the same as the views that appeal to the more diverse audience Channel 4 is designed to appeal to and represent. Populist governments appeal to one particular view as 'the will of the people'. A media organization that sees its purpose as promoting and celebrating diversity may make it harder for a populist leader to homogenize the will of the people into one clear voice represented by that populist leader.

The proposed reform of Channel 4 also illustrates a pattern of the Johnson government of presenting a particular outcome, seeking consultation on that outcome, and then sticking to its original plan despite facing widespread criticism by those who responded to the government's consultation exercise. This pattern can be found in the government's response to the independent review of administrative law and the ensuing consultation exercise on judicial review, and its response to the independent Human Rights Act review and the ensuing consultation exercise on human rights. Why bother listening to the views of others if you are part of a populist government representing the wishes of the people? If the government knows that the people wish to privatize Channel 4, then this should be achieved, even if stakeholders and other experts who are likely to respond to these consultation exercises strongly disagree. Surely only experts and not the public can be bothered to respond to consultation exercises, so they cannot represent the wishes of the people in the same way as the government.

However, this can also be explained in terms of a fit with government policies. Conservative governments have traditionally favoured privatization and market regulation over publicly owned corporations. There is also more minimal interference with the media than can be seen in other states where populist governments have been more willing to control and regulate the media. The plans to privatize Channel 4 were ultimately reversed by Michelle Donelan, who replaced Nadine Dorries as Culture Secretary.

At least as far as the media is concerned, although the situation may not be perfect, there is little evidence of drastic changes suggesting a populist takeover of the media. Indeed, the widespread media reporting on Partygate arguably shows that the media is still able to perform its function as a constitutional watchdog.

The reaction to the temporary suspension of BBC sports presenter Gary Lineker following his tweet about the government's immigration policies demonstrates the extent to which reactions on social media, and support from other colleagues in the media and politicians, may be used to push back against any form of limit on the freedom of those working in the media to present their personal views. The BBC will now revisit its guidance as to the extent to which its presenters, other than those involved in the news where more neutrality is required, may tweet views that might question the independence of the BBC. It is important to ensure that the correct balance is drawn so the BBC can uphold its reputation for neutrality and the ability to enable those working for the BBC to express their personal views. Both are needed to ensure the media can perform its watchdog role.

However, the ease with which any government can introduce a policy that flies in the face of the majority outcome of a consultation exercise also shows that we cannot become complacent. It can be all too easy for any populist government, should it wish to do so, to undermine the media's function as a constitutional watchdog.

Reform of the Electoral Commission: oversight or control?

The Electoral Commission is an independent body tasked with overseeing the conduct of elections, including referendums, and party funding. It was established in 2000. Prior to its establishment, there were concerns about party funding, particularly about donations to political parties from foreign nationals. These concerns were raised by the Committee on Standards in Public Life. The Electoral Commission oversees funding; political parties and registered campaigners have to submit annual accounts and reports to the Electoral Commission. They must also notify the Electoral Commission of large donations and loans to political parties. The Electoral Commission maintains a register of these donations and of statements of accounts and reports. The public can access these registers. This facilitates transparency, enabling the public to know who is funding a particular political party.

The Electoral Commission oversees voting in elections and referendums and provides advice and guidance to ensure that elections function effectively and fairly. It also has the task of publicizing elections, and encouraging increased voter participation, particularly through encouraging individuals to register to vote. The Electoral Commission has the power to impose financial penalties on political parties and campaigners who fail to register their accounts or donations. It can also require that donations be forfeited. When there are more serious cases, these can be referred to the police.

The Electoral Commission, therefore, plays an important role in the democratic process. It encourages larger voter turnout by ensuring there is sufficient information on upcoming elections and referendums and by encouraging as many of the electorate as possible to ensure they are registered to vote and can exercise their right to vote. It also ensures fairness in the electoral process by checking that there are no irregularities in the financing of campaigns, as well as overseeing fairness in election campaigns.

Given its important role, it is necessary to ensure that it is independent of political influence. There could be criticism of its regulation of political donations, campaigns and campaign expenditures if it were perceived that the Electoral Commission was linked to a particular political party. However, the importance of its role also means that it is essential there is oversight of how it performs this role. Democracy can also be harmed if the Electoral Commission is unable to perform its job effectively, or if it carries out its activities in too draconian a manner. A failure to oversee fairness in campaigns and expenditure runs the risk that larger political parties with more resources may dominate a political campaign. To exercise control too stringently may make it harder for new parties with fewer resources to campaign effectively, as their lack of experience or ability to pay for expert help may mean they inadvertently fail to fully comply with the rules.

The recent Elections Act 2022 modified the oversight of the Electoral Commission. Before the 2022 Act, the Electoral Commission was subject to parliamentary oversight by the Speaker's Committee on the Electoral Commission. This committee is chaired by the Speaker of the House of Commons, who is joined by nine other MPs. Five of the MPs are non-ministerial MPs who are appointed by the speaker. A further member is a minister with responsibility for local government who is appointed by the prime minister. The rest of the members of the committee are ex officio members, meaning they are members of the committee because of official positions they hold elsewhere; they include chairs of other committees responsible for constitutional affairs and local elections, two relevant ministers and the speaker who chairs the committee.

The speaker's committee oversees the process of recruiting and appointing new electoral commissioners. Parliament must approve the nominees before they are appointed by the Monarch. There are ten electoral commissioners, of whom four are drawn from nominations by political parties. The speaker's committee also oversees the budget of the Electoral Commission and its five-year plan, and answers questions about the Electoral Commission from MPs.

The Elections Act 2022 changes the oversight of the Electoral Commission. First, rather than the Electoral Commission determining its five-year plan, the government may set a strategy and policy statement for the Electoral Commission. This statement sets out the strategic and policy priorities of the government regarding elections, referendums and other aspects of the role of the Electoral Commission. It also sets out the role and responsibilities of the Electoral Commission in achieving these priorities. The statement is made by a minister after consulting with relevant stakeholders, including the Electoral Commission. The statement also has to be approved by Parliament. It has to be renewed at least every five years and may also be revised. The Electoral Commission is required to have regard to the statement when carrying out its functions.

Second, the Elections Act 2022 changes how the Electoral Commission is overseen by the Speaker's Committee on the Electoral Commission. The Electoral Commission has to produce an annual report on its activities and how they relate to the strategic and policy priorities set out in the government's statement. The speaker's committee may then examine how far the Electoral Commission has performed its functions in line with its duty to have regard to the government's statement of strategic and policy priorities. The Electoral Commission may be required to provide the speaker's committee with information to enable the committee to carry out its oversight function.

There are concerns that these changes undermine the independence of the Electoral Commission. Rather than being able to set its own priorities to ensure the fairness of elections, its priorities are being set by the government. Although there is parliamentary oversight of the government's statement of these priorities, the political reality means that the government will find it easy to achieve a majority vote, given that any government will normally possess a working majority in the House of Commons. The setting of priorities by one of the political parties subject to oversight by the Electoral Commission may undermine the ability of the Electoral Commission to ensure fairness in the electoral process. Any government might set priorities or strategies that facilitate its chances of success, or which undermine the tactics of its political rivals.

This change fits a populist narrative. The Electoral Commission may oversee fairness in the electoral process, but it is also a group of elite individuals with expertise in elections. Members of the Electoral Commission tend to either be former politicians (those nominated by political parties) or former senior figures in government or academia. Why should the rules and procedures set out by experts get in the way of the will of the people? The events at the White House on 6 January 2021 provide a stark illustration of how far some may be prepared to go when they feel that those administering election processes have not reached the right outcome, thereby thwarting the will of the people. On 6 January 2021, supporters of President Trump, who had recently lost the presidential election, stormed Capitol Hill in protest at the election result. They sought to keep Donald Trump in power by preventing a joint session of Congress from certifying Joe Biden's election victory as the new US president. Populist leaders wishing to stay in power may also modify election rules to favour their re-election.

The changes achieved through the Elections Act 2022 do not go this far. In many respects, they are a modest change. A lot will depend on the content of the strategy statement. At the time of writing, the first draft statement had been prepared by the government and sent for consultation. Several concerns were raised by the parliamentary committees tasked with being consulted on the statement. First, there are concerns that the statement strays too far in interfering with the Electoral Commission's operational independence. The statement is meant to set strategic and policy priorities. However, aspects of the statement go beyond this, setting out detailed instructions as to how the Electoral Commission is meant to carry out its job.

Second, the statement sets out an account of the roles and responsibilities of the Electoral Commission in wording that is different from the statute which provides the legal definition of these roles and responsibilities. The use of different and occasionally contradictory language could give rise to confusion. This may cause problems when it comes to overseeing the Electoral Commission. In particular, there were concerns that the Electoral Commission may face legal actions and potentially even vexatious litigation that would hamper the commission from performing its functions. Differences in wording may provide an opportunity to bring legal action when the Electoral Commission complies with the wording set out in one source but is contradicted by the wording in a different source.

Third, there are concerns that the statement requires the Electoral Commission to prioritize goals of the government that have not yet been approved by Parliament and which may not even be official government policy. For example, the draft statement sets out that the Electoral Commission should 'support the Government's delivery of legitimate executive priorities in relation to elections during this Parliament, including changes brought by the Elections Act 2022'.[5]

If this statement were merely to set out that the Electoral Commission was required to deliver the changes brought by the Elections Act 2022, this would not be problematic. However, the statement is not limited to this purpose. It may imply, therefore, that the Electoral Commission is meant to facilitate government policy; however, it may be difficult to check that this is the policy of the government and not that of the particular political party in power at the time. It is also preferable for the Electoral Commission to be implementing the policies set out in legislation, or approved by a parliamentary committee, not those set out by whatever political party happens to be in government at the time.

These problems led the Speaker's Committee on the Electoral Commission to conclude that the statement was 'not fit for purpose'.[6] The committee also concluded that the statement would 'introduce uncertainty, confusion, and new legal risks which are likely to reduce the Commission's efficiency, economy and effectiveness, in return for no material benefit to the democratic process'.[7]

The speaker's committee considered that, given that the current arrangements were working well and that there was only a power and not a duty to create a statement, the best course of action may be not to produce a statement and, if a statement was desired, that the current statement should be radically redrafted in light of the criticisms from the relevant parliamentary committees. It concluded its report with the following strong words:

> We also note that, just as the Secretary of State's power to designate a Statement is optional, the power of the Speaker's Committee to hold the Commission accountable for its duty to have regard to that Statement is also optional. Were the Government to proceed to designate a Statement which we consider not fit for purpose, we would need to consider carefully what account we could take of such a Statement, and whether we could legitimately hold the Commission to account for their duty in relation to it.
>
> The Government should therefore be mindful not to set a precedent of disregarding concerns during consultations on draft Statements; doing so could, ultimately, be to the detriment of our electoral integrity and public confidence in the UK's democratic processes.[8]

Concerns as to how a policy is produced, particularly the lack of regard for the views of experts expressed in a consultation process, also fit a populist narrative. There is no need to take these views into account if they are only going to get in the way of the will of the people, as expressed through the government's policies.

It is also possible to see further evidence of the influence of populism in the motivation behind the changes to the role of the Electoral Commission. The Electoral Commission had issued several fines to those campaigning in the Brexit referendum. These fines had been issued to those on both sides of the campaign. However, a lot of attention was drawn to the fines imposed on some members of the Vote Leave and the BeLeave campaign groups, which had criticized the intervention of the Electoral Commission. Two matters were referred to the police. The campaigners whose conduct had been referred to the police accused the Electoral Commission of bias. One campaigner was successful in his legal challenge. However, while this did lead to criticism of the Electoral Commission, there is no evidence of a clear causal link between this criticism and the proposed reforms.

Unlike the proposed changes to privatize Channel 4, there has not, to date, been a change made to the government's statement of policy and strategy for the Electoral Commission. However, it also appears to merely remain a draft statement. There would appear to be a danger that the proposed statement will undermine the ability of the Electoral Commission to perform its essential watchdog role. It is to be hoped that the content of this statement will either be modified in the light of the strongly worded criticisms, particularly those of the Speaker's Committee on the Electoral Commission which has the main role of overseeing the Electoral Commission, or dropped.

People power?

For many, the only way in which to ensure your voice is heard is through the use of your right to peaceful protest. Marches and assemblies in public have played a key part in raising awareness which, in turn, can sometimes lead to change. Marches, protests and Pride events, for example, played a key role in legal changes to provide greater protections for LGBTQ+ (lesbian, gay, bi, trans, queer, questioning and ace) rights. Marches have also raised awareness of environmental issues, from fossil fuels to fracking, climate change to pollution. The right to peaceful protest is sometimes referred to as the lifeblood of democracy. It is an effective means to raise awareness of issues, ensure a diverse range of voices are heard in society and even bring about policy change.

The right to peaceful protest is protected in the UK. Prior to the Human Rights Act 1998 coming into force, this was through a series of negative liberties. In other words, individuals were free to protest, unless there was a law preventing this activity. The scope of the right to protest, therefore, depended on the scope of laws enacted that would restrict this right. The Human Rights Act 1998 means that human rights are now protected as positive rights and not just as negative liberties. In particular, this means that laws that might restrict the right to protest are interpreted, so far as it is possible to do so, to protect the human rights found in the European Convention on Human Rights (ECHR). In particular, UK courts can refer to two convention rights: the right to freedom of expression (set out in Article 10 ECHR) and the right to freedom of association (set out in Article 11 ECHR). These rights can protect peaceful protest, enabling individuals to come together in support of a particular cause or to advocate a particular policy change.

A recent decision of the Supreme Court demonstrates the changes that the Human Rights Act 1998 has made. In September 2017, the Excel Centre in East London was used as the venue for the biennial Defence and Security International Fair. The fair provides an opportunity for defence contractors to demonstrate their goods to those wishing to purchase military equipment, including weapons. Mr Ziegler and others wished to protest against the arms trade. To do so, they laid down in the middle of one of the main access roads to the fair in the days before the fair opened. They also attached themselves to two lock boxes with pipes. Protesters put their arms into the pipes and then locked themselves to the box. It took considerable time to remove the protesters from the road, particularly given that the boxes they had locked themselves to were designed to be difficult to remove. The protesters were charged with the offence of wilfully obstructing the highway without lawful excuse.[9]

Before the Human Rights Act 1998 came into force, the court would have assessed whether the protesters had committed the offence of obstructing the highway by looking at whether their use of the highway was reasonable. If it was, then this would provide a lawful excuse for obstructing the highway, meaning that they were not guilty of the offence. This could include taking account of the common law protections of the right to freedom of speech and the right to peaceful protest, provided that this was consistent with the general right of the public to pass and repass along the highway. The question that arose before the Supreme Court was whether this situation had changed. Should the court consider reasonable excuse differently, paying more attention to convention rights?

The Supreme Court concluded that, as the offence of obstructing the highway without reasonable excuse is set out in a statute, its provisions have to be read and given effect in a manner that is compatible with convention rights. This is required by section 3 of the Human Rights Act 1998. For Mr Ziegler and the other protesters, this meant that the courts had to determine whether the removal of the protesters was a proportionate restriction on their right to protest. If this was a proportionate restriction, then they would not have a lawful excuse to obstruct the highway and so their removal from the street was lawful, and they could also be prosecuted for obstructing the highway. If, however, the removal of the protesters was a disproportionate restriction on their right to protest, then this would mean that there was a lawful excuse for their conduct as they were merely exercising their right to peaceful protest. This lawful excuse could include protests where protesters deliberately physically obstructed others from using the highway. As the first court that had looked at whether the protestors had committed an offence had not looked at whether they had a lawful excuse for obstructing the highway, their original conviction was quashed.

As a later decision of the Supreme Court makes clear, this does not mean that the impact of the Human Rights Act 1998 provides a means through which any protest designed to physically obstruct people from using a highway will provide protesters with a lawful excuse for obstructing the highway.[10] These assessments depend on the facts of each protest, assessed by the courts to determine whether there has been a disproportionate breach of the right to protest. It is also important to note that there are limits to when the courts will allow protesters to rely on their convention rights. This is because Articles 10 and 11 of the ECHR are designed to protect peaceful protest. They do not include protests that are intentionally designed to cause serious disruption for a long time, or which incite or use violence.

UK law does provide good protection of the right to peaceful protest, as well as setting out specific legal restrictions designed, predominantly, to ensure that protests are peaceful. However, recent developments show a weakening of the protection of the right to peaceful protest in the post-Brexit constitution. The changes were made in the Police, Crime, Sentencing and Courts Act 2022. Before this Act, the police had powers to place conditions on gatherings or processions if this appeared necessary to the senior police officer present at that protest or procession to prevent serious disorder, serious damage to property or serious disruption. For example, the police might decide to reroute a procession or move a gathering to a different location if protesters started damaging property or threatening passers-by.

Also, conditions could be placed on a gathering or protest if these conditions appeared necessary to the senior police officer present when the gathering or procession aimed to intimidate others either not to do something they had a right to do, or to do something they did not have a right to do. For example, the police may ask protesters not to physically prevent or threaten to physically prevent people from going to a bank because the protesters believed that the bank in question invested in the oil trade.

These provisions also created offences for when a protester, or the organizer of the procession or gathering, knowingly fails to follow a direction from a police officer. There was also a defence for those who failed to comply because of circumstances beyond their control. If convicted of this offence, a protester could face a fine or a prison sentence of up to three months.[11]

The focus of these conditions is to stop gatherings and processions that are no longer peaceful and which, instead, are becoming or are about to become violent protests or protests that move beyond persuasion into intimidation. They aim to ensure that those who wish to can protest peacefully while hoping to mitigate protests from becoming violent by using conditions on a step-by-step basis to diffuse tension and prevent violence. However, it can be a difficult job for police officers to achieve this on the ground when faced with ever-changing situations during what may start as a peaceful protest.

The new law makes three significant changes. First, and most controversially, it broadens the situation in which a senior police officer can place a condition on a gathering or a procession, focusing in particular on noisy protests. Conditions can now be placed on gatherings and processions where 'the noise generated by persons taking part in the procession may result in serious disruption to the activities of an organization which are carried out in the vicinity' of either the procession or the gathering,[12] or where 'noise generated may have a relevant impact on persons in the vicinity'.[13] These are quite broadly defined; how can the police determine when noise will result in serious disruption, or have 'relevant impact' on others in the vicinity of a protest?

The new law provides an example of serious disruption as being where the noise disrupts the activities of an organization such that the organization is not 'reasonably able, for a prolonged period of time' to carry out its activities.[14] This is still very broad; it is not clear, for example, what is meant by a 'prolonged time' or how noisy a protest or gathering has to be to stop an organization from carrying out its activities. This may well depend on the facts; for example, organizations producing goods in a noisy factory, selling products in a supermarket with background music, or teaching yoga and meditation, will all be affected differently by noise from a nearby protest.

The new law also defines what is meant by 'relevant impact'. This occurs if it will 'result in the intimidation or harassment of persons of reasonable firmness with the characteristics of persons likely to be in the vicinity' or 'cause such person to suffer alarm or distress'. [15] This probably seems like odd wording to those not used to reading legislation. 'Intimidation', 'harassment', 'alarm' and 'distress' are used in other offences relating to public order; for example, to prevent those taking part in processions or gatherings from using words or behaviour that would have this effect. The section also makes it clear that whether noise intimidates, harasses, alarms or distresses others is to be assessed in a reasonable manner. It may be the case that an overly sensitive person may be alarmed by the level of noise. However, the law makes it clear that this would not be enough. It has to be the case that a person of reasonable firmness would be alarmed. However, the law does take account of the types of persons in the vicinity; for example, if the protest was close to a school or a hospital the standard would be different from the one used if the protest was close to a bank or supermarket. To assess whether this impact is serious, the police have to take into account how many people are affected by the noise, the duration and the intensity of the impact.[16]

As well as extending to noisy protests, the new law provides for a new set of particular circumstances in which a gathering or protest may cause 'serious disruption to the life of the community'.[17] This will now clearly include when protests may cause significant delays to the distribution of a time-sensitive product – for example, fresh food. It also includes 'prolonged disruption of access to any essential goods or any essential service'; for example, money, fuel, water or communication systems, as well as disruptions to access to places of worship, transport facilities, schools, hospitals and others providing health services.[18]

Second, the Police, Crime, Sentencing and Courts Act 2022 makes it easier for a protester or an organizer to be convicted of an offence when they fail to follow a direction of a police officer. Under the old law, protesters or organizers were prosecuted when they knowingly failed to comply with a condition, unless this was due to circumstances beyond their control. Under the provisions of the 2022 Act, a protester or organizer can be guilty of an offence if they fail to comply with a condition that they knew about or ought to have known about. This may make it easier to prosecute protesters and organizers who fail to follow police directions. The new law does retain the ability for the protester or organizer to show that their lack of compliance was due to circumstances beyond their control. Third, the new law increases the maximum penalty for this offence, from three months' to 51 weeks' imprisonment, although the maximum-level fine that may be imposed remains the same.

It is understandable why some were seriously concerned about these new laws. They have the potential to narrow the scope of peaceful protests. Rather than focusing on ensuring gatherings and processions do not become violent or intimidating, there is also a need to ensure that protests do not become so noisy that they may prevent others from carrying out their activities, or which may give rise to intimidation, harassment, alarm or distress due solely to the noise levels. This seems to modify our understanding of peaceful protest. A protest is no longer peaceful merely because it does not give rise to harm to others or to property. A protest is peaceful because it is relatively quiet.

When considering the impact of this change in the law on the right to peaceful protest, we also need to take account of the 'chilling effect'. This happens when protesters err on the side of caution, deciding not to hold or take part in a meeting or gathering that would be lawful because they fear that it might be unlawful. Vague and broadly worded offences are likely to increase this chilling effect. If it is not clear what is and what is not an offence, or a march or a protest that may give rise to the police being able to impose conditions on a gathering or procession, then protesters may be more likely to define these as broadly as possible to ensure they do not break the law.

Protesters are also more likely to err on the side of caution because they may be prosecuted for failing to comply with a condition they ought to have known about. How easy is it for other protesters to know about conditions placed on a procession or gathering if they did not see or hear the police officer making this condition? It may be difficult for the message to be communicated to all protesters. The increase in the penalty to a maximum prison sentence of 51 weeks raises the stakes of getting it wrong. This, again, may induce protesters to err on the side of caution, for fear that they may otherwise face a prison sentence rather than a fine.

The changes in the law, therefore, have the potential to have a larger impact on the right to peaceful protest than may appear from merely looking at how the law has changed. Moreover, they are not the only proposed changes to the right to protest. During the enactment of the Police, Crime, Sentencing and Courts Act 2022, the government proposed further restrictions on the right to protest by proposing amendments to the legislation in the House of Lords. The House of Lords rejected these amendments. As they were introduced in the House of Lords, the government could not reintroduce and insist on these amendments in the House of Commons. As we saw in Chapter 3, however, some of these rejected measures were nevertheless reintroduced through delegated legislation. This, in particular, will empower the police to prevent slow marches.

Also, a new Bill has been introduced to Parliament: the Public Order Bill 2022–23, now the Public Order Act 2023. This creates a further set of new offences. What is particularly concerning about these offences is how they relate to situations in which courts have used convention rights to interpret current legislation in a manner that ensures it does not undermine the right to peaceful protest; for example, by creating new offences of locking-on and of causing serious disruption through tunnelling. The first new offence responds to *Ziegler*, discussed above. The actions of the protesters of locking themselves to a box is now an offence. As is travelling to the protest site with equipment to facilitate locking-on. Although there is a defence of reasonable excuse, this is linked to the act of locking-on and not a reasonable excuse linked to the protest in which the locking-on will take place. The offence carries a maximum sentence of 51 weeks' imprisonment. The second new offence responds to other court cases where it proved difficult to find the relevant offence committed by those tunnelling on the grounds of land owned by HS2 in protest at the HS2 rail link.

As with our other examples, these modifications may fit a populist narrative. They may make it harder for those who do not fit the homogenized 'will of the people' – particularly those with minority views or from minority communities – to express their views and make their voices heard. This may make it harder to challenge the 'will of the people' by pointing out that this may not represent the wishes of a majority of the electorate, or that it fails to represent a range of views in any particular society. How do we know of these other voices if they are effectively silenced, or their protests are frequently disrupted for being too noisy, or never held in the first place? This may make it easier for populist leaders to remain in power as it is easier to demonstrate that a populist government's view of the 'will of the people' is accurate.

However, not all of the current and proposed changes fit this narrative. These changes may well have other justifications. For example, while protests need to be effective, the right to peaceful protest should be limited if this protest means that essential goods or services are unable to reach individuals who need them for a prolonged period; for example, fuel, medicine and, for most of us, the internet or wireless telecommunications networks. There may well be other ways in which protests can raise issues or seek to influence policies without serious disruption. However, as with most elements of the law relating to the right to peaceful protest, the devil is in the detail and the potential chilling effect. It may be reasonable for those protesting against climate change to provide some disruption to fuel supplies to demonstrate how much society depends on fossil fuels. Drawing the line between a reasonable protest, and one which causes serious disruption to the supply of essential goods and services, is not easy in practice.

As with the other aspects of recent changes to constitutional watchdogs, the impact of these changes will depend on how they are put into practice. For the right to peaceful protest, this may have a larger impact on protesters who do not have ready and affordable access to legal advice to help them to negotiate these new legal provisions without erring too greatly on the side of caution and cancelling lawful protests for fear that they or those taking part in the protest may face criminal charges. This may have a larger impact on diverse as opposed to mainstream interests.

Conclusion

Constitutional watchdogs perform an important function in any constitution. Their role becomes all the more important in the UK's predominantly political constitution, where we rely on political controls, self-restraint and mutual respect. They may also be the main means through which the people can check the activities of the government or play a role in policy decisions.

As with our other examples, there may not be enough evidence here to support a populist narrative. However, nor can we argue that these changes are designed to return the UK to its more orthodox system of political as opposed to legal checks. The private ownership of Channel 4 is not part of the orthodox UK constitution, as is perhaps recognized by the fact that this no longer appears to be government policy. The right to peaceful protest has long been protected in the UK as a negative liberty, before being a positive right following the enactment of the Human Rights Act 1998. Recent changes to the law may make it harder for protesters to make their voice heard. Erring on the side of caution, they avoid gatherings and processions for fear that they become too noisy, leading to arrests of protesters who did not know, but where it was deemed that they should have known, that conditions had been placed on their protest to minimize the disruptive impact of the noise of their protest.

Of particular concern are the changes to the oversight of the Electoral Commission, particularly in light of the strong words of the Speaker's Committee on the Electoral Commission over the government's first proposed policy and strategy document for the Electoral Commission. This does fit with a populist narrative, potentially interfering with an independent watchdog in a manner that might favour the policies of a particular political party in government. It is to be hoped that the criticism of parliamentary committees on this draft statement will cause the government to rethink this policy. What is all the more concerning, however, is how both the original policy to privatize Channel 4 and to modify the independence of the Electoral Commission were undertaken by the government despite this being contrary to the outcomes of consultation exercises. This provides further evidence to fit a populist narrative, where the wishes of the people should always outweigh those of experts.

8

Should We Be Afraid and If So What Should We Do about It?

We have been examining the changes that have taken place in the UK constitution post Brexit. Our main focus has been the Westminster Parliament, particularly on the checks over the powers of the UK government. In particular, we have asked whether there is evidence of a change in the powers of the Westminster government. Have they grown post Brexit? Are there still the same checks and balances in place over these powers from Parliament, the electorate, the courts and other constitutional watchdogs, or have these checks been diminished?

Unchecked power?

It is hard to deny that the UK's constitution is changing. Brexit has had a huge impact on the structure of the UK and its relationship with the European Union. This book has not looked at the many changes to the constitution that have been required to implement Brexit. Rather, it has focused on other constitutional changes. While Brexit may have been the catalyst for some of these changes, they were not needed to achieve the UK's withdrawal from the EU treaties, or to establish the UK's new relationship with the EU, or to assess which of the remaining EU provisions that still have direct effect in UK law we want to keep and which we want to change. These changes may, however, have been prompted by a reaction to the use of a referendum. Some were a reaction to the perception that Parliament in 2019 tried to thwart the will of the people expressed in that referendum by delaying Brexit to prevent the UK from leaving the EU with no deal.

Some of these changes have come from legislation, implementing promises set out in the Conservative Party's manifesto for the 2019 general election.[1] These include the repeal of the Fixed-term Parliaments Act 2011 and its replacement with the Dissolution and Calling of Parliament Act 2022, as well as changes implemented by the Elections Act 2022 – for example, to broaden the franchise to include expats who have lived outside the UK for more than 15 years and to introduce voter ID.

Some changes to legislation did not go as far as might have been implied from the Conservative Party's manifesto. The Judicial Review and Courts Act 2022, for example, did not remove checks and balances over the government by the courts, focusing instead on creating, or reinforcing, new remedies and limiting one narrow example of judicial review. Some changes have gone further. For example, the changes mentioned in the manifesto to protect democracy did not include the changes made to the oversight of the Electoral Commission. Other changes were not part of the manifesto, for example, changes to the right to protest found in the Police, Crime, Sentencing and Courts Act 2022.

Some appear to have been weakened. The Bill of Rights Bill, for example, is no longer part of the legislative agenda. Yet, as the Illegal Migration Bill 2022–23 demonstrates, there is evidence of Bills which are designed to limit or remove the protection of convention rights to certain aspects of UK law. We may also question to what extent policy choices are good ones if they can depend so radically on the personal choices of ministers and the relative support they receive from the prime minister, the Bill of Rights Bill having been removed following the replacement of Dominic Raab as Lord Chancellor by Alex Chalk.

Constitutional change initiated in this way is nothing new. As we have frequently noted, the Westminster Parliament is sovereign. Any parliament can change the constitution through the enactment of Acts of Parliament. Future parliaments can initiate their own changes to the constitution, including reversing earlier constitutional changes. However, as there is no requirement for these constitutional changes to stem from a manifesto promise, and no requirement to consult the electorate before changing the constitution, it is not always the case that these changes are merely implementing the will of the people. Even when manifesto promises are implemented, the manifesto may not be fully followed. Manifestos set out broad aims rather than specific policies. Like referendums, manifestos may also homogenize the will of the people. Did you read any manifestos before voting in the 2019 general election, or any other election? If you did, how far did it influence you when you cast your vote and are you holding the political party you voted for to account in terms of how far they are sticking to their manifesto commitments?

We have also seen changes to other sources of the constitution. First, we saw changes made to the Ministerial Code by both Boris Johnson and Rishi Sunak. This is nothing new. Prime ministers are expected to reissue the Ministerial Code when they take office. While Johnson changed the code to include the ability of the independent adviser on minister's interests to play a larger role in initiating investigations, these changes mostly reflect what had become the practice and did not go as far as those suggested by the Committee on Standards in Public Life to provide more effective political checks on ministers. The changes to the nature of the penalties that may be imposed may also have weakened the ability of the Ministerial Code to hold ministers to account for their actions. Rishi Sunak's changes to the Ministerial Code were mostly cosmetic rather than substantive. However, he too decided not to fully implement the changes to the Ministerial Code suggested by the Committee on Standards in Public Life.

The Owen Paterson affair prompted the House of Commons select committee on standards to propose changes to clarify codes of conduct. These changes extend to clarification over lobbying, as well as the procedures used to investigate allegations that Members of Parliament have breached codes of conduct. These changes followed an independent inquiry and may provide a more effective means of holding MPs to account while ensuring fairness in investigations.

There have also been more informal changes to the UK constitution. These are changes to how those in government exercise their powers, as opposed to changes to the law or the internal rules that MPs and those in government should follow. They are more subtle and harder to pin down. We've noted a rise in the use of delegated legislation, including skeleton legislation which achieves policy objectives by granting broad powers to the government to finalize and implement policy choices. We've also seen a greater use of guidance and advice as a way of setting the rules, rather than a means of clarifying legal obligations and responsibilities made by, or overseen by, Parliament.

There have also been what appear to be examples of a lack of self-restraint and a loss of mutual respect by some members of the government for other institutions of the constitution. The Owen Paterson affair, for example, saw the government originally move to reject the conclusions of the House of Commons select committee on standards, intermingling general concerns about the procedures used by that committee with specific concerns as to the outcome of their conclusion. More worryingly, we've seen a lack of self-restraint that could give rise to the undermining of the rule of law. The government seems less constrained by international law, being willing to propose legislation that breaches the UK's international law obligations. Although the Northern Ireland Protocol Bill was withdrawn in light of the Windsor Framework, the Illegal Migration Bill, if enacted, will require the UK to act contrary to its obligations in international law to abide by interim judgments made by the European Court of Human Rights.

Other examples of when those in government have appeared to be less constrained by the legal limits over their powers include the possibility that either civil servants or ministers may be found to have committed contempt of court by producing guidance which would have induced those following it to commit contempt of court by failing to comply with orders of the Parole Board.

There are also examples of a possible lack of respect by the government for the role of the courts. We noted an example of where a minister ignored a court order, as well as an example of the failure of the government to implement a declaratory order. We have also seen how a government department failed to comply with the duty of candour, such that inaccurate information was shared with those bringing an action for judicial review against the government, making it harder for them to bring their case and ensure the government acted within the law.

A further example of a more general lack of respect and a willingness to ignore the views of experts is seen in the willingness of the government to forge ahead with constitutional changes, even when these are contrary to, or go further than, those recommended by independent reports or responses to government consultation exercises. We saw this with the government's response to changes to human rights reform and the now-stalled Bill of Rights Bill.

We've also looked at whether Boris Johnson's prime ministership in particular saw a change in behaviour towards a greater use of rhetoric rather than deliberation. We noted that rhetoric seems to be a general feature of the UK constitution, particularly at Prime Minister's Questions (PMQs) and when introducing Bills for their second reading in the House of Commons. Nevertheless, Boris Johnson tended to use more colourful phrases and a more informal style of presenting information to the public. We've also noted how far Boris Johnson's government and other governments had developed a habit of announcing major policy changes to the public as opposed to Parliament, most recently the government's plans in the Illegal Migration Bill for those who arrive in the UK by crossing the Channel in small boats and changes to the modification of retained EU law. We argued that this fits more with a presidential as opposed to a prime ministerial system of government. It also undermines the role of Parliament by preventing parliamentary scrutiny and replacing it with a direct appeal to the public. This, in turn, can undermine checks and balances.

However, some changes have either been withdrawn or have been checked by other institutions, reducing the impact of proposed changes to the UK constitution and the potential reduction in checks and balances. The privatization of Channel 4 will now no longer take place. Some of the reforms to judicial review in the Judicial Review and Courts Bill 2022 were prevented by the House of Lords. The attempt to legislate contrary to international law in the Internal Market Bill 2020 led to two high-profile resignations, amendments from the House of Lords and pressure from EU institutions during negotiations for the UK's future trade agreement with the EU. These checks combined to lead the government to remove the offending provisions from the Act. The Northern Ireland Protocol Bill 2022, which also proposed to suspend the operation of the Northern Ireland Protocol in domestic law, was argued by the government to be a legally justifiable breach of international law. The Bill was dropped following a negotiated settlement with the EU set out in the Windsor Framework.

Parliamentary and public outrage meant that Owen Paterson did resign. The media were able to report on Partygate and the allegations made against Chris Pincher. These, in part, led to the resignation of Boris Johnson as Prime Minister. The House of Commons Committee on Privileges concluded that Boris Johnson had knowingly misled Parliament and recommended that he be suspended from Parliament for 90 days and his parliamentary pass as a former MP be removed. This was later confirmed by a majority vote in the House of Commons. There were two prime ministerial resignations in 2022. The media, again, played a part in publicizing what was going on in Parliament and facilitating debate on Liz Truss's government's economic policies. These occurrences, in particular, may seem hard to tally with an assessment of a constitution where there are no effective checks on the powers of the government. It also suggests that we should not worry even if a prime minister seems to act like a populist leader. After all, he or she can be removed.

These changes do not conclusively show that the checks over the power of the government have been drastically reduced. They do not show that the UK has been dominated by a form of populism that is in danger of producing authoritarianism. There are some examples of when checks on the power of the government have been effective, particularly when it comes to holding the prime minister to account.

I do, however, remain concerned. It would be wrong to argue that these changes are merely returning the UK constitution to its more orthodox understanding, a sovereign parliament that provides effective political checks over governmental power. This is because these changes are not merely redressing an imbalance of power, reducing legal checks over the government and reinforcing political checks. There are reductions in political checks as well as legal checks. There are also changes in behaviour. More fundamentally, the orthodox understanding regards Parliament as the most important institution of the constitution. Parliament, on behalf of the people, is meant to provide the most effective check on the power of the government. Yet, recent events would suggest that the most effective check on the government is not Parliament, but the members of the political party from which the government is formed, particularly those who are MPs.

Even if we could argue that these changes are just a return to business as usual, I am concerned that business as usual is not good enough. The UK constitution may have sufficient checks and balances in place during a time of constitutional crisis. We saw this through the rollercoaster events of 2019, where Parliament was able to check the power of the government. The courts were able to strike down an unlawful prorogation of Parliament. But those checks are not always there for the day-to-day business of government. Lord Hailsham's accusation that the UK constitution was best described as an elective dictatorship is just as accurate today.

Moreover, while the checks and balances in place may be effective in a crisis or when a large change is proposed to the constitution, they are less effective when faced with a series of incremental changes that shift the balance of power in favour of the government and reduce legal and political checks over the government's powers. This places the UK in danger of democratic and constitutional decline through continual, gradual attrition of checks and balances designed to uphold principles of good constitutional government. It can leave the UK constitution constantly standing on a cliff edge which is gradually being eroded. While there may be means of stopping the constitution from falling off the cliff edge, there may not be the means to stop erosion of the ground on which the constitution stands. Yet this gradual erosion may have the same consequence as a major constitutional crisis. Why do I think this? And what, if anything, can we do to stop it?

Populism or business as usual?

This book has looked at two possible narratives to explain the changes made to the UK's post-Brexit constitution. The first argues that the UK is becoming populist. The second states that these changes merely restore balance to the UK constitution, returning the UK constitution to its traditional system of political as opposed to legal checks.

As we've seen, populism is difficult to define. Any accusation that a system is, or has become, populist is difficult to prove. Populism believes that the people and not Parliament are sovereign. It pitches the will of the people against the will of the elites. In this contest, there can be only one winner – the people. There is no space for compromise or consensus. The will of the people is also homogenized. The will of the people is not composed of a range of diverse groups in society, all of whom have different interests and values. Nor does the will of the people seek to find a consensus across this range of diverse voices. Rather, there is only one clear voice of the people. One subset of society is the real and only will of the people. This will of the people is only championed by a populist leader. Populist leaders also tend to use rhetoric rather than deliberation. There's no need to listen to experts, or the opinions of other MPs, particularly as they may stop a populist leader from implementing the will of the people.

Defined in this way, populism harms democracy. It undermines participatory democracy by making it harder for those who do not agree with the will of the people from having their voices heard. It undermines deliberative democracy by undermining discussion through the use of rhetoric and failing to listen to expert guidance. The will of the people has to triumph. There is no room for achieving consensus across a range of interests.

We also argued that populism can lead to a further undermining of democracy, particularly when populist leaders make changes which move towards authoritarianism: taking more power, for longer, and removing effective checks and balances. Populist leaders also tend to change the constitution to reduce checks and balances over the government. These changes make sense to populists. After all, the government represents the will of the people. The will of the people should be implemented, not checked by Parliament, the courts or other constitutional watchdogs.

We have seen signs of some changes that fit this pattern. However, the evidence is not conclusive. This is for two reasons. First, while we have seen changes that have undermined checks and balances, we've also seen how these checks and balances have worked effectively. Second, for every change, we've been able to present a narrative that shows that these changes could also be seen as nothing other than business as usual for the UK constitution, changes designed to restore the UK's predominantly political constitution.

Perhaps the clearest example of this duality is the repeal of the Fixed-term Parliaments Act 2011 and its replacement with the Dissolution and Calling of Parliament Act 2022. On the one hand, this change fits a populist narrative. It transfers power from Parliament to the government. The justification for this transfer also fits a populist narrative. The Dissolution and Calling of Parliament Act returns power to the people because it makes it easier for the government to request a general election. The people will ultimately decide if the government chose a good or bad day for a general election. The debate on the Bill also provided some clear examples of the use of rhetoric. There were lots of mentions of the 'zombie Parliament' of 2019, regarded as having been caused by the Fixed-term Parliaments Act 2011.

On the other hand, this change also fits our narrative of a return to business as usual. The 2022 Act turns back the clock to the constitutional position before the Fixed-term Parliaments Act 2011 was made. It revives the prerogative power of the Monarch to dissolve Parliament and returns the Westminster Parliament to maximum terms as opposed to fixed terms. It makes it easier for the government to call a general election if it loses a vote of no confidence, restoring the key constitutional convention that a government only remains in power for as long as it has the confidence of the House of Commons. This also makes it easier for the government to decide that a vote on a Bill is a matter of confidence, to ensure support for a Bill from its backbench MPs.

Given this possibility of being able to read the post-Brexit constitution both as showing signs of succumbing to populism and of merely restoring orthodoxy, how should we evaluate these changes? First, we need to look for similarities and differences between the orthodox account of the UK constitution and populism. Second, we need to assess how far any change to checks and balances over the government by Parliament and the people provides for an effective check, as opposed to a check by the political party from which the government is formed.

There are similarities between populism and orthodox accounts of the UK constitution. Populism advocates adversarial and antagonistic debate, often deploying rhetoric rather than deliberation, which seeks to find consensus. The Westminster Parliament is often regarded as an arena parliament. The government sets out its policies and is challenged by the opposition. The opposition sets out its alternative policies as to what it would do, were it in power. The government and the opposition sit opposite each other as rivals in this debate. The spectacle of PMQs prioritizes rhetoric over deliberation. The Westminster Parliament does not look like the place where we would find consensus across political divides. It's a showdown where one side wins and the other loses.

The first-past-the-post voting system and the use of the manifesto may also homogenize the will of the people. This voting system is designed to produce strong governments. A government with a strong majority in the House of Commons can usually command the votes it needs to enact its legislative agenda. There is no need to seek consensus. There is one voice from the government, backed up by the constitutional convention of collective ministerial responsibility. This convention means that ministers who do not agree with the government's policies keep silent about their disagreement outside cabinet discussion, which is kept private. Ministers either support the government or resign. While there may be discussion within the cabinet behind closed doors, the extent to which this facilitates deliberation and consensus may well depend on the personalities of those in government, particularly the personality of the prime minister. The manifesto presents one view of the political party, again potentially homogenizing the will of those in that party. The Salisbury-Addison convention in the House of Lords means that the second chamber of the Westminster legislature will neither veto nor propose wrecking amendments to Bills implementing the manifesto. All of these elements may make it easy to form one will of the people for the government to implement.

The use of delegated legislation is nothing new. Nor is the lack of detailed scrutiny over its provisions. Standing Order No. 14, prioritizing the business of the government, is still present. Programme motions are used to enable the government to ensure its legislation is enacted, even if this means cutting down on the time that can be used to debate and scrutinize a Bill's provisions.

However, there are also some elements of the orthodox account of the Westminster Parliament and the UK constitution that do not fit with a populist narrative. The UK constitution is based on the sovereignty of Parliament, not the people. The role of the people is mostly limited to general elections, electing MPs who then become members of the sovereign Parliament. Referendums are a relatively new phenomenon in the UK constitution. Although, post Brexit, and in light of the recent decision of the UK Supreme Court that the Scottish Parliament does not have the power to enact legislation to hold a second Scottish independence referendum, it may be that there are few, if any, referendums in the UK in the near future.[2]

Second, the UK constitution does have a system of checks and balances. The government is held to account in the political arena by Parliament and, ultimately, by the people, as well as being held to account in the legal arena by the courts. These checks and balances arguably justify the prioritization of governmental power in the UK. The government's actions are also overseen by other institutions, particularly the media, who play the role of constitutional watchdogs. These facilitate the ability of the people to hold the government to account.

These similarities and differences between populism and the orthodox account of the UK constitution hint at both the relative strengths and the relative weaknesses of the UK constitution. In terms of its strength, if the checks and balances over the government are healthy, particularly if they enable Parliament and the people to check the actions of the government, then the UK constitution and democracy in the Westminster Parliament should remain relatively healthy. However, if these checks are predominantly performed by the political party from which the government is formed, thereby minimizing the role of Parliament and the people, then there are reasons to be concerned about the state of democracy and the maintenance of good principles of constitutional government in the UK.

The similarities between aspects of orthodox constitutionalism in the UK and populism may also explain why it has been possible to provide two competing narratives about the constitutional changes taking place in the UK's post-Brexit constitution, where each seems feasible, but neither seems conclusive. The problem is that this may also make it easier for populism to be disguised as a normally functioning democracy. In particular, it may make it difficult to determine when a series of small changes, all of which can be justified as a return to orthodox constitutionalism in the UK, push the UK's constitution closer towards the cliff edge, undermining democracy and constitutional principles of good government.

Parliament, the party and the people

We've often referred to how checks over the government that take place in the political arena can come from Parliament, the people and the political party from which the government is formed.

When these checks work well, they enable the people to hold the government to account and ensure the government acts within the law. But when these checks tend to come more from members of the political party from which the government is formed, this may make it harder for the people to hold the government to account. It may also make it easier to prioritize gaining and holding on to political power over and above acting in a manner that upholds good principles of constitutional government, particularly as, in the UK, this depends on institutions acting with self-restraint and upholding mutual respect. Has the balance between these checks changed, such that the roles of Parliament and the people have been reduced, and that of the political party has increased?

The ability of the people to check the actions of the government continues to be, predominantly, indirect. The people vote in general elections. Constituency MPs represent the views of the electorate, voicing their concerns and asking questions. Ultimately, any check from the people relies on the extent to which MPs believe there is a need to appeal to the electorate to continue in government or receive sufficient parliamentary seats following a general election to form an alternative government that can command the confidence of the House of Commons. How far this may affect the behaviour of MPs, particularly to uphold self-restraint and mutual respect, may well depend on how close the country is to the next general election. It may also depend on how large a majority the government has in the House of Commons. The greater a political party's majority, the harder it may be to believe that they could lose support at the next general election. It may also be easier to justify acting in a manner that ignores self-restraint and mutual respect. After all, a large majority must mean that the political party has the support of the people, whose will should prevail.

There are also signs of constitutional changes in the post-Brexit constitution that may weaken the ability of the people to check the powers of the government. The Dissolution and Calling of Parliament Act 2022 may provide more of an opportunity for a prime minister to gameplay the calling of the next general election, choosing a time that is advantageous for their political party. The increased oversight of the government over the Electoral Commission may, if abused, potentially undermine the ability of this commission to ensure the fairness of general elections. Restrictions on the right to peaceful protest and the potential restrictions on human rights may also make it harder for the electorate to communicate their views on policy change to the government and Parliament.

The institution that can provide the most effective check over a government in the post-Brexit constitution would appear to be the political party from which the government is formed. It was the strength of feeling of backbench MPs over, among other things, the Patterson affair, Partygate and the Pincher affair that led to the resignation of Boris Johnson. The perceived lack of confidence of backbench MPs in Liz Truss, given her handling of the economy and votes on fracking, also played a large role in her resignation. Legislative amendments are more successful if they are backed by backbench MPs, who can communicate their concerns to the government. The government may then initiate their amendments to legislation in line with the suggestions of backbench MPs to ensure their support. In other words, what may appear to be a government amendment may well have been initiated by a backbench MP checking proposed legislative provisions.

None of the recent constitutional changes have weakened the power of the political party to check the actions of the government. If anything, the change in the process for choosing a new leader of the Conservative Party for the leadership contest that took place following the resignation of Liz Truss shows a strengthening of the role of backbench MPs and a relative weakening of the role of the broader members of the political party in question. This, itself, was a choice of members of the Conservative Party.

Yet, while the strongest and most resilient political check over the government comes from the political party, this is the body that has the smallest claim to democratic legitimacy. The percentage of the population that are members of a political party is dwindling. While the electorate may tend to vote on party lines, most of the electorate have little say over the content of a party's manifesto. This is not to argue that political parties are an illegitimate institution of the constitution. Their role is necessary in modern democracies. Rather, it is to question the extent to which any political party should play the main role in ensuring there are effective checks and balances over the government. Surely Parliament, composed of representatives from a range of political parties and none, is a better representative of the people than the members of one political party.

The importance of the role of political parties in providing effective checks over the government questions the justification for granting power to the government. It is hard to conclude that the government is the most democratic institution in the constitution if the only effective political check on its power comes not from Parliament, nor the people, but from the members of its political party, particularly its backbench MPs.

Those who argue that the government should have more power would point to what they regard as the key principle of the UK constitution – that the government only holds power for as long as it has the confidence of the House of Commons, composed of MPs who are directly accountable to the electorate through general elections. However, if we are to accept this argument, we need to understand how votes of no confidence work in practice, particularly given how rare it is for the government to lose a vote of no confidence. A government with a majority in the House of Commons will only lose a vote of no confidence if members of its own political party vote against the government. The stick of party discipline and the carrot of promotion within the political party makes this unlikely. This can make it less of a check and more of means for those in government to check on the actions of their backbench MPs.

Not only are political parties less representative than Parliament, but also the check provided by political parties may be less likely to ensure that members of the government act in a manner that upholds the constitutional guardrails of self-restraint and mutual trust. Any political party aims to win the next general election. For those political parties in government, the aim is to remain in power. Members of political parties may have the incentive to ignore when the government fails to act in a manner that upholds constitutional guardrails when the government is popular. After all, why bother upholding good principles of constitutional government if this does not win votes?

This is arguably demonstrated by how backbench MPs effectively forced the resignations of Boris Johnson and Liz Truss. Boris Johnson originally survived a challenge to his leadership of the Conservative Party in the aftermath of the Partygate scandal. However, he resigned over the Pincher affair. We can read this as a case of too many scandals leading to a prime ministerial resignation because the electorate had had enough. Or we can interpret this as tables turning because members of Boris Johnson's own cabinet and backbench MPs no longer felt they could trust the Prime Minister and did not think he could win the next general election. Similarly, Liz Truss was forced to resign over her economic policies, but also because she mishandled whether the vote on fracking was a confidence vote. Would she have had to resign if she had handled the vote of confidence more carefully, retaining the trust of the Conservative backbench MPs?

In other words – how far do checks and balances hold the government to account for their actions and how far do they merely try and ensure that any government holds on to power for as long as possible?

This becomes all the more concerning when we assess whether the UK constitution can resist democratic backsliding and the dangers of populism. It can be all too easy for a charismatic leader to use populist tactics to appeal to the will of the people to gain and maintain political power. While Parliament and the people may be able to check extreme abuses of power, they may be powerless to stop a series of small changes, each one seemingly minor, whose cumulative effect is just as devastating on democracy and constitutionalism as an extreme example of an abuse of power. It is also harder for the courts to provide a constitutional backstop in such situations. Courts can provide an effective check against abuse of power in extreme circumstances, as seen in particular in the prorogation case, and can challenge extreme examples of when the government acts in a manner that does not respect the mutual trust between the government and the courts. It is much harder for courts to push back against a series of smaller, incremental changes, where each one has a veneer of legitimacy.

We should be worried about the extent to which a government, of any political persuasion, may use populist tactics to gain power and then use this power to undermine democracy and constitutionalism, particularly by reducing the extent to which Parliament, the courts and other constitutional watchdogs can hold the government to account for its actions. It may be easy to justify each small change as merely a return to constitutional orthodoxy, protecting democracy by ensuring the government acts in line with the will of the people. It may also be difficult for Parliament and the people to stop these changes. A political party that is winning in the polls is unlikely to check the actions of a leader that may guarantee future electoral success. Any check over the power of any government using populist tactics may be unlikely to succeed if that government can claim that it is right for the government to have more power than any other institution in the constitution, given its democratic credentials and its claim to be the only institution that truly represents the will of the people.

What, if anything, can we do to reduce this potential weakness in the UK constitution?

Should we reform the UK constitution?

Whenever there are discussions as to possible changes to the UK constitution, the obvious reform is for the UK to move away from parliamentary sovereignty and a political constitution and adopt a codified constitution, where courts can strike down actions of the legislature and the executive that breach constitutional principles. Unsurprisingly, I'm often asked if this is the solution to all sorts of constitutional ills. My response is: not necessarily. Codification may help to provide clarity. A constitution that can protect constitutional principles from erosion by legislation as well as acts of the government may make it harder for a populist leader to modify long-standing constitutional principles. The courts may also have more powers to prevent the erosion of democracy and constitutional principles from a series of small, incremental changes, and not just to prevent larger erosions caused by a constitutional crisis.

However, the devil is in the detail. A lot depends on the constitutional principles that we decide to codify, and how we identify these principles. Difficulties can also arise if these principles are insufficiently flexible to allow for change as circumstances change. A codified constitution is also no guarantee that a populist leader is unable to gain power and use that power to undermine democracy. A populist leader with a large majority can change the constitution, including changing the procedures through which a constitution is modified, weakening or even removing constitutional safeguards. Populist leaders can remove independent judiciaries and replace them with a judiciary that is more likely to decide cases to agree with the preferred outcomes of a populist leader. A codified constitution may not prevent populism. Nor is it necessarily the solution to the UK's situation.

If we are to solve any problem, we have to understand its cause. Why am I worried that weaknesses in the UK constitution may make the UK vulnerable to populism and what, in particular, is concerning about the direction of travel of the UK's post-Brexit constitution? Some of my concerns stem from how the UK constitution prioritizes and legitimizes strong government. This is not to argue that governments should be weak. However, I am concerned that strong governments can become unchecked governments. I'm also concerned that, in practice, the most effective checks and balances seem to come from the political party to which a prime minister belongs, rather than coming from Parliament as a whole.

Every political party wishes to get elected and, to this extent, will take account of possible reactions from the electorate when making decisions, whether in government or opposition. However, if a political party has a large majority, this potential future check may be ineffective. Why worry about the wishes of the electorate if you have such a large majority that it seems unthinkable that you would not be able to win the next general election? This check may also focus more on power than on upholding good principles of constitutional government. Any backbench MP wishing to challenge the government on its policies or behaviour will need to consider how this may affect their future career in politics. We tend to vote on party lines. Upholding good principles of constitutional government is not that high on the list of priorities when it comes to voting. Political parties will also pay more attention to winning the votes of a handful of voters in contestable seats. That is how elections are won. Only a few of us are members of political parties. Even fewer of us have a large enough role in or over political parties to be able to influence their policies.

It is hard to see, therefore, how any political party can claim to have better democratic credentials than Parliament as a whole. Parliament also has a specific role to hold any government to account for its actions. This is why the House of Commons has select committees designed to oversee and report on the activities of particular ministerial departments. It is why we have written and oral questions in Parliament, again enabling Parliament to hold ministers to account for their actions. It is also why we have committees in the House of Lords and joint committees of the House of Commons and the House of Lords. The electorate only has the blunt tool of voting in elections.

This dominance of the role of political parties in providing effective checks on the government would suggest a need to think about how the UK constitution could be changed to strengthen parliamentary controls. There are several options. We may want to think about changing the voting system. First-past-the-post creates strong governments. However, it disincentivizes these governments from seeking consensus, or, as we have seen, from listening to and responding constructively to consultation exercises rather than forging ahead with a government's original policies. While strong governments may need to seek consensus from within their political party, or at least the MPs who are members of that political party, a government with a large majority in the House of Commons need not seek consensus across Parliament. This means that it can be easy, and arguably acceptable, to homogenize the will of the people, seeing this as effectively represented by the government that gained the most seats in Parliament, which should have free reign to implement its policies as set out in the manifesto.

This is not necessarily to argue in favour of proportional representation. The Scottish Parliament and the Senedd Cymru are elected through an additional member system. This has not led to a situation in which the governments formed in either of these parliaments have found it impossible to enact legislation. While there are problems in forming an executive in Northern Ireland, which also uses the additional member system, these are not caused by the electoral system alone. Northern Ireland is based on consociationalism, a form of democratic power sharing. Any executive formed in Northern Ireland must have representatives from political parties who wish Northern Ireland to be part of the United Kingdom and those who wish Northern Ireland to be part of Ireland. This is not always easy to achieve, with current divisions arising, at least in part, due to problems over the Northern Ireland Protocol and the extent to which these have been resolved by the Windsor Framework.

Given an alternative system of elections can work for other parliaments in the UK, it is at least worth thinking about whether changes to the electoral system used to form the Westminster

Parliament could help to provide a better balance between strong and representative governments, minimizing the possibility of any government being able to use the blurred lines between democracy and populism to undermine necessary checks and balances over their powers.

It may also be worth looking at the internal rules of the Westminster Parliament. In particular, is there a need for Standing Order No. 14 to prioritize government business to such an extent? Should the government be able to determine what is debated in Parliament, and when, and to propose a legislative timetable that may minimize legislative scrutiny? It is exceptional for the House of Commons to vote against a programme motion for a Bill. Would it be better to set up a specific committee in the House of Commons that could propose the business of the House, looking at the agenda proposed by the government and balancing that against the need for democratic scrutiny over legislation, as well as time for business raised by other MPs? This may also provide a better means for the people to raise matters that they wish to see discussed, using the intermediary of their constituency MP. It may also be possible for the current system of e-petitions, which may lead to a debate in Westminster Hall, to also be used to prompt debate in the main chamber of the House of Commons.

As well as helping to facilitate deliberation and consensus, changes to these internal rules may help Parliament to provide more effective checks and balances over the government, particularly when governments with large majorities may have less of an incentive to adhere to principles of self-restraint and mutual respect. We may also wish to think about whether the Ministerial Code should only be enforced by the prime minister. The code could be amended to grant greater freedom to the independent adviser on ministerial interests to initiate investigations. The code could also be amended such that reports from the independent adviser should normally be adopted by the prime minister unless there are exceptional public interest reasons for the prime minister to not follow the independent adviser's recommendation.

Similarly, changes could be made to ensure that reports of departmental select committees are normally debated, providing Parliament with a chance to discuss the issues raised, as well as facilitating greater publicity for these reports, with hopefully more accountability of ministers to the electorate. It may also be possible to think about whether select committees can propose specific motions to be debated in Parliament, based on their recommendations, particularly if they are recommending changes to the internal rules of Parliament, the Ministerial Code or the Code of Conduct for MPs.

More also needs to be done to improve the level of scrutiny over delegated legislation. This can be done by providing more time in Parliament, as well as through enacting legislation which requires the affirmative as opposed to the negative resolution procedure to be used to make delegated legislation, or which allows Parliament to propose amendments to draft delegated legislation. More could also be done to provide a more effective check over whether parent legislation provides for too much power to enact delegated legislation, or delegates power that should not be delegated to the government. This check is currently carried out by the Delegated Powers and Regulation Reform Committee in the House of Lords. This committee writes reports on all legislation before the committee stage in the House of Lords. It may be possible for this committee to become a joint committee of the House of Commons and the House of Lords. In this way, their scrutiny over parent legislation could come in time to inform debate in the House of Commons as well as in the House of Lords. This may also help to raise the profile of this issue, as has been the case regarding human rights given the work of the Joint Committee on Human Rights, which scrutinizes legislation as regards its compatibility with the European Convention on Human Rights, as well as providing reports on broader human rights issues. It may be better for the reports of this committee to be made available earlier to assist the House of Commons as well as the House of Lords in their deliberations, providing a closer check on whether legislation is granting too much power to the government.

Another area of possible reform is the role of political parties. There is very little legislation which specifically regulates political parties, save for provisions relating to election campaigns and party finances. More could be done to facilitate debate within political parties, perhaps requiring greater consultation between the leaders and the members of political parties over the formation of policies. This may help political parties to foster deliberation and consensus. Any requirements, however, would have to ensure that they did not constrain freedom of association, or place a disincentive on the formation of political parties, or their ability to recruit new members.

What about the courts? As discussed, the UK does have good protection of judicial independence. Parliamentary sovereignty means that courts cannot strike down legislation. However, courts can interpret legislation to guard human rights protected by the European Convention on Human Rights and common law rights, including constitutional principles. It can also quash the unlawful exercise of governmental powers. This was illustrated most clearly in the second *Miller* case, where the Supreme Court struck down the Prime Minister's request to prorogue Parliament given that the prorogation of Parliament for such a long period at such a time of constitutional importance, with no justification, would harm both parliamentary sovereignty and parliamentary accountability.

The courts are best able to provide this form of constitutional backstop in exceptional circumstances. There are also statements in court decisions suggesting that, in exceptional circumstances, courts may decide not to enforce legislation. This may arise in circumstances where a strong executive has dominated Parliament and enabled legislation to be enacted that removes constitutional principles designed to provide effective checks and balances – for example, removing the role of the courts.[3] Similarly, statements made in cases by judges of the Supreme Court suggest that courts should not enforce legislation enacted by a strong government that seriously undermines the franchise or the right to vote.[4]

Should courts do more? I would argue that the most legitimate role of the courts is to act as a form of constitutional backstop, stepping in when, given exceptional circumstances, Parliament has not been able to provide effective checks over the government, or when self-restraint and mutual trust have completely broken down. It is also important to ensure that courts do not act in a manner that would undermine their independence, making them vulnerable to challenge. Courts, too, need to act in a manner that respects their proper role in the constitution, particularly to ensure that they do not take political decisions.

However, there are still some areas where courts can be more aware of the potential dangers of populism and unchecked executive power when deciding cases. We have seen that the courts have been willing to point out when the government has failed to adhere to principles of mutual trust underpinning the UK constitution. The courts have reminded the government of its legal duty to obey court orders, as well as reminding the government that it is expected to adhere to declaratory orders and to comply with the duty of candour to ensure the protection of the rule of law. This is an important role that the court should continue to perform.

I also think that courts should take into account the reality of the powers of the government. Courts already read down broad legislative powers to ensure that they do not empower the government to enact delegated legislation that contravenes fundamental common law rights. This is called the principle of legality.[5] Courts also read down broad Henry VIII clauses – clauses which empower the executive to amend or repeal Acts of Parliament.[6] Again, this is to ensure that these powers are limited. Courts could also be aware of how much scrutiny has been given to a provision found in primary or secondary legislation when determining how much weight to give to the government's decisions when determining whether their actions are reasonable, or whether restrictions on the rights found in the European Convention of Human Rights, protected by the Human Rights Act 1998, are proportionate.

Courts should also think more carefully about how to provide a check over the discretionary decisions of ministers when a minister is empowered to act when he or she considers it appropriate to do so. Should this merely be a subjective test, or are there more objective standards that we would expect a minister to adhere to when determining whether it is appropriate to act?

What can I do?

The changes listed above may take time to achieve. Some of them require legislation. Others do not. Some of them require changes to how Parliament, political parties or the government act. Others may rely on courts developing principles of the common law, running the risk that they may be criticized by a populist government for going too far. These changes are not, however, enough.

If populism is able to take hold in any constitutional system, it is not merely because weaknesses in how the constitution is structured, or how democracy is protected, leave sufficient space for populism to take hold. Nor is it because there is a consensus that institutions of the constitution have gone too far – the out-of-touch elites ignoring the wishes of the people. If populism succeeds, it is because there is a lack of awareness and acceptance of the values of democracy, accountability and diversity.

It is easy to become complacent and take these values for granted. We do not tend to discuss why society should be democratic. It is either assumed that it should be or assumed that it is, and so is not discussed. We only tend to talk about the value of democracy when we think democracy has broken down. We may be quick to criticize the rise of populism or remark on democratic backsliding. But we are often slow to explain why democracy is a good idea in the first place. Similarly, we are slow to discuss why seeking consensus is valuable, or why we value a society that has a range of voices and diverse groups. We are also slow to discuss the value of democratic deliberation and participation.

This is not to criticize the electorate. It is to recognize that, as a society, we have not taken enough steps to ensure that everyone learns about how the government and Parliament work, the benefits and costs of the UK's unique constitutional arrangements, and why we value democracy, diversity, good principles of constitutional government and human rights. The UK constitution tends to evolve by fixing practical problems as and when they arise. This more practical approach to constitutional reform means that reforms are judged on whether they have fixed a perceived problem. There tends to be very little discussion of why the problem arose, or of the values underpinning our constitution and how they can be used to fix this problem.

Perhaps, as an individual whose job it is to educate people about the UK constitution, it was predictable that I would conclude by arguing that education is important. After all, everyone might expect me to protect my job! However, it is more fundamental than this. If we are to ensure that the people are the political sovereign, then the people need to know what is going on in the UK constitution and be encouraged and facilitated to play their part.

It will be hard for any populist leader to claim they are representing the will of the people if the people know that this 'will of the people' is the view of only one group in society, where any voices of dissent are effectively silenced. If the will of the people is to be the voice of democracy, then it needs to be formed from a consensus of a range of diverse voices and not the homogenized will of one group. This can only happen if there is free and fair democratic deliberation for all, where the electorate not only knows about the constitution but can talk about the values the constitution upholds and why they are important. If the people are to be the political sovereign, they need to take part in political deliberations and care about the principles of good constitutional government. Only then can the people ensure that power does not go unchecked.

Notes

Chapter 1

1   www.indy100.com/politics/boris-johnson-peter-hennessy-bbc
2   https://hansard.parliament.uk/commons/2021-12-01/debates/A0E282CF-039D-4F26-8F16-946B8C6E2ABC/Engagements
3   www.itv.com/news/2021-12-07/no-10-staff-joke-in-leaked-recording-about-christmas-party-they-later-denied
4   https://hansard.parliament.uk/commons/2021-12-08/debates/DB36FDA8-C784-4AEE-8D0C-F95FBB5345E9/Engagements
5   https://hansard.parliament.uk/commons/2022-01-12/debates/CEFD521F-BECA-495E-8650-C4FF8E2C5428/Engagements
6   Cabinet Office, 'Investigation into alleged gatherings on government premises during covid restrictions – update', 31 January 2022
7   https://hansard.parliament.uk/commons/2022-01-31/debates/6B412B49-AB7D-4FE3-9F82-B9EAE93FB6AC/SueGrayReport
8   Cabinet Office, 'Findings of Second Permanent Secretary's investigation into alleged gatherings on government premises during Covid restrictions', 25 May 2022, p. 36, https://assets.publishing.service.gov.uk/government/uploads/system/uploads/attachment_data/file/1078404/2022-05-25_FINAL_FINDINGS_OF_SECOND_PERMANENT_SECRETARY_INTO_ALLEGED_GATHERINGS.pdf
9   Cabinet Office, Ministerial Code 2022, https://assets.publishing.service.gov.uk/government/uploads/system/uploads/attachment_data/file/1126632/Ministerial_Code.pdf
10 R (FDA) v Prime Minister and Minister for the Civil Service [2021] EWHC 3279 (Admin), www.judiciary.uk/wp-content/uploads/2022/07/FDA-v-Prime-Minister-judgment-061221.pdf
11 Cabinet Office, Ministerial Code December 2022, para 1.6, https://assets.publishing.service.gov.uk/government/uploads/system/uploads/attachment_data/file/1126632/Ministerial_Code.pdf
12 Ministerial Code, para 1.4.b
13 Ministerial Code, para 1.7
14 HC Deb, vol 292, cols 1046–7, 19 March 1997, https://publications.parliament.uk/pa/cm199697/cmhansrd/vo970319/debtext/70319-67.htm
15 www.bbc.co.uk/news/uk-politics-65863336

[16] House of Commons, Committee of Privileges, 'Matter referred on 21 April 2022 (conduct of Rt Hon Boris Johnson) Final Report', Fifth Report of Session 2022–23, HC 564, 15 June 2023, https://committees.parliament. uk/publications/40412/documents/197897/default, para 14

[17] HC Deb vol 734, cols 662–4, 19 June 2023, https://hansard.parliament. uk/commons/2023-06-19/debates/E15A1DF8-31A1-4FEF-B007-3CBF444BAA11/PrivilegeConductOfRightHonBorisJohnson

[18] www.gov.uk/government/speeches/pm-statement-12-april-2022

[19] HC Deb, vol 712, cols 48–9, 19 April 2022, https://hansard.parliament. uk/Commons/2022-04-19/debates/2C3E878D-6ECB-4FF2-9E3A-7B134989EAA6/EasterRecessGovernmentUpdate

[20] The Prime Minister's statement in Downing Street, 7 July 2022, www.gov. uk/government/speeches/prime-minister-boris-johnsons-statement-in-downing-street-7-july-2022

[21] HC Deb, vol 718, col 726, 18 July 2022, https://hansard.parliament. uk/commons/2022-07-18/debates/EA7DB1BF-EC36-4C3B-8F73-D47B2523BA53/ConfidenceInHerMajesty%E2%80%99SGovernment

[22] HC Deb, vol 718, col 730, 18 July 2022, https://hansard.parliament. uk/commons/2022-07-18/debates/EA7DB1BF-EC36-4C3B-8F73-D47B2523BA53/ConfidenceInHerMajesty%E2%80%99SGovernment

[23] A Blick and P Hennessy, *Good Chaps No More? Safeguarding the Constitution in Stressful Times*, 2019, The Constitution Society, https://consoc.org.uk/ wp-content/uploads/2019/11/FINAL-Blick-Hennessy-Good-Chaps-No-More.pdf

[24] www.bbc.co.uk/news/uk-politics-61134002

[25] www.bbc.co.uk/news/uk-politics-61134002

Chapter 2

[1] These provisions are set out in the Constitutional Reform and Governance Act 2010, sections 20–5

[2] This was often referred to as the 'meaningful vote'. It was set out in section 13 of the European Union (Withdrawal) Act 2018. This provision was later amended so as not to apply to the second withdrawal agreement.

[3] HC Deb, Vol 664, col 775, 25 September 2019, https://hansard.parliament. uk/commons/2019-09-25/debates/AD2A07E5-9741-4EBA-997A-97776F80AA38/PrimeMinisterSUpdate

[4] HC Deb, Vol 664, cols 775–6, 25 September 2019, https://hansard. parliament.uk/commons/2019-09-25/debates/AD2A07E5-9741-4EBA-997A-97776F80AA38/PrimeMinisterSUpdate

[5] HC Deb, Vol 664, col 780, 25 September 2019, https://hansard.parliament. uk/commons/2019-09-25/debates/AD2A07E5-9741-4EBA-997A-97776F80AA38/PrimeMinisterSUpdate

[6] www.dailymail.co.uk/news/article-3903436/Enemies-people-Fury-touch-judges-defied-17-4m-Brexit-voters-trigger-constitutional-crisis.html

[7] J-W Müller, *What is Populism?*, University of Pennsylvania Press: 2016

Chapter 3

1 These figures are based on the House of Commons Library paper, 'UK election statistics: 1918–2021: a century of elections', CBP 7529, 18 August 2021, https://researchbriefings.files.parliament.uk/documents/CBP-7529/CBP-7529.pdf

2 This is referred to as the Salisbury or the Salisbury-Addison convention. There is some dispute among members of the Liberal Democrat Party in the House of Lords as to whether they are bound by this convention.

3 Ministerial and Other Salaries Act 1975 sets the limit of paid ministerial posts. The House of Commons Disqualification Act 1975 sets the limit of holders of ministerial posts who can vote in the House of Commons.

4 House of Lords, Secondary Legislation Scrutiny Committee, 'Government by diktat: a call to return power to Parliament', 20th report of session 2021–2022, HL Paper 105, https://committees.parliament.uk/publications/7941/documents/82225/default

5 'Strathclyde Review: secondary legislation and the primacy of the House of Commons', December 2015, CM 9177, https://assets.publishing.service.gov.uk/government/uploads/system/uploads/attachment_data/file/486791/53088_Cm_9177_PRINT.pdf

6 House of Lords, Secondary Legislation Scrutiny Committee, 'Government by diktat: a call to return power to Parliament', 20th report of session 2021–2022, HL Paper 105, https://committees.parliament.uk/publications/7941/documents/82225/default and House of Lords, Delegated Powers and Regulatory Reform Committee, 'Democracy denied? The urgent need to rebalance the power between Parliament and the executive', 12th Report of Session 2021–22, HL Paper 106, https://committees.parliament.uk/publications/7960/documents/82286/default

7 www.hansardsociety.org.uk/publications/data/coronavirus-statutory-instruments-dashboard

8 www.parliament.uk/about/how/laws/secondary-legislation/#:~:text=They%20are%20published%20with%20an,to%20be%20considered%20by%20Parliament

9 HC Deb, vol 681, col 331, 30 September 2020, https://hansard.parliament.uk//commons/2020-09-30/debates/8160262B-DA85-4D6C-B7FF-86717C8261B2/Speaker'SStatement#contribution-0F1BA845-676B-4F06-AF93-97BE1A22BFEB

10 www.gov.uk/government/news/coronavirus-sms-messages

11 *Dolan, Monks and AB v Secretary of State for Health and Social Care and Secretary of State for Education* [2020] EWHC 1786 (Admin), www.bailii.org/ew/cases/EWHC/Admin/2020/1786.html. The decision was appealed to the Court of Appeal, which dismissed the argument that Covid regulations were unlawful: *Dolan, Monks and AB v Secretary of State for Health and Social Care and Secretary of State for Education* [2020] EWCA Civ 1605, www.bailii.org/ew/cases/EWCA/Civ/2020/1605.html

12 'It's Time for Real Change. The Labour Party Manifesto 2019', https://labour.org.uk/wp-content/uploads/2019/11/Real-Change-Labour-Manifesto-2019.pdf

13 HL Deb, vol 830, Tuesday 13 June 2023, by Lord Coaker, cols 1915–16, Lord Pannick, cols 1921, 1922, 1923, Baroness Hayman, col 1923, and Lord Paddick col 1933. https://hansard.parliament.uk/lords/2023-06-13/debates/7C52CB74-6B52-4DB9-9363-28AAB6678B51/PublicOrderAct1986(SeriousDisruptionToTheLifeOfTheCommunity)Regulations2023

Chapter 4

1 Confidence and Supply Agreement between the Conservative and Unionist Party and the Democratic Unionist Party, www.gov.uk/government/publications/conservative-and-dup-agreement-and-uk-government-financial-support-for-northern-ireland/agreement-between-the-conservative-and-unionist-party-and-the-democratic-unionist-party-on-support-for-the-government-in-parliament

2 *R (Miller) v Prime Minister; Cherry v Advocate General for Scotland* [2019] UKSC 41, www.supremecourt.uk/cases/docs/uksc-2019-0192-judgment.pdf. You can find this statement in paragraph 50 of the judgment, on page 18.

3 *R (Miller) v Prime Minister; Cherry v Advocate General for Scotland* [2019] UKSC 41, www.supremecourt.uk/cases/docs/uksc-2019-0192-judgment.pdf. You can find this statement in paragraph 61 of the judgment, on page 22.

4 HC Deb, vol 664, col 163, 4 September 2019, https://hansard.parliament.uk/commons/2019-09-04/debates/917B81A6-57F8-48C3-AABE-63224897F16E/Engagements

5 HC Deb, vol 664, col 164, 4 September 2019, https://hansard.parliament.uk/commons/2019-09-04/debates/917B81A6-57F8-48C3-AABE-63224897F16E/Engagements

6 HC Deb, vol 718, col 949, 20 July 2022, https://hansard.parliament.uk/commons/2022-07-20/debates/63F450D4-6D44-4D0B-915A-8D06DCDD7E4A/Engagements

7 HC Deb, vol 718, col 950, 20 July 2022, https://hansard.parliament.uk/commons/2022-07-20/debates/63F450D4-6D44-4D0B-915A-8D06DCDD7E4A/Engagements

8 HC Deb, vol 718, cols 939–48, 20 July 2022, https://hansard.parliament.uk/commons/2022-07-20/debates/63F450D4-6D44-4D0B-915A-8D06DCDD7E4A/Engagements

9 House of Commons, Committee on Standards, 'Mr Owen Paterson', Third report of session 2021–22, HC 797, 26 October 2021

10 HC Deb, vol 702, cols 938–73, 3 November 2021, https://hansard.parliament.uk/Commons/2021-11-03/debates/EA7E30B2-F0D0-4FC8-A608-9845CE43CF28/CommitteeOnStandards

11 HC Deb, vol 703, cols 33–82, 8 November 2021, https://hansard. parliament.uk/Commons/2021-11-08/debates/6E81CD0D-33C6-4796- B224-5D88EFAC8F07/CommitteeOnStandardsDecisionOfTheHouse

12 HC Deb, vol 703, cols 426–7, 15 November 2021, https://hansard. parliament.uk/Commons/2021-11-15/debates/AAB40FF9-A432-4E06- B5BA-2967713CEA6F/BusinessWithoutDebate

13 HC Deb, vol 703, cols 624–93, 17 November 2021, https://hansard. parliament.uk/Commons/2021-11-17/debates/09622FB9-93D2-4FBA- A177-9787E0454DD7/StrengtheningStandardsInPublicLife

14 These reports can be found on the website of the Committee on Standards at: https://committees.parliament.uk/committee/290/committee-on- standards/publications/reports-responses

15 House of Commons, 'Procedural protocol in respect of the Code of Conduct', HC 875, 10 November 2022, https://publications.parliament. uk/pa/cm5803/cmcode/875/875.pdf

16 For more information, see House of Commons Committee on Standards, 'Owen Paterson', Third report of session 2021–22, HC 797, 26 October 2021, https://committees.parliament.uk/publications/7644/documents/ 79907/default

17 https://researchbriefings.files.parliament.uk/documents/SN03750/ SN03750.pdf

18 Cabinet Office, Ministerial Code December 2022, https://assets.publishing. service.gov.uk/government/uploads/system/uploads/attachment_data/ file/1126632/Ministerial_Code.pdf

19 www.gov.uk/government/publications/ministerial-code/ministerial-code

20 You can read his report here: https://assets.publishing.service.gov.uk/ government/uploads/system/uploads/attachment_data/file/1152026/ 2023.04.20_Investigation_Report_to_the_Prime_Minister.pdf

21 You can find the full text of the resignation letter here: www.bbc.co.uk/ news/uk-politics-65333734

22 Conservative Party 2019 Manifesto, page 48, www.conservatives.com/our- plan/conservative-party-manifesto-2019

23 *R (Miller) v The Prime Minister; Cherry v Advocate General for Scotland* [2019] UKSC 41, [69]

24 https://assets.publishing.service.gov.uk/government/uploads/system/ uploads/attachment_data/file/975301/judicial-review-reform-consultation- document.pdf, para 2

25 Lord Buckland's statement to Parliament on IRAL, HC Deb, vol 691, cols 504– 6, 18 March 2021, https://hansard.parliament.uk/commons/2021-03- 18/debates/8629246C-68B7-48DE-B601-FB80866A4CEA/Independent ReviewOfAdministrativeLaw

26 ECHR Memorandum, Illegal Migration Bill, https://publications. parliament.uk/pa/bills/cbill/58-03/0262/ECHR%20memo%20Illegal%20 Migration%20Bill%20FINAL.pdf

[27] ECHR Memorandum, Illegal Migration Bill, https://publications. parliament.uk/pa/bills/cbill/58-03/0262/ECHR%20memo%20Illegal%20 Migration%20Bill%20FINAL.pdf, para 47

Chapter 5

[1] A Blick and P Hennessy, *Good Chaps No More? Safeguarding the Constitution in Stressful Times*, 2022, The Constitution Society, https://consoc.org. uk/publications/good-chaps-no-more-safeguarding-the-constitution-in-instressful-times-by-andrew-blick-and-peter-hennessy and *The Bonfire of the Decencies: Repairing and Restoring the British Constitution*, Haus: 2022

[2] S Levitsky and D Ziblatt, *How Democracies Die*, Viking: 2018

[3] See, for example, the statement of Lord Faulks, then Minister for Justice, confirming this interpretation HL Deb, 28 October 2015, cols 1170–1 and *R (Gulf Centre for Human Rights) v The Prime Minister and the Chancellor of the Duchy of Lancaster* [2018] ECWA Civ 1855

[4] HC Deb, vol 679, cols 508–9, 8 September 2020, https://hansard. parliament.uk/commons/2020-09-08/debates/2F32EBC3-6692-402C-93E6-76B4CF1BC6E3/NorthernIrelandProtocolUKLegalObligations

[5] HC Deb, vol 679, col 509, 8 September 2020, https://hansard.parliament. uk/commons/2020-09-08/debates/2F32EBC3-6692-402C-93E6-76B4CF1BC6E3/NorthernIrelandProtocolUKLegalObligations

[6] HL Deb, vol 805, col 1286, 19 October 2020, https://hansard.parliament.uk/ lords/2020-10-19/debates/EE01801B-5883-4BDD-9809-B860F5BA6120/ UnitedKingdomInternalMarketBill

[7] You can read the government's legal position here: www.gov.uk/ government/publications/northern-ireland-protocol-bill-uk-government-legal-position/northern-ireland-protocol-bill-uk-government-legal-position

[8] See for example, the House of Lords Select Committee on the Constitution, 'Northern Ireland Protocol Bill' 6th report of session 2022–23, HL Paper 78, https://committees.parliament.uk/publications/30438/documents/175587/ default

[9] HC Deb, vol 728, col 576, 27 February 2023, https://hansard.parliament. uk/Commons/2023-02-27/debates/145ECA09-85E8-40C9-B631-5795DCABFA93/NorthernIrelandProtocol

[10] HC Deb, vol 620, col 287, 25 January 2017, https://hansard.parliament. uk/Commons/2017-01-25/debates/2C0D6980-7BD9-49A3-A401-61B9DCB7B803/Engagements

[11] HC Deb, vol 620, cols 818–9, 31 January 2017, https://hansard.parliament. uk/Commons/2017-01-31/debates/C2852E15-21D3-4F03-B8C3-F7E05F2276B0/EuropeanUnion(NotificationOfWithdrawal)Bill

[12] *Craig v Her Majesty's Advocate* [2022] UKSC 6, www.supremecourt.uk/cases/ docs/uksc-2020-0185-judgment.pdf

[13] *Craig v Her Majesty's Advocate* [2022] UKSC 6, www.supremecourt.uk/cases/ docs/uksc-2020-0185-judgment.pdf, para [44]

[14] *Craig v Her Majesty's Advocate* [2022] UKSC 6, www.supremecourt.uk/cases/ docs/uksc-2020-0185-judgment.pdf, para [46]

15 *R (HM) v Secretary of State for the Home Department* [2022] EWHC 695 (Admin), www.bailii.org/ew/cases/EWHC/Admin/2022/695.html

16 *R (HM) v Secretary of State for the Home Department* [2022] EWHC 2729 (Admin), www.bailii.org/ew/cases/EWHC/Admin/2022/2729.html

17 *R (HM) v Secretary of State for the Home Department* [2022] EWHC 2729 (Admin), www.bailii.org/ew/cases/EWHC/Admin/2022/2729.html, at para [10]

18 *R (Majera) v Secretary of State for the Home Department* [2021] UKSC 46, at para [44]

19 *R (Bailey) v Secretary of State for Justice* [2023] EWHC 555 (Admin), https://caselaw.nationalarchives.gov.uk/ewhc/admin/2023/555/data.pdf

20 *R (Bailey) v Secretary of State for Justice* [2023] EWHC 821 (Admin), www.judiciary.uk/wp-content/uploads/2023/04/Bailey-and-Morris-Final-Judgment-2-final.pdf

21 A Blick and P Hennessy, *Good Chaps No More? Safeguarding the Constitution in Stressful Times*, 2022, The Constitution Society, https://consoc.org.uk/wp-content/uploads/2019/11/FINAL-Blick-Hennessy-Good-Chaps-No-More.pdf

Chapter 6

1 HC Deb, vol 664, col 163, 4 September 2019, https://hansard.parliament.uk/Commons/2019-09-04/debates/917B81A6-57F8-48C3-AABE-63224897F16E/Engagements

2 HC Deb, vol 664, col 165, 4 September 2019, https://hansard.parliament.uk/Commons/2019-09-04/debates/917B81A6-57F8-48C3-AABE-63224897F16E/Engagements

3 HC Deb, vol 664, col 165, 4 September 2019, https://hansard.parliament.uk/Commons/2019-09-04/debates/917B81A6-57F8-48C3-AABE-63224897F16E/Engagements

4 HC Deb, vol 664, col 164, 4 September 2019, https://hansard.parliament.uk/Commons/2019-09-04/debates/917B81A6-57F8-48C3-AABE-63224897F16E/Engagements

5 HC Deb, vol 664, col 172, 4 September 2019, https://hansard.parliament.uk/Commons/2019-09-04/debates/A7A1E43B-AD26-4F52-BB21-E7715164C5B4/Engagements

6 HC Deb, vol 664, col 164, 4 September 2019, https://hansard.parliament.uk/Commons/2019-09-04/debates/A7A1E43B-AD26-4F52-BB21-E7715164C5B4/Engagements

7 HC Deb, vol 664, col 166, 4 September 2019, https://hansard.parliament.uk/Commons/2019-09-04/debates/917B81A6-57F8-48C3-AABE-63224897F16E/Engagements

8 HC Deb, vol 664, col 168, 4 September 2019, https://hansard.parliament.uk/Commons/2019-09-04/debates/A7A1E43B-AD26-4F52-BB21-E7715164C5B4/Engagements

9   HC Deb, vol 664, col 172, 4 September 2019, https://hansard.parliament.
    uk/Commons/2019-09-04/debates/A7A1E43B-AD26-4F52-BB21-
    E7715164C5B4/Engagements
10 HC Deb, vol 718, col 952, 20 July 2022, https://hansard.parliament.
    uk/Commons/2022-07-20/debates/63F450D4-6D44-4D0B-915A-
    8D06DCDD7E4A/Engagements
11 HC Deb, vol 718, col 952, 20 July 2022, https://hansard.parliament.
    uk/Commons/2022-07-20/debates/63F450D4-6D44-4D0B-915A-
    8D06DCDD7E4A/Engagements
12 HC Deb, vol 718, col 953, 20 July 2022, https://hansard.parliament.
    uk/Commons/2022-07-20/debates/63F450D4-6D44-4D0B-915A-
    8D06DCDD7E4A/Engagements
13 HC Deb, vol 718, col 953, 20 July 2022, https://hansard.parliament.
    uk/Commons/2022-07-20/debates/63F450D4-6D44-4D0B-915A-
    8D06DCDD7E4A/Engagements
14 HC Deb, vol 718, col 954, 20 July 2022, https://hansard.parliament.
    uk/Commons/2022-07-20/debates/63F450D4-6D44-4D0B-915A-
    8D06DCDD7E4A/Engagements
15 HC Deb, vol 718, col 962, 20 July 2022, https://hansard.parliament.
    uk/Commons/2022-07-20/debates/63F450D4-6D44-4D0B-915A-
    8D06DCDD7E4A/Engagements
16 N Polsby, 'Legislatures', In F.I. Greenstein and N.W. Polsby (eds), *Handbook of Political Science, V*, Addison-Wesley: 1975, pp. 257–319
17 HC Deb, vol 698, col 788, 6 July 2021, https://hansard.parliament.
    uk/Commons/2021-07-06/debates/6FE2AA38-3302-423F-82D3-
    968692BA6C06/DissolutionAndCallingOfParliamentBill
18 HC Deb, vol 698, col 791, 6 July 2021, https://hansard.parliament.
    uk/Commons/2021-07-06/debates/6FE2AA38-3302-423F-82D3-
    968692BA6C06/DissolutionAndCallingOfParliamentBill
19 HC Deb vol 700, col 733, 13 September 2021, https://hansard.parliament.
    uk/Commons/2021-09-13/debates/F9066A76-C751-4BE9-BFAF-
    6A0095261AA3/DissolutionAndCallingOfParliamentBill
20 HC Deb vol 700, col 733, 13 September 2021, https://hansard.parliament.
    uk/Commons/2021-09-13/debates/F9066A76-C751-4BE9-BFAF-
    6A0095261AA3/DissolutionAndCallingOfParliamentBill
21 HC Deb, vol 698, col 791, 6 July 2021, https://hansard.parliament.
    uk/Commons/2021-07-06/debates/6FE2AA38-3302-423F-82D3-
    968692BA6C06/DissolutionAndCallingOfParliamentBill
22 HC Deb, vol 698, col 791, 6 July 2021, https://hansard.parliament.
    uk/Commons/2021-07-06/debates/6FE2AA38-3302-423F-82D3-
    968692BA6C06/DissolutionAndCallingOfParliamentBill
23 HC Deb, vol 698, col 791, 6 July 2021, https://hansard.parliament.
    uk/Commons/2021-07-06/debates/6FE2AA38-3302-423F-82D3-
    968692BA6C06/DissolutionAndCallingOfParliamentBill

24   HC Deb, vol 700, col 720, 13 September 2021, https://hansard.parliament. uk/Commons/2021-09-13/debates/F9066A76-C751-4BE9-BFAF-6A0095261AA3/DissolutionAndCallingOfParliamentBill

25   HC Deb, vol 700, col 740, 13 September 2021, https://hansard.parliament. uk/Commons/2021-09-13/debates/F9066A76-C751-4BE9-BFAF-6A0095261AA3/DissolutionAndCallingOfParliamentBill

26   HC Deb, vol 710, col 652, 14 March 2022, https://hansard.parliament. uk/Commons/2022-03-14/debates/885EE1A2-32C5-44EE-B3F0-4A6F2824C743/DissolutionAndCallingOfParliamentBill

27   Joint Committee on the Fixed-Term Parliaments Act, 'Report', Session 2019–21, HC 1046, HL Paper 253, 24 March 2021, https://committees. parliament.uk/publications/5190/documents/52402/default

28   Public Administration and Constitutional Affairs Committee, 'The Fixed-Term Parliaments Act 2011', Sixth report of session 2019–21, HC 167, 15 September 2020, https://committees.parliament.uk/publications/2550/documents/26167/default

29   House of Lords Select Committee on the Constitution, 'A Question of Confidence? The Fixed-Term Parliaments Act 2011', 12th report of session, 2019–21, HL Paper 121, 4 September 2020, https://publications.parliament. uk/pa/ld5801/ldselect/ldconst/121/121.pdf

30   HC Deb, vol 700, col 815, 13 September 2021, https://hansard.parliament. uk/Commons/2021-09-13/debates/F9066A76-C751-4BE9-BFAF-6A0095261AA3/DissolutionAndCallingOfParliamentBill

31   Cabinet Office, Ministerial Code December 2022, para 9.1, https:// assets.publishing.service.gov.uk/government/uploads/system/uploads/attachment_data/file/1126632/Ministerial_Code.pdf

32   Cabinet Office, Ministerial Code December 2022, para 9.5, https:// assets.publishing.service.gov.uk/government/uploads/system/uploads/attachment_data/file/1126632/Ministerial_Code.pdf

33   HC Deb, vol 679, col 619, 9 September 2020, https://hansard.parliament. uk/commons/2020-09-09/debates/0CEEB81E-F31C-4447-B0F4-E7E3EE8D2F4C/PointsOfOrder

34   HC Deb, vol 697, col 22, 14 June 2021, https://hansard.parliament. uk/commons/2021-06-14/debates/DEEBE3E2-7787-48FF-948F-E4FC53F30211/PointsOfOrder

35   HC Deb, vol 697, col 23, 14 June 2021, https://hansard.parliament. uk/commons/2021-06-14/debates/DEEBE3E2-7787-48FF-948F-E4FC53F30211/PointsOfOrder

36   HC Deb, vol 680, col 641, 21 September 2020, https://hansard.parliament. uk/commons/2020-09-21/debates/82079059-849B-40AD-B657-FF49F5DF00ED/PointOfOrder

37   HC Deb, vol 680, col 641, 21 September 2020, https://hansard.parliament. uk/commons/2020-09-21/debates/82079059-849B-40AD-B657-FF49F5DF00ED/PointOfOrder

38 HC Deb, vol 652, cols 695-6, 11 January 2019, https://hansard.parliament. uk/commons/2019-01-11/debates/DEC2B854-E86E-4837-BC7B-5D4341AE44F9/PointsOfOrder

39 HC Deb, vol 709, col 1045, 2 March 2022, https://hansard.parliament. uk/Commons/2022-03-02/debates/B9E0411F-DD26-4ECB-94A4-249FB21EBCE9/PointsOfOrder

40 HC Deb, vol 732, col 437, 11 May 2023, https://hansard.parliament. uk/commons/2023-05-11/debates/151534D5-FE5C-42A2-B95C-195EA5353DC7/RetainedEULaw(RevocationAndReform)Bill

41 Vote Leave, 'Why Vote Leave', www.voteleavetakecontrol.org/why_vote_leave.html

Chapter 7

1 You can read the report here: https://publicappointmentscommissioner. independent.gov.uk/wp-content/uploads/2023/04/2023-04-28-OCPA-DECISION-NOTICE-IN-RELATION-TO-THE-APPOINTMENT-OF-CHAIR-OF-THE-BBC-BOARD-MR-RICHARD-SHARP.pdf

2 para 21

3 para 32

4 paras 47–50

5 Draft Electoral Commission Strategy and Policy Statement, para 8, 22 August 2022, www.gov.uk/government/publications/draft-electoral-commission-strategy-and-policy-statement/draft-electoral-commission-strategy-and-policy-statement

6 The Speaker's Committee on the Electoral Commission, 'Response to the government's consultation on the draft strategy and policy statement for the Electoral Commission', Third report 2022, HC 967, 22 December 2022, para 30, https://committees.parliament.uk/publications/33350/documents/180486/default

7 The Speaker's Committee on the Electoral Commission, 'Response to the government's consultation on the draft strategy and policy statement for the Electoral Commission', Third report 2022, HC 967, 22 December 2022, para 31

8 The Speaker's Committee on the Electoral Commission, 'Response to the government's consultation on the draft strategy and policy statement for the Electoral Commission', Third report 2022, HC 967, 22 December 2022, paras 34–5

9 Director of Public Prosecutions v Ziegler [2021] UKSC 23, www.supremecourt. uk/cases/docs/uksc-2019-0106-judgment.pdf

10 Reference by the Attorney General for Northern Ireland – Abortion Services (Safe Access Zones) (Northern Ireland) Bill [2022] UKSC 32, www.supremecourt. uk/cases/docs/uksc-2022-0077-judgment.pdf

11 These were found in the Public Order Act 1986. Section 12 sets out the provisions relating to processions and section 14 sets out the provisions for gatherings.

¹² These can be found in two new sections of the Public Order Act 1986, section 12(1)(aa) and section 14(1)(aa)

¹³ These can be found in two new sections of the Public Order Act 1986, section 12(1)(ab) and section 14(1)(ab)

¹⁴ These can be found in two new sections of the Public Order Act 1986, section 12(2C) and section 14(2C)

¹⁵ These can be found in two new sections of the Public Order Act 1986, section 12(2D) and section 14(2D)

¹⁶ These can be found in two new sections of the Public Order Act 1986, section 12(2E) and section 14(2E)

¹⁷ Police Crime and Sentencing Act 2022, section 73, which changes section 12 of the Public Order Act 1986

¹⁸ These can be found in two new sections of the Public Order Act 1986, section 12(2A) and section 14(2A)

Chapter 8

1 'Get Brexit Done. Unleash Britain's potential. The Conservative and Unionist Party Manifesto 2019', pp 47–8, www.conservatives.com/our-plan/conservative-party-manifesto-2019

2 *Reference by the Lord Advocate of devolution issues under paragraph 34 of Schedule 6 of the Scotland Act 1998* [2022] UKSC 31, www.supremecourt.uk/cases/docs/uksc-2022-0098-judgment.pdf

3 See, for example, the statement of Lord Steyn in *R (Jackson) v Attorney General* [2005] UKHL 56, [2006] 1 AC 262 (https://publications.parliament.uk/pa/ld200506/ldjudgmt/jd051013/jack.pdf) and the statement of Lord Hope in *AXA General Insurance v the Lord Advocate* [2011] UKSC 46, [2012] 1 AC 868 (https://www.supremecourt.uk/cases/docs/uksc-2011-0108-judgment.pdf)

4 See the statement of Lord Hodge in *Moohan v The Lord Advocate* [2014] UKSC 67, [2015] AC 901, www.supremecourt.uk/cases/docs/uksc-2014-0183-judgment.pdf

5 See *R v Secretary of State for the Home Department, ex parte Simms* [1999] UKHL 33, [2000] 2 AC 115, https://publications.parliament.uk/pa/ld199899/ldjudgmt/jd990708/obrien01.htm

6 See *R (Public Law Project) v Lord Chancellor* [2016] UKSC 39, [2016] AC 1531 (www.supremecourt.uk/cases/docs/uksc-2015-0255-judgment.pdf) and *R (Ingenious Media) v Commissioners for HMRC* [2016] UKSC 54, [2016] 1 WLR 4164 (www.supremecourt.uk/cases/docs/uksc-2015-0082-judgment.pdf)

Index